IMAGES
of America

Southern Colorado
O.T. Davis Collection

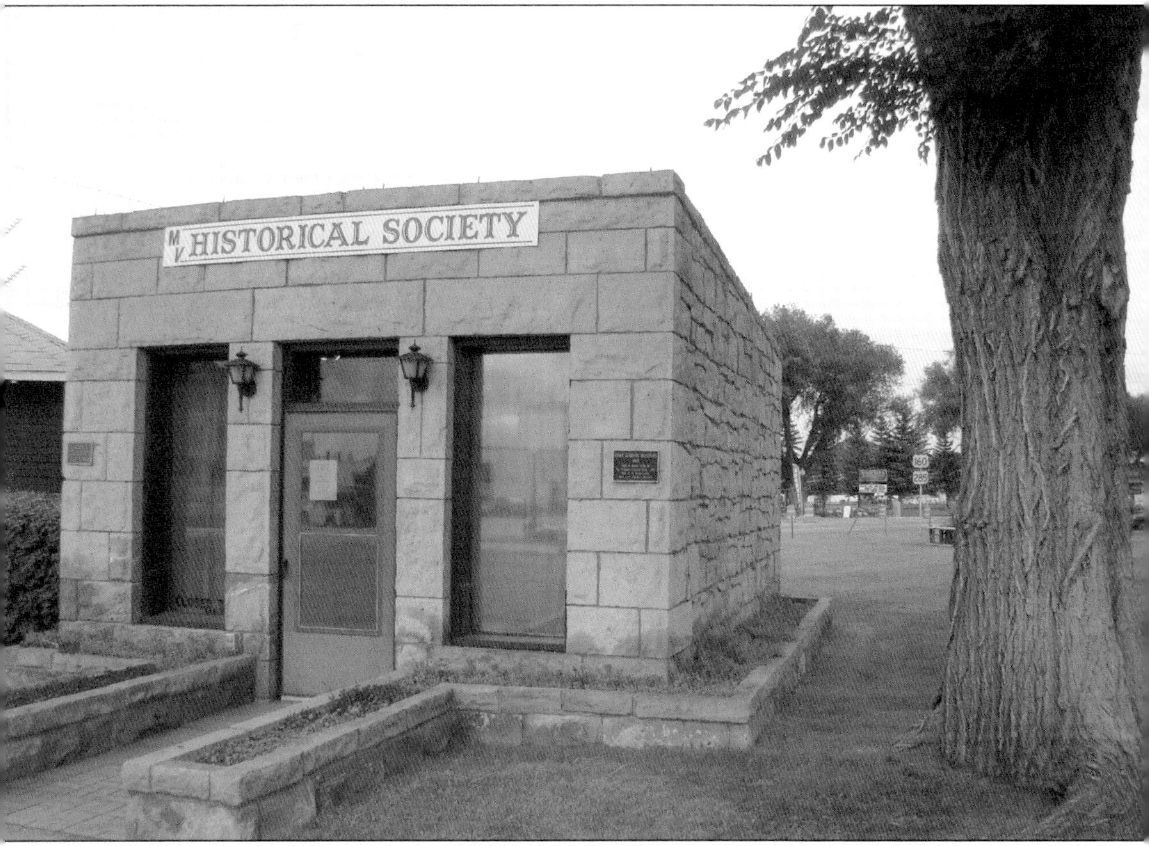

Monte Vista Historical Society, 2013. The Monte Vista Historical Society occupies this small stone building at 111 Jefferson Street. The building was constructed in 1895 and originally housed the Monte Vista Library. The O.T. Davis photographic collection resides here. (Photograph by author.)

On the Cover: The Shippey Ranch, pictured here on August 2, 1911, belonged to Dr. Orland P. Shippey and was located two miles east of Villa Grove. See page 59 for more information. (Courtesy of the O.T. Davis collection of the Monte Vista Historical Society.)

IMAGES
of America

SOUTHERN COLORADO O.T. DAVIS COLLECTION

Mike Butler and
Monte Vista Historical Society

ARCADIA
PUBLISHING

ISBN 978-1-4671-3173-5

Published by Arcadia Publishing
Charleston, South Carolina

Printed in the United States of America

Library of Congress Control Number: 2014932940

For all general information, please contact Arcadia Publishing:
Telephone 843-853-2070
Fax 843-853-0044
E-mail sales@arcadiapublishing.com
For customer service and orders:
Toll-Free 1-888-313-2665

Visit us on the Internet at www.arcadiapublishing.com

This book is dedicated to the pioneers of southern Colorado and to the Monte Vista Historical Society for keeping memories of the pioneers alive.

Contents

ACKNOWLEDGMENTS

The photographs of O.T. Davis presented in this book are from the collection of the Monte Vista Historical Society in Monte Vista, Colorado. Davis family heirs made the collection available to the historical society to share with the public, and the historical society has partnered with the author to publish the photographs in this book. Out of the hundreds of Davis photographs in the collection, the historical society selected 250 to be printed. Those prints are on display in archival notebooks at the historical society's headquarters at 111 Jefferson Street in Monte Vista. It is from those prints that the photographs in this book were selected.

The Monte Vista Historical Society was founded in 1987 as an outgrowth of the Monte Vista centennial celebration of 1986. The purpose of the historical society is to promote the historical development and preservation of the city of Monte Vista and the San Luis Valley. The historical society has been instrumental in helping acquire National Register of Historic Places and Colorado State Register of Historic Properties designation for 15 buildings in downtown Monte Vista.

The author would like to thank Peg Schall of the Monte Vista Historical Society for her assistance in providing access to the O.T. Davis photographs. Any errors or omissions in the photographic captions and historical text provided in this book are completely the responsibility of the author. Unless otherwise noted in the text, all photographs in the book are from the O.T. Davis collection of the Monte Vista Historical Society.

INTRODUCTION

When Colorado became a state on August 1, 1876, the southern portion of the state from Walsenburg west to Wolf Creek Pass (approximately 130 miles) was still a raw frontier, served only by stage lines and wagon roads. The first town in southern Colorado, San Luis, had only been established 25 years earlier, in 1851, when Spanish settlers arrived from New Mexico. Mexican land grants in the 1830s and 1840s had encouraged settlers to move into what was to become Colorado, but Ute Indian raids kept most settlers out of the area until the 1850s. The establishment of Fort Massachusetts in 1852 (it was replaced by Fort Garland in 1858) brought US troops to the area to help subdue the Ute raids, and Hispanic and Anglo settlers arrived in greater numbers after that.

Originally a part of Mexico, southern Colorado became a possession of the United States after the Mexican War ended in defeat for the Mexicans in 1848. When the Colorado Territory was carved out of the New Mexico Territory in 1861 with a southern border along the 37th parallel, the present-day boundaries of the state were set. Colorado became embroiled in the Civil War as a Union territory and was even called upon to send troops from Fort Garland to help quell a Texas Confederate invasion of New Mexico at Glorieta Pass, just east of Santa Fe. After the war, veterans from both sides of the conflict moved west in great numbers, seeking their fortunes in mining, ranching, and railroad building.

Not long after this early frontier period, Iowan Ory Thomas "O.T." Davis came on the scene in 1888 to record photographic views of mines, railroads, settlements, and people of southern Colorado. Much like his famous counterpart, frontier photographer William Henry Jackson, Davis hauled his huge box camera and darkroom supplies on the back of a mule into the high mountain passes and valleys. Unlike Jackson, however, Davis's photographic work was almost entirely focused on southern Colorado.

O.T. Davis was born in Oskaloosa, Iowa, on October 17, 1859, to parents Sylvester J. Davis (1835–1912) and Lavina Thomas Frantz Davis (1837–1915). Taking advantage of the Homestead Act of 1862, the Davis family moved to eastern Nebraska to claim 160 acres of farmland. As he grew up on the farm, O.T. developed a desire to join the thousands of people moving west to the Rockies. In 1881, at the age of 22, Davis joined a construction team building a rail line along the Republican River in southern Nebraska toward Denver. When he finally made it to Colorado in 1885, O.T. joined the operation of a copper mine on Pass Creek, just northwest of the small town of La Veta. Unfortunately, the mine soon played out, and Davis was forced to seek a new career.

In 1888, Davis obtained corporate commissions to photograph mines and railroads in the area. His first commission was to photograph the coal mines at Hastings, 20 miles south of Walsenburg. Later, the Denver & Rio Grande (D&RG) Railroad commissioned Davis to photograph the construction of its new standard-gauge line over La Veta Pass in 1899. (Davis had missed the construction of the D&RG narrow-gauge line over Veta Pass in 1877.) Davis supplemented his corporate income with income from portrait photography throughout his career.

From 1888 to 1893, Davis often set up his "roving" photography studio tent at either Walsenburg or La Veta. After marrying Rosalie Braun of Pueblo on November 21, 1888, he and his bride moved to La Veta. Rosalie, also known as Rosa, was a widow with three children, and O.T. gladly accepted these children into his family. He and Rosa had one child of their own, Edmond Theodore Davis, born on September 9, 1889. In 1893, O.T. and Rosa divorced, and Rosa moved to California, taking all four children with her. Heartbroken, O.T. moved to Walsenburg, where he started his Davis Home Gallery. There, he took photographs documenting the town's early development. On June 11, 1895, O.T. married Viola Wheeler of Walsenburg, and, although they had no children, they remained married until death.

In January 1906, O.T. and Viola moved from Walsenburg to Alamosa. As reported in the *Alamosa Journal*, O.T. set up his photography studio in a room over Ambler's real estate office. At the time, Alamosa was a boomtown, the center of the D&RG's railroad operations in the San Luis Valley, and opportunities for O.T.'s photography business expanded greatly. Davis was on hand to photograph scenes of Alamosa's railroad depot burning down in 1907, the construction of Adams State Normal School in 1923, and the building of a beautiful new US post office in 1935. Davis roamed across the San Luis Valley taking photographs of mines, ranches, irrigation networks, crops, and scenic roads. In May 1917, he moved his studio to the Emperius Building in downtown Alamosa, purchasing the photography business previously operated by C.B. Shepard. Later, he moved his studio to its final place of business, on Fourth Street, which was open until just before his death in 1945.

The photographs of O.T. Davis are an invaluable historical record of the development of the southern Colorado frontier. No other photographer produced as many photographs of the area. He captured scenes from early-day Walsenburg and La Veta; followed the D&RG Railroad over La Veta Pass and Cumbres Pass; photographed mines in the San Juan Mountains; traveled with road builders on Wolf Creek Pass in 1916; and recorded scenes of towns across the San Luis Valley. As the *Denver Post* once stated, "History comes alive in his photos."

As previously mentioned, O.T. Davis's career began with commissions to photograph mines and railroads in southern Colorado. Thus, his career depended upon the expansion of the Denver & Rio Grande Railroad across southern Colorado as it built lines south from Denver to the coalfields of Walsenburg and west to the silver mines of the San Juan Mountains. The D&RG Railroad was the brainchild of Gen. William Jackson Palmer, a Union veteran of the Civil War decorated with the Medal of Honor. Born in Delaware in 1836, Palmer grew up in Philadelphia, eventually working on the Pennsylvania Railroad, where he developed his railroad expertise. After the Civil War, Palmer was the construction manager for the Kansas Pacific Railroad as it built west from Kansas City, Missouri, to Denver. Upon reaching Denver, Palmer explored routes south hoping to fulfill his dream of building a railroad from Denver to Mexico City.

Backed by wealthy New York investors, Palmer incorporated the Denver & Rio Grande Railroad in 1870. He planned to build a narrow-gauge rail line three feet in width, as opposed to the standard gauge of four feet, eight and one-half inches. The narrow gauge would allow for construction on the steeper grades and tighter curves that Palmer knew he would encounter in the mountains of southern Colorado. In 1871, a total of 75.5 miles of rail were laid from Denver south to the new town of Colorado Springs. In 1872, an additional 44 miles were completed south to Pueblo. Construction was then halted by the financial panic of 1873 and did not begin again until 1876, with the completion of 50 miles to Walsenburg and another 16 miles west to La Veta. From there, the tortuous grade west over Veta Pass was conquered, and the narrow-gauge rails reached the new town of Alamosa, in the San Luis Valley, in 1878. The railroad then followed its namesake, the Rio Grande, west to the San Juan Mountains mining country. Another branch led south from Alamosa to Antonito and then west over Cumbres Pass, reaching Durango in 1881 and the fabulously rich silver mines of Silverton in 1882.

New towns followed the development of the D&RG Railroad westward, and already established settlements grew larger. West from Veta Pass, the towns of Fort Garland, Blanca, Alamosa, Monte Vista, Del Norte, and South Fork developed along the railroad. O.T. Davis photographed all of these towns in their infancy. The D&RG also built a line across Poncha Pass, at the north end of the San Luis Valley, south to Villa Grove in 1881. When the line expanded farther south to Alamosa in 1890, the new towns of Moffat, Hooper, and Mosca sprang up along the line. O.T. Davis was there to photograph these new towns. As the railroad reached mines in the San Juan Mountains, Davis was on hand to photograph mines in places as far-flung as Jasper on the west, Creede on the north, and Orient on the east. Mining and the D&RG Railroad went hand in hand, and Davis was there to record this historic development.

O.T. Davis's photography studio in Alamosa was near the center of the vast San Luis Valley, which stretches approximately 100 miles from north to south and about 60 miles from east to west. It is bordered on the west by the San Juan Mountains and on the east by the Sangre de Cristo Mountains, both ranges that have some of Colorado's highest peaks, at over 14,000 feet of elevation. The average elevation of this high mountain valley is 7,500 feet. A unique feature of the valley is the Great Sand Dunes, created by wind blowing from west to east across the valley, carrying sand particles that deposited at the base of the Sangre de Cristos, creating America's tallest sand dunes, which can reach 750 feet high. Annual precipitation in the valley is 10 inches or less, officially qualifying it as a desert climatic region. However, underground water is abundant, and artesian wells bring water to the surface for irrigation. Canals dug from the Rio Grande and other surface streams also provide irrigation. All of this irrigation produces abundant crops in the San Luis Valley, including lettuce, potatoes, cauliflower, barley, wheat, and peas. O.T. Davis produced wonderful photographs of these crops and their transportation on the D&RG. His photographs of artesian wells spewing water illustrate the abundance of groundwater available.

Southern Colorado possesses some of the state's finest mountain scenery, and O.T. Davis captured spectacular mountain views in his photographs. His scenes of the north side of Blanca Peak are particularly striking. As automobiles gradually replaced horses and wagons in the early 1900s, Davis exhibited a particular fascination with the new contraptions. He followed automobiles across the San Luis Valley, snapping photographs of them crossing irrigation ditches and navigating impossibly narrow mountain roads in the high country. Davis was also on hand to record the opening of the road over Wolf Creek Pass in 1916.

O.T. Davis was indeed fortunate to be located in southern Colorado at the time of its frontier development, and we are likewise fortunate to have these lovely photographs preserved by the Monte Vista Historical Society, which has allowed their reproduction in this book.

For more information on Walsenburg and La Veta, please see the author's Arcadia book Images of America: *Around the Spanish Peaks*. For more information on mining and ranching in the area around the Great Sand Dunes in the San Luis Valley, please see the author's Arcadia book Images of America: *Great Sand Dunes National Park*.

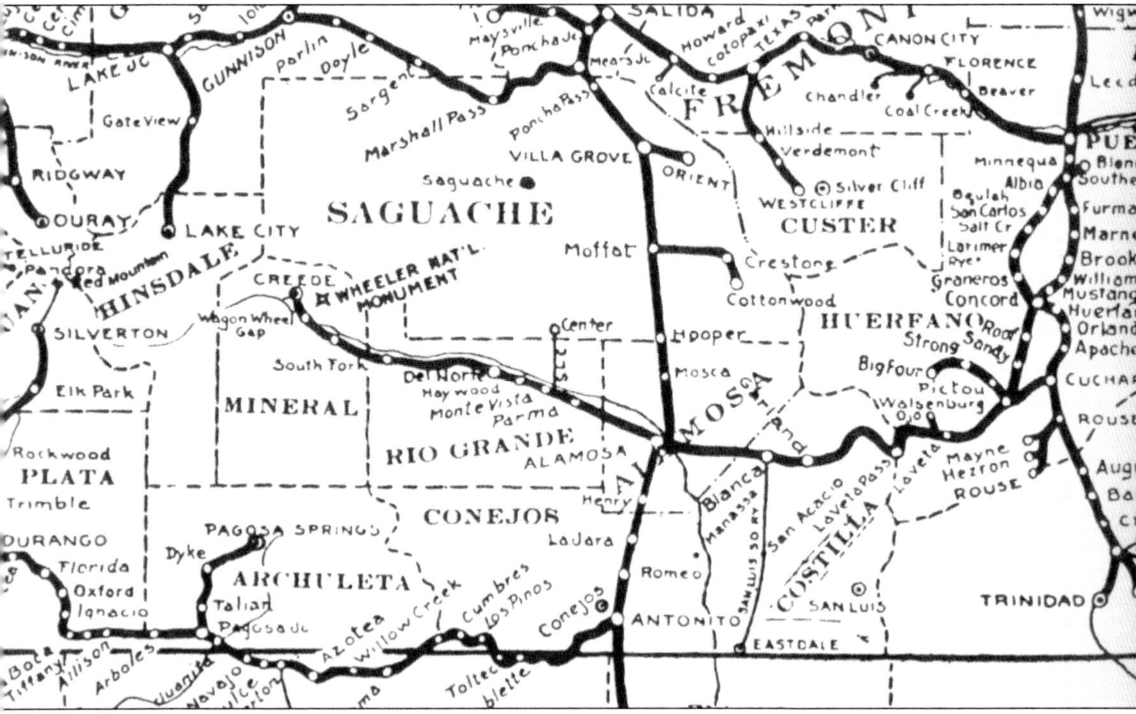

1916 Denver & Rio Grande Railroad Map. Almost all of the places mentioned in this book are shown on this map. (Author's collection.)

One

Ory T. Davis
"A Real Live Wire"

When O.T. Davis came to Colorado to work in the Pass Creek copper mines in 1885, his family came with him. His father, Sylvester, and mother, Lavina, gave up farming in Nebraska to join Ory in Colorado. Also in the traveling party were Sylvester's brothers Isaac and Merrick and their wives. O.T.'s brother Corin and his wife, Martha "Mattie," also appear in early photographs of the Davis family on Pass Creek. O.T.'s parents eventually moved to La Veta in 1896. O.T. married Rosalie Braun of Pueblo on November 21, 1888, and they made their home in La Veta after the Pass Creek copper mines played out. O.T. began his photography business at that time. Davis gained a family when he married Rosalie, as she was a widow with three children. Davis and Rosalie had one child of their own, Edmond Theodore Davis, born on September 9, 1889. Unfortunately, O.T. and Rosalie divorced in 1893. Davis then set up a permanent studio, known as the Davis Home Gallery, in Walsenburg, where he married his second wife, Viola Wheeler, in 1895.

Davis was paid by mining corporations and railroads to photograph their business enterprises, and he also had a thriving portrait business wherever he set up his studio. He made his living as a photographer from 1888 until his death in 1945, and he supplemented his income by working in various mines along the way. In anticipation of Davis moving his photography studio to Alamosa in 1906, the *Alamosa Journal* wrote on December 22, 1905, that "his work ranks with the best in southern Colorado." By 1917, the *Journal*'s opinion of Davis had greatly increased, as they wrote on May 10 of that year, "O.T. is a live wire and is one of the best photographers in the state." His photographic record of the southern Colorado frontier certainly backs up that compliment from the *Journal*.

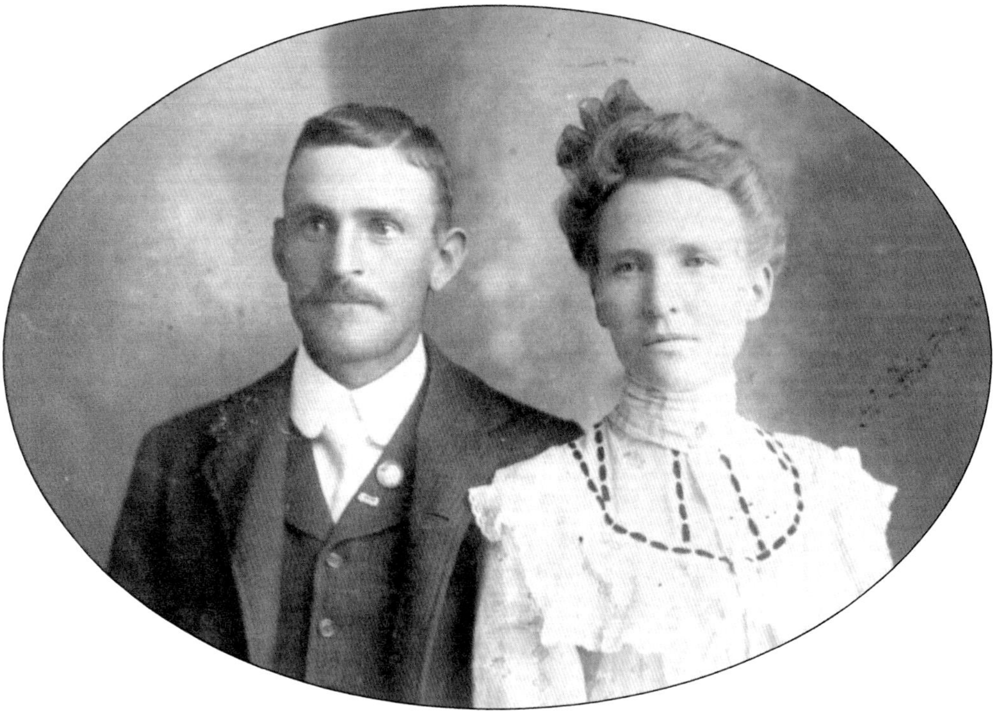

Wedding Portrait, 1888. O.T. Davis and his bride, Rosalie Braun, of Pueblo, were married on November 21, 1888. Rosa was a widow with three children whom O.T. welcomed into his family. O.T. and Rosa had one child of their own, Edmond Theodore Davis, born on September 9, 1889.

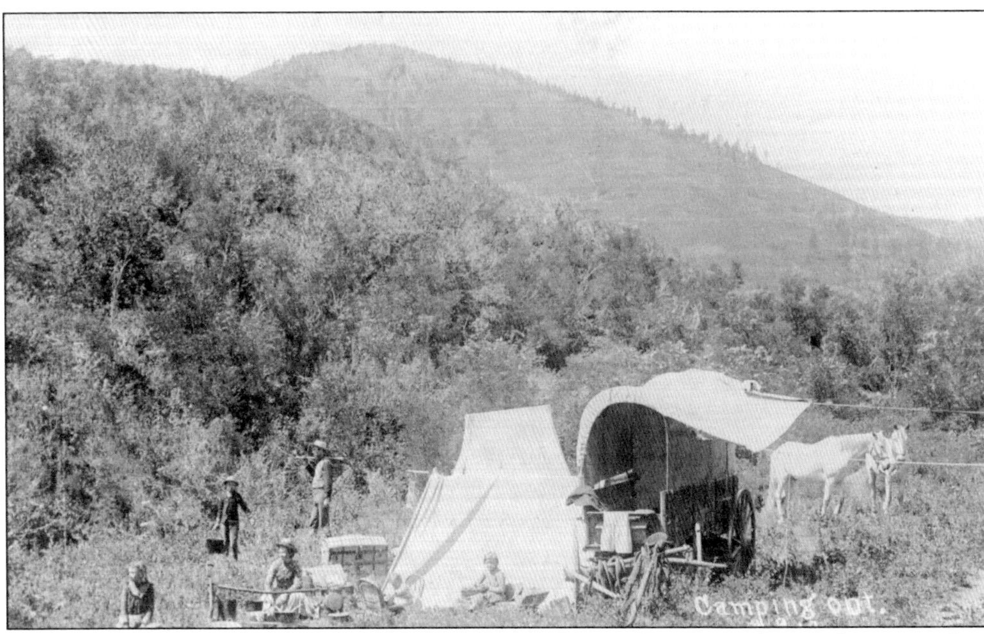

Davis Family Campout, 1891. This is likely near the Pass Creek area, northwest of La Veta, where O.T. first settled in 1885 when he worked in the Pass Creek copper mines. Pictured here are O.T. and his wife, Rosa, her three children, and their young son Edmond (at bottom left of tent).

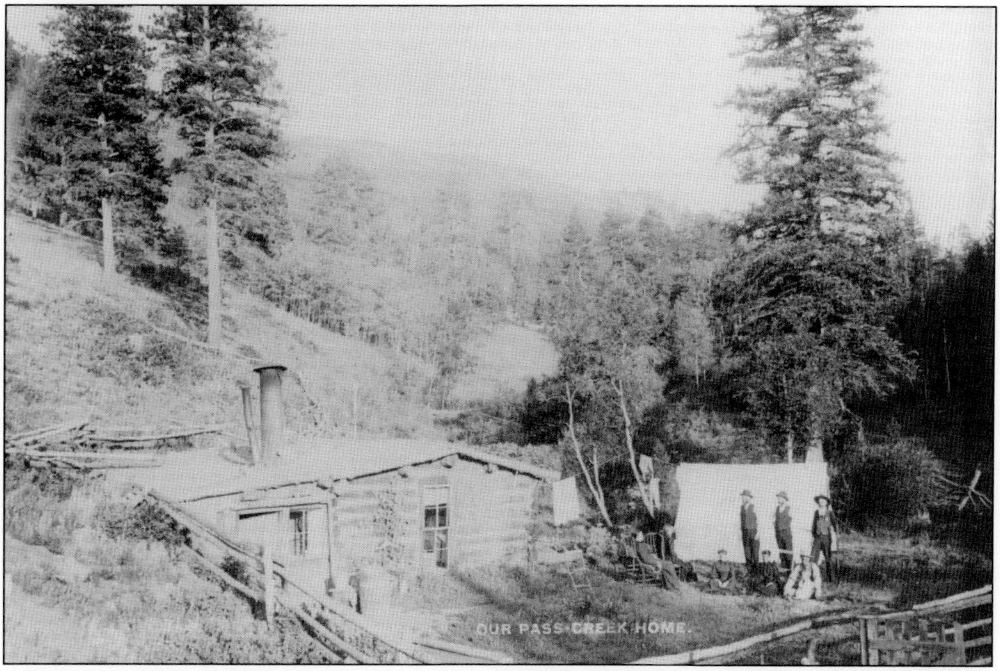

Pass Creek Home, 1893. This was home for many of O.T.'s relatives who moved to Colorado with him in 1885. In the photograph, the following relatives are identified, from left to right, along with their relationship to O.T.: (sitting in the chairs) Sue Davis (aunt) and Ruth Brown Davis (grandmother); (sitting on ground) Abbie Davis (aunt), Mattie Davis (sister-in-law), and Corin Davis (brother), holding his son Floyd; (standing) two unidentified men and Merrick Davis (uncle).

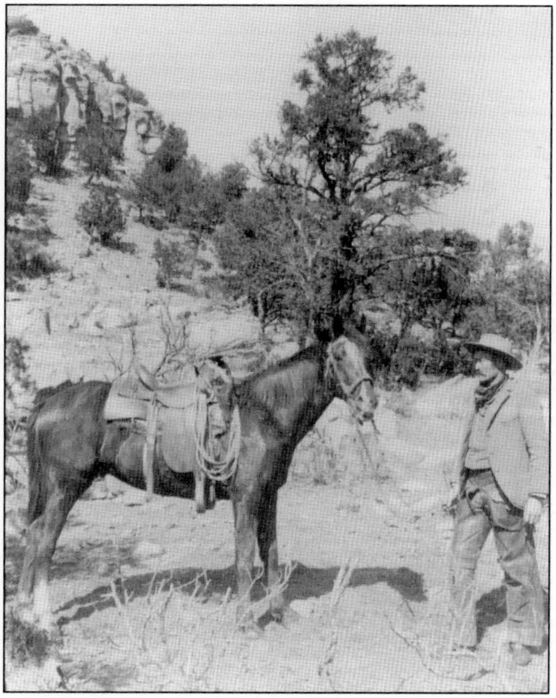

Near Hastings Coal Mines, 1893. O.T. stands with his horse near the coal mines where he was first commissioned to take photographs. Hastings was about 20 miles south of Walsenburg. The area from Walsenburg south to Trinidad was the home of many large underground coal mines during this time period.

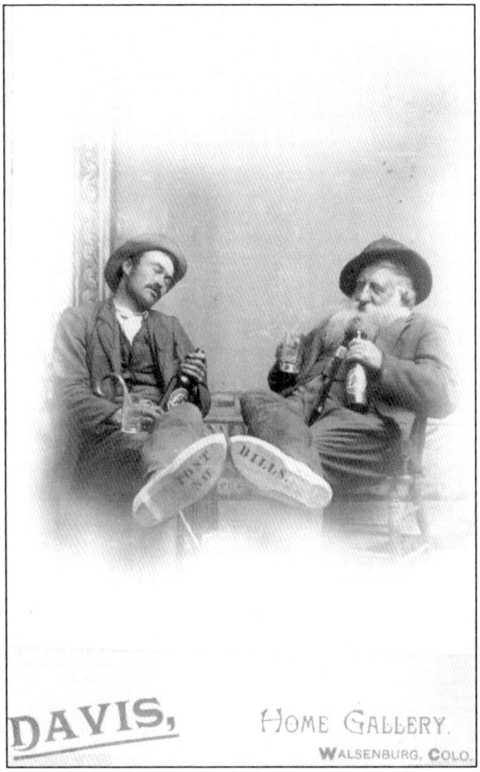

"JUST GOOFING AROUND," C. 1893. In 1893, O.T. (left), recently divorced from his wife, Rosa, set up his Davis Home Gallery in Walsenburg. Perhaps he was drowning his marital sorrows by sharing a drink with his grandfather Sylvester Davis. The message on the bottom of their boots is "Post No Bills."

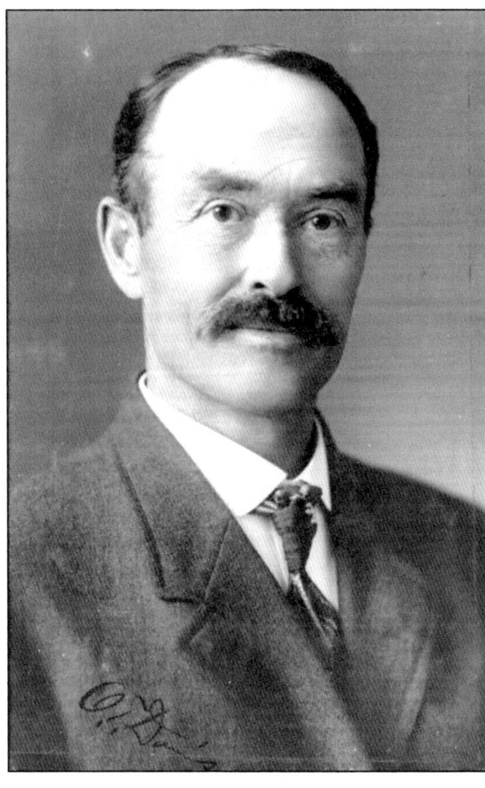

O.T. DAVIS PORTRAIT, C. 1906. The photographer of this splendid portrait of O.T. Davis is unidentified. It was probably taken in 1906 or later in Davis's Alamosa studio by a capable assistant in his business.

Two

Railroads
"Sluggin' It Out on La Veta Pass"

O.T. Davis followed the progress of the Denver & Rio Grande Railroad across southern Colorado. In 1899, he was commissioned by the railroad to photograph the construction of the new standard-gauge line west from La Veta. The route followed Middle Creek and crossed a pass that became known as La Veta Pass; the old narrow-gauge route had crossed Veta Pass just a bit to the north. The new route had a maximum grade of 3 percent, compared to 4.7 percent on the narrow-gauge line, and it shaved a mile off of the old route. The D&RG converted the mainline from the northeast into La Veta to standard gauge in 1890. Thus, from 1890 to 1899, freight loads had to be transferred from standard-gauge cars to narrow-gauge cars in La Veta for the trip west over Veta Pass. This was extremely inefficient and costly, creating the need for the new standard-gauge line west over the new La Veta Pass in 1899.

Freight shipments on the D&RG continued to increase throughout the 1890s and early 1900s. The railroad shipped mineral products east from the San Juan Mountains and foodstuffs east from the San Luis Valley, while manufactured goods and mining equipment were shipped west. There was so much freight traffic over La Veta Pass that the battle of the steam engines to haul the loads over the steep pass was referred to by author Stephen Rasmussen in his book *The Rio Grande's La Veta Pass Route* as "sluggin' it out on La Veta Pass."

After moving his studio to Alamosa in 1906, O.T. Davis continued photographing the D&RG across the San Luis Valley and into the mountains. New towns sprang up along the rail lines, and Davis photographed Moffat, Hooper, and Mosca in the northern portion of the San Luis Valley. To the south, he photographed scenes of the rail line over Cumbres Pass. West from Alamosa, the towns of Monte Vista, Del Norte, South Fork, and Creede were also featured in his photographs.

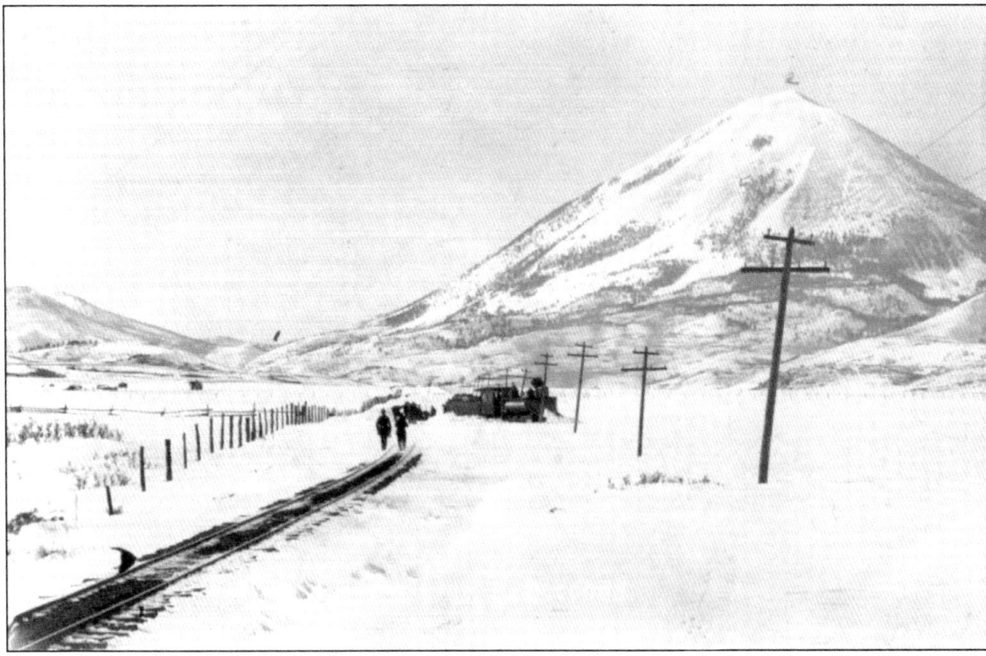

Off the Tracks, February 13, 1896. D&RG narrow-gauge locomotive No. 54 slid off the tracks west of La Veta when a rail broke loose. O.T. Davis wrote the following identifying numbers on the photograph: 1. Veta Pass and 2. Veta Mountain, also known as "Old Baldy." Today, the area of this scene is easily viewed from US Highway 160 west.

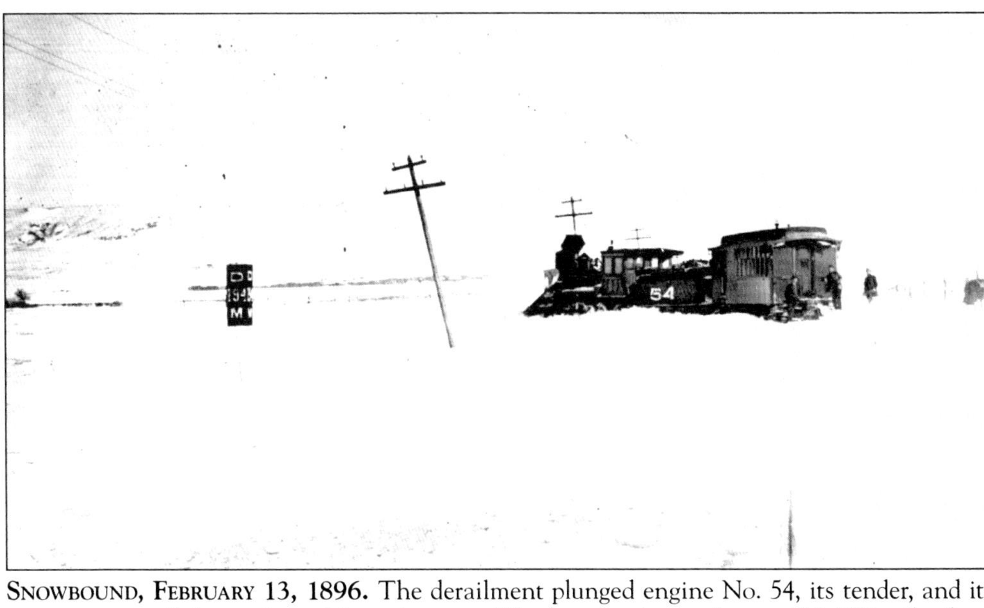

Snowbound, February 13, 1896. The derailment plunged engine No. 54, its tender, and its passenger car off the tracks and into the snow. The location is at milepost 194 (194 miles from Denver). Davis noted that this snowstorm closed Veta Pass for almost two months.

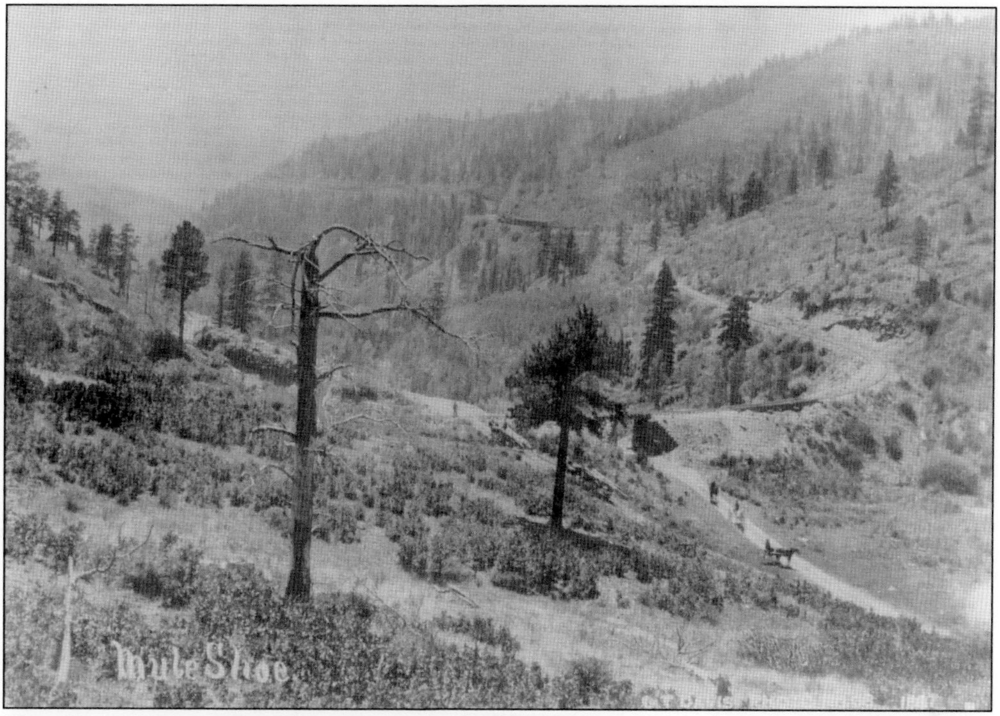

Mule Shoe Curve, 1887. The narrow-gauge railroad gained elevation as it switched back around Mule Shoe Curve heading west to Veta Pass. This view looking southeast shows travelers on Baldy Scott's toll road, which passed under the railroad bridge on the curve. The toll road was completed over Veta Pass in 1870, seven years before the railroad.

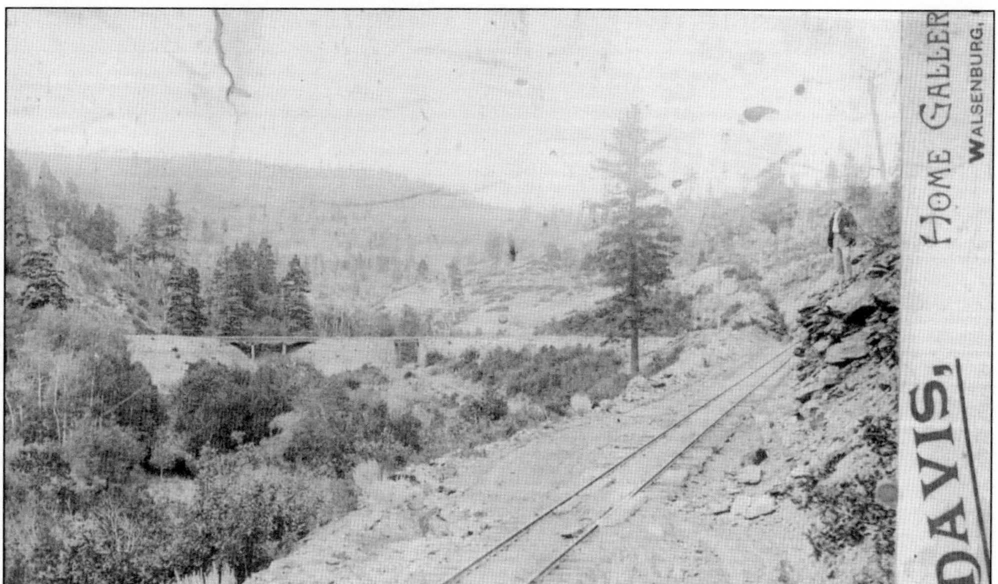

Mule Shoe Curve, 1896. This northwest view of Mule Shoe Curve illustrates the obstacles that had to be overcome in building a railroad over the mountains. This difficult route was replaced in 1899 by a standard-gauge route farther south. Mule Shoe Curve can be traversed by car today on a gravel road crossing old La Veta Pass.

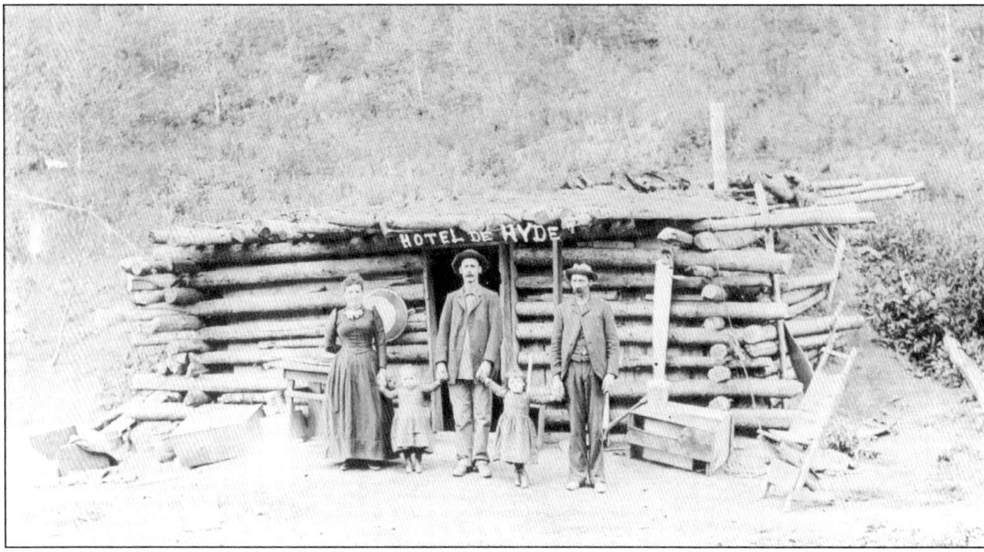

"Hotel De Hyde," 1889. This hostelry was located at Camp Berry on Mule Shoe Curve. O.T. Davis was having a bit of fun with this photograph, as this "hotel" would not have served D&RG passengers, who would have traveled straight through from La Veta to Alamosa. The family is unidentified.

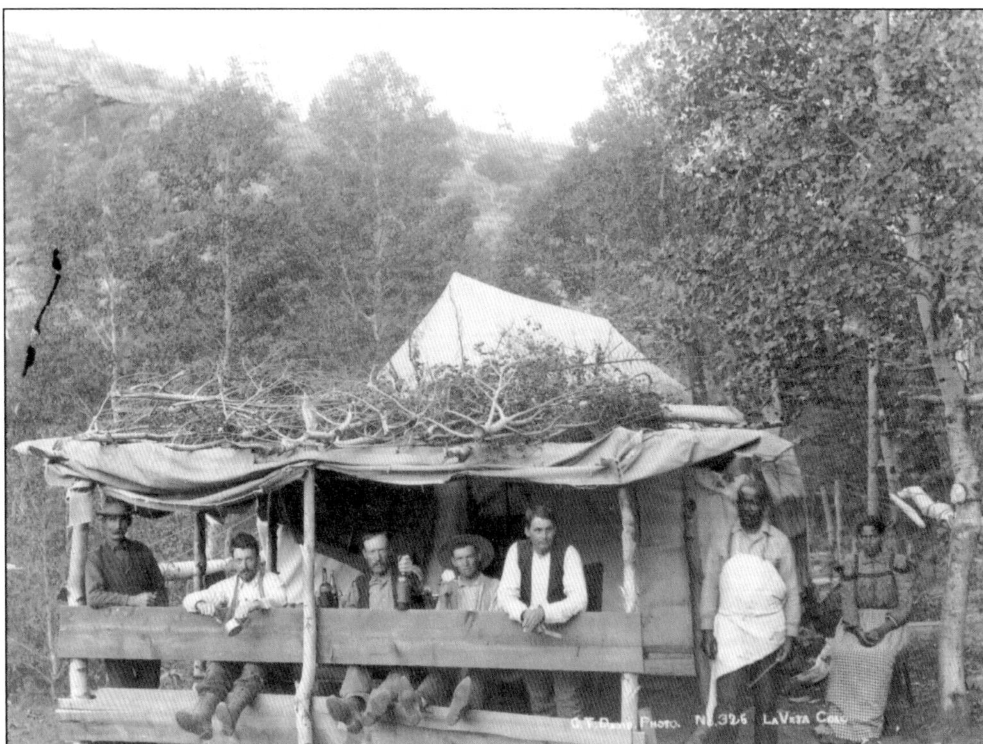

D&RG Construction Camp, 1899. During the construction of the standard-gauge line over La Veta Pass in 1899, construction workers were housed in tent camps. O.T. Davis noted that "they endured hard living conditions, but look happy." Note the black couple on the right, who may have served as camp cooks.

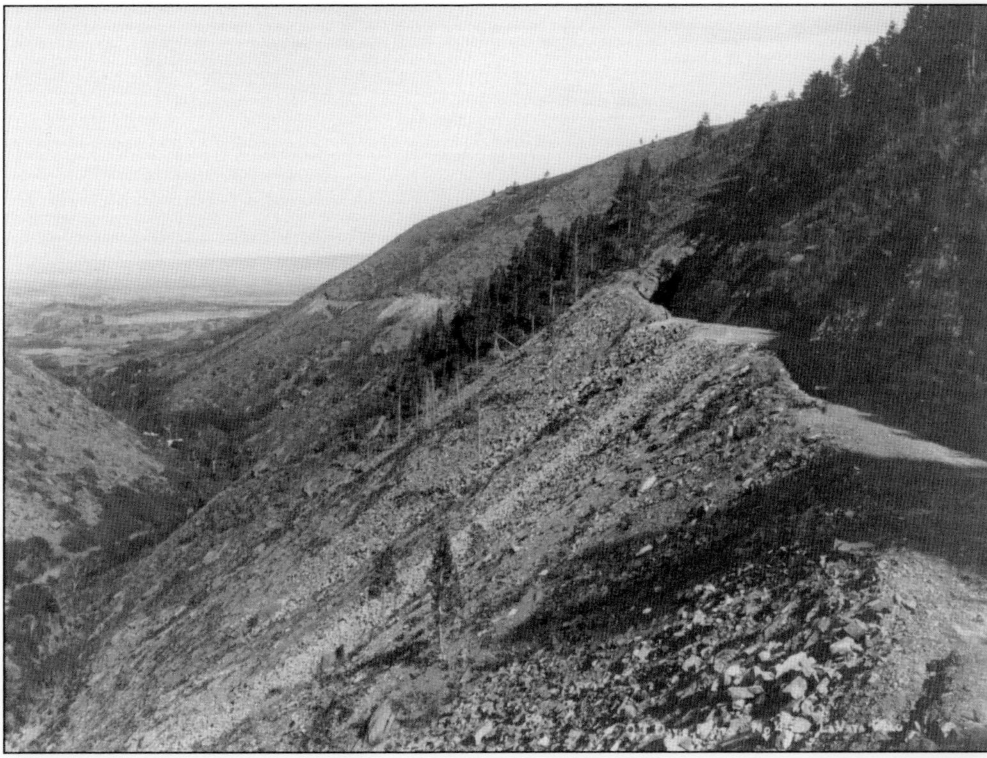

D&RG LINE CONSTRUCTION, 1899. The new standard-gauge line over La Veta Pass required three tunnels. In this view east toward La Veta, the lower tunnel can be seen toward the upper right. It is 655 feet in length. Construction worker tents are located along Middle Creek to the left.

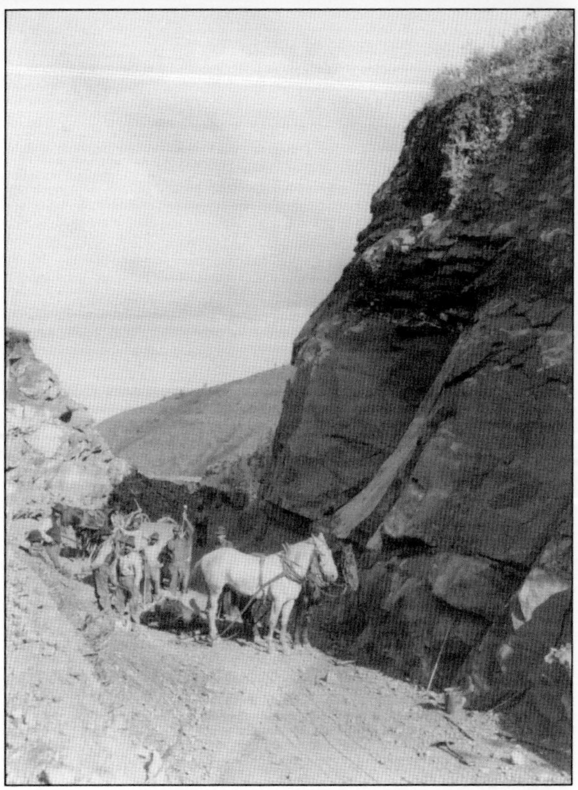

NICOLETT'S CUT, 1899. This cut through the rocks was located west of the lower tunnel. To create the cut, the construction crew used horses, mules, wagons, shovels, and black powder. O.T. Davis was commissioned by the D&RG to photograph the construction of the line.

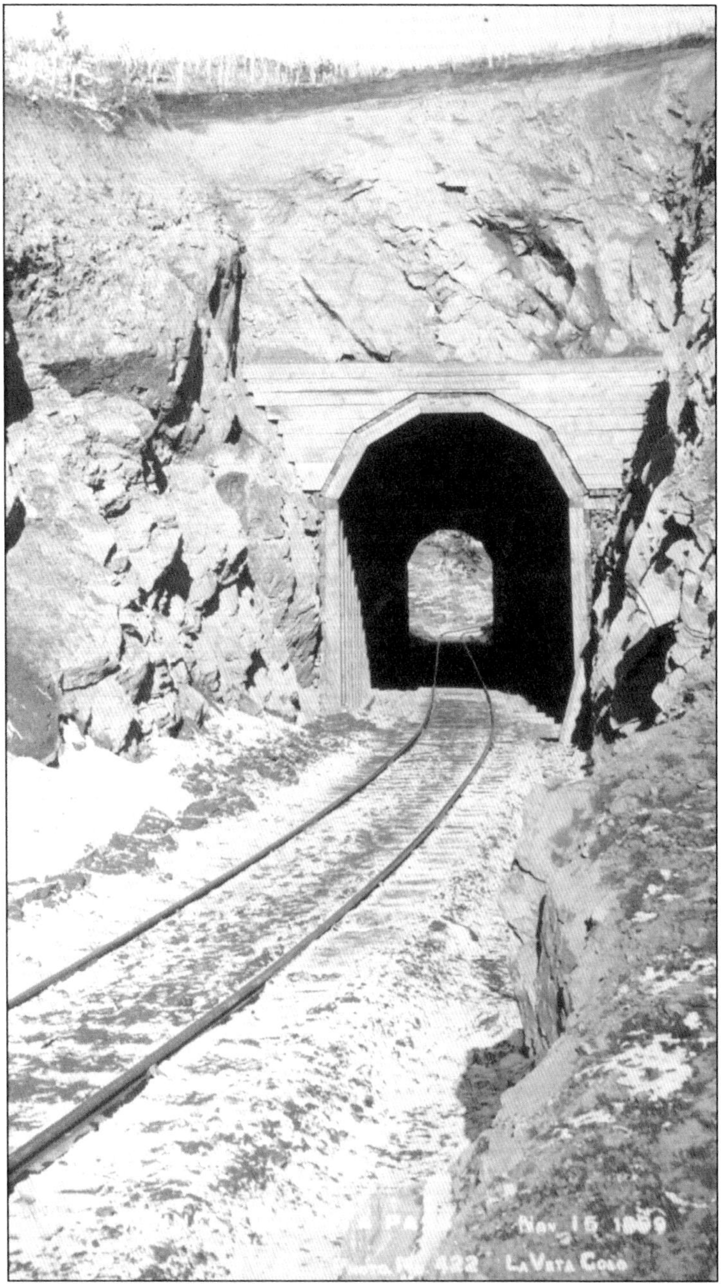

La Veta Pass Tunnel, November 15, 1899. O.T. Davis did not identify which of the three tunnels this was. Its short length suggests that it is the upper tunnel, which was 234 feet long, while the middle tunnel was 338 feet long. Construction at the upper tunnel is shown on the following two pages. The upper tunnel was a "problem child" for the D&RG. It was plagued by roof cave-ins, one of which killed a worker. Then, on January 13, 1915, the wooden lining of the tunnel caught fire from the sparks of a passenger train. The raging fire destroyed the interior of the tunnel, closing the line for a month. Finally, in 1929, the railroad gave up the battle with the upper tunnel and "daylighted" it. Davis took this photograph three days after the line opened on November 12, 1899.

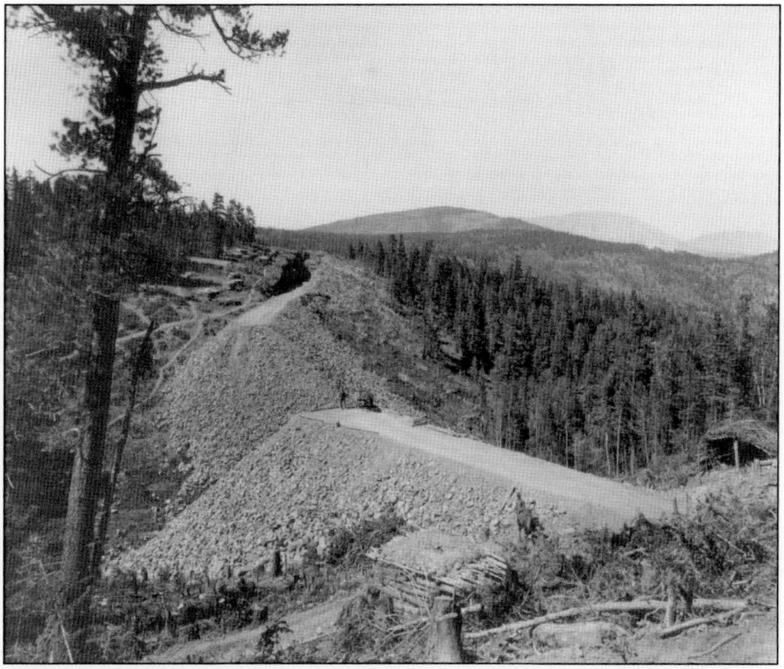

UPPER TUNNEL, 1899. The upper tunnel was constructed at an elevation of 9,160 feet at milepost 206.3. Devil's Gulch had to be bridged to reach the tunnel. Davis's photograph shows the amount of rock fill used in the gulch for approaches to the bridge, which would cross the remaining gap.

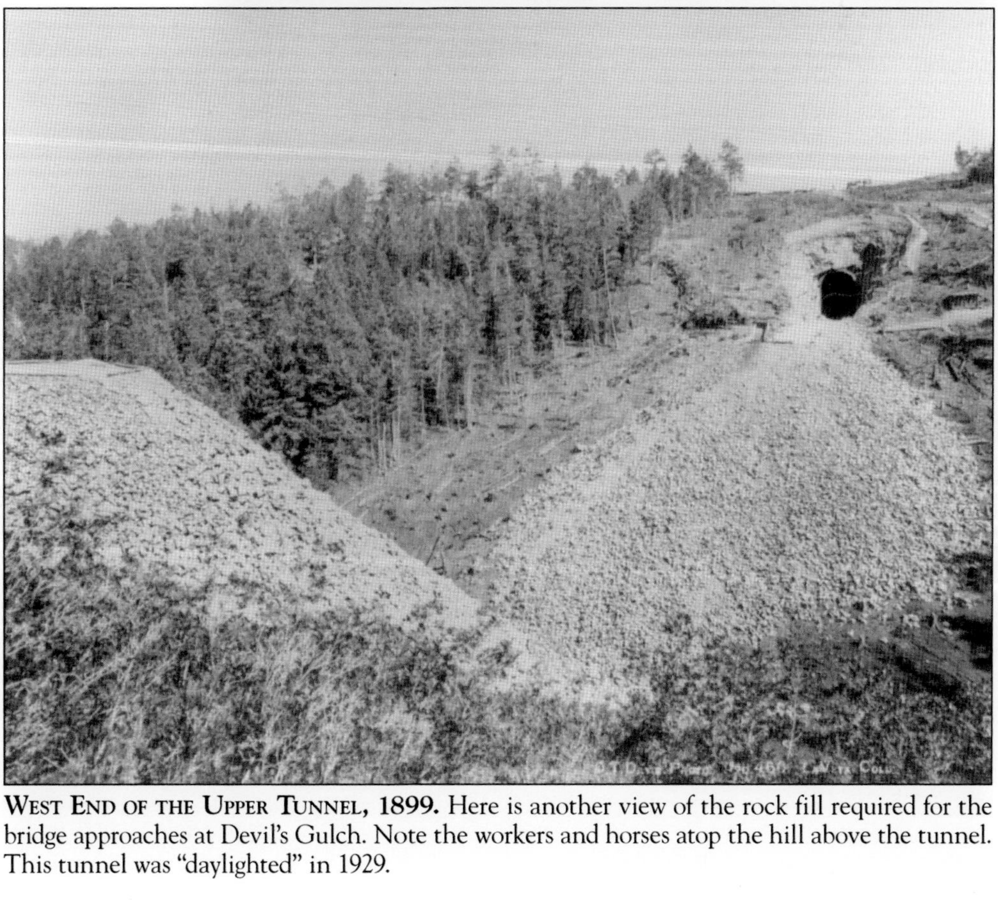

WEST END OF THE UPPER TUNNEL, 1899. Here is another view of the rock fill required for the bridge approaches at Devil's Gulch. Note the workers and horses atop the hill above the tunnel. This tunnel was "daylighted" in 1929.

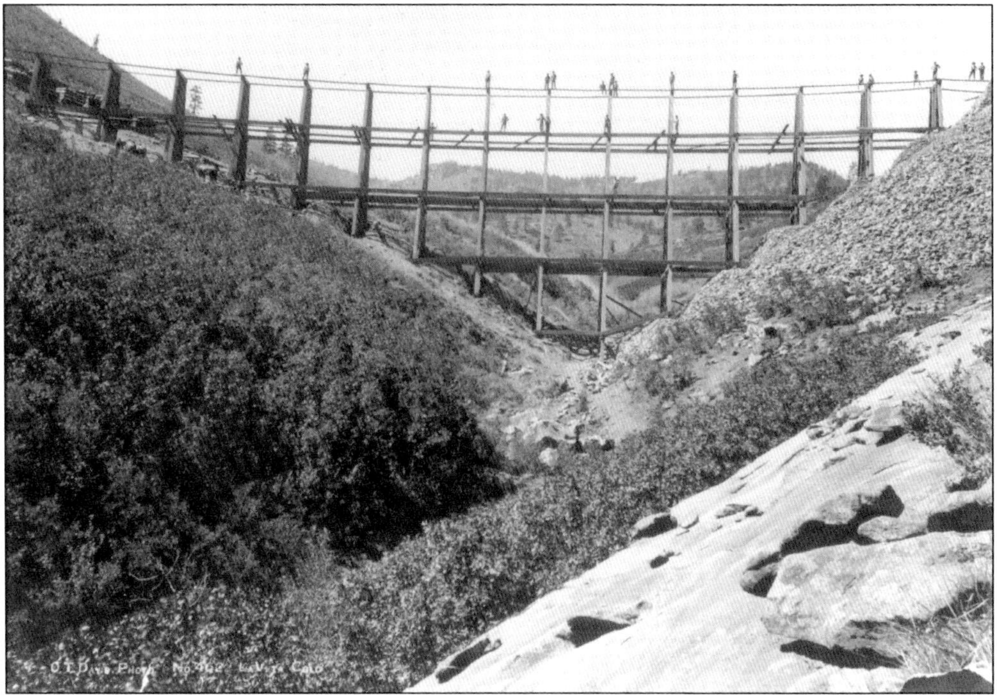

DEVIL'S GULCH TRESTLE, 1899. O.T. Davis stood in the dry gulch with his camera and took this photograph of 22 workers on the trestle. The D&RG built 26 wooden trestles in 27 miles over La Veta Pass.

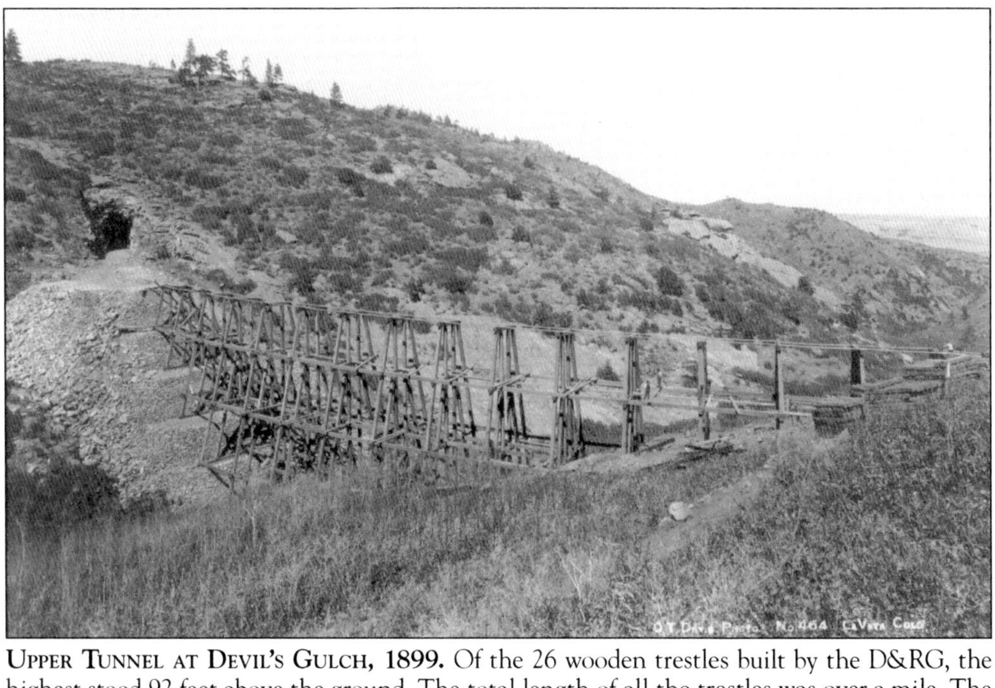

UPPER TUNNEL AT DEVIL'S GULCH, 1899. Of the 26 wooden trestles built by the D&RG, the highest stood 92 feet above the ground. The total length of all the trestles was over a mile. The trestles were costly to build and maintain. The D&RG began a program of filling in the trestles in 1912; by 1927, they had all been filled in.

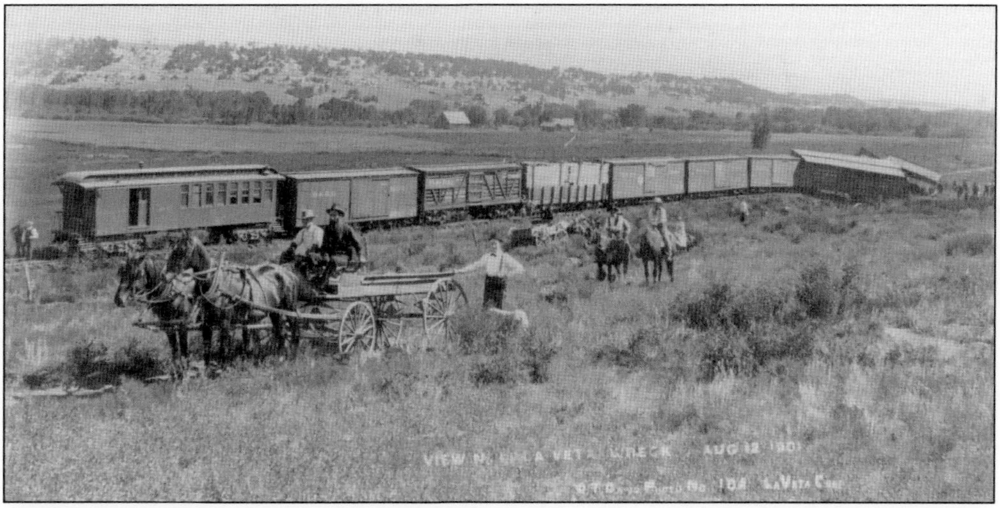

D&RG Train Wreck, August 12, 1901. This catastrophic wreck one mile east of La Veta was caused when the boiler of the locomotive exploded. The corpse of engineer Wood is in the wagon. Fireman Maples, found nearby, survived for eight hours before perishing from his injuries.

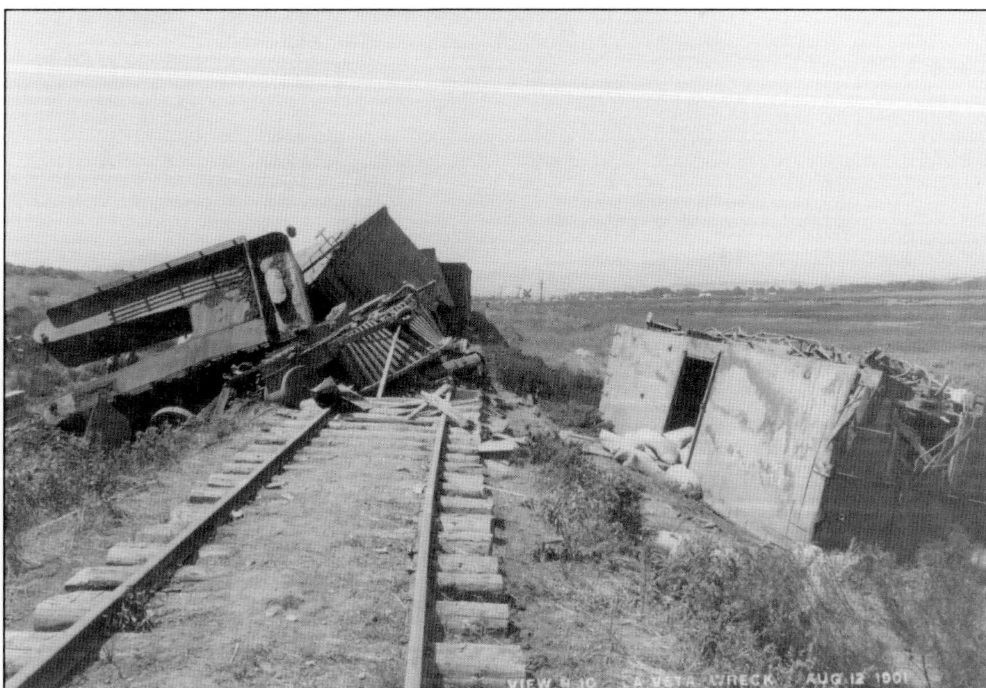

Remains of Train Wreck, August 12, 1901. The view from the front end of the train shows the cowcatcher tilting off the tracks, with the upended tender to the left. A boxcar is to the right, spilling its contents. Buildings in La Veta can be seen in the right background.

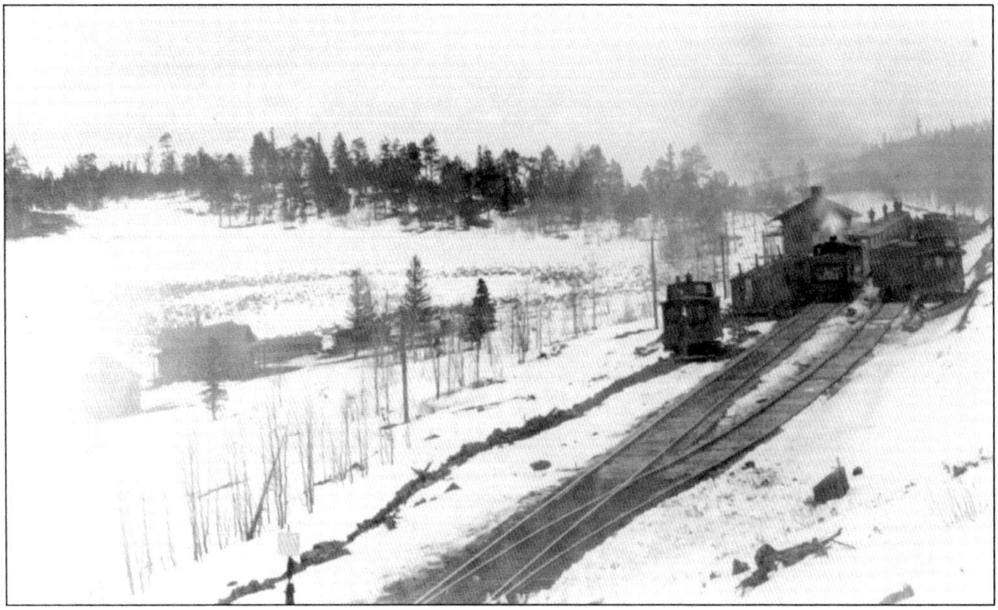

La Veta Pass, 1899. Not long after the opening of the standard-gauge line on November 12, 1899, O.T. Davis took this photograph of the depot at the pass. This view looking east shows a passenger train stopped at the depot. The depot building had previously stood at Placer, on the old narrow-gauge line, and the D&RG hauled it up to La Veta Pass.

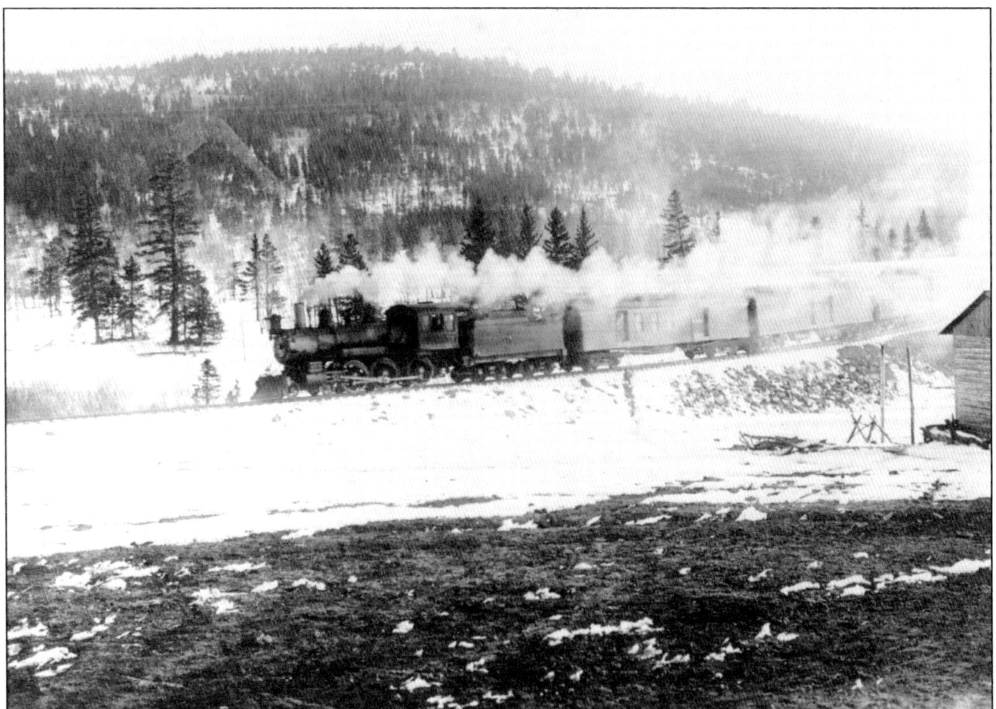

La Veta Pass, c. 1912. O.T. Davis returned to the pass several years later and took this terrific shot of a 4-6-0 steam engine barreling west with a passenger train consist. La Veta Pass, at an elevation of 9,242 feet, was lower than the narrow-gauge route over Veta Pass (elevation 9,400 feet).

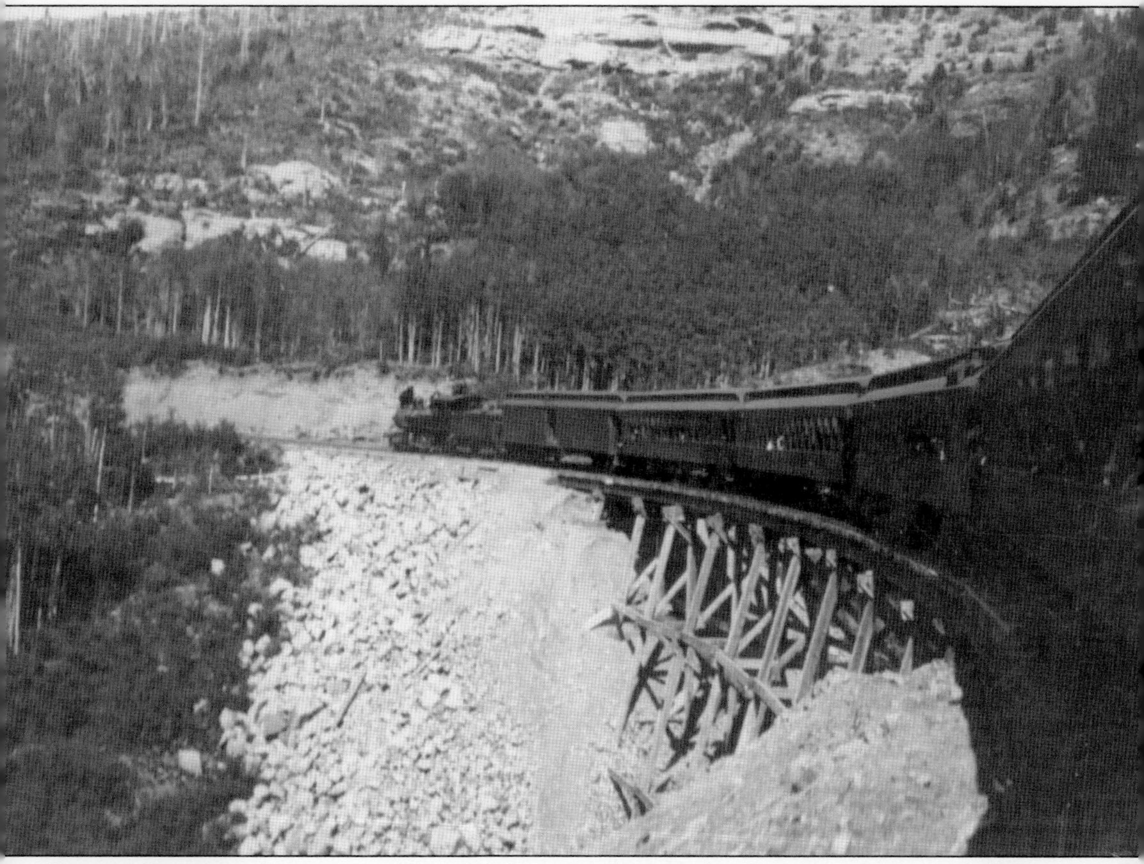

DAYTIME PASSENGER SERVICE, C. 1900–1910. Daytime photographs of passenger service on La Veta Pass, such as this one, are extremely rare. From the very beginning of service in 1899, almost all passenger train service was routed over the pass at night. Passenger trains left Denver about 6:30 p.m. and arrived in Walsenburg about 1:00 a.m. They then left La Veta at 2:20 a.m. and arrived in Alamosa at 5:35 a.m. From there, passengers could continue on to Durango, arriving at 5:00 p.m. From December 1901 to May 1909, "accommodation" trains ran from La Veta to Alamosa and back in daylight to serve local passengers. This undated Davis photograph could be such a train. Or it could be the *San Luis Valley Express*, which crossed the pass in daylight hours for only four months in 1910. Freight traffic was so heavy on the line that locomotive power was taken away from daylight passenger trains and assigned to freight trains. Daylight passenger service over La Veta Pass did not begin again until February 1, 1951.

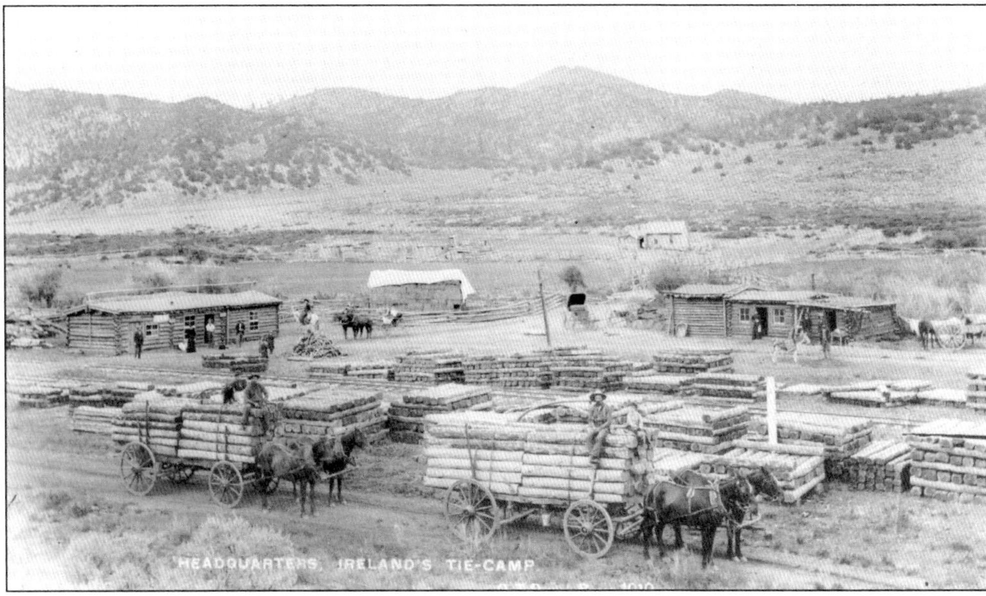

IRELAND'S TIE CAMP, C. 1910. Timber from the Trinchera Estate (see page 54) was harvested for railroad ties and processed at Ireland's tie camp at Mortimer. A siding on the D&RG located at the former site of Garland City (six miles northeast of Fort Garland), Mortimer flourished in 1877 and 1878 during construction of the narrow gauge to Alamosa.

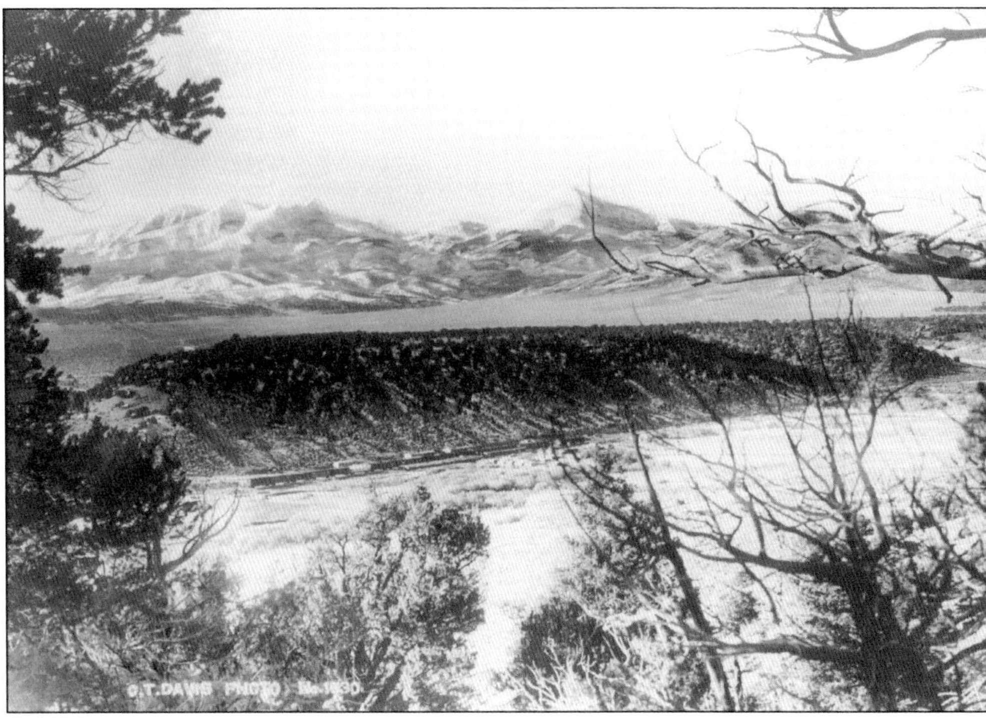

MORTIMER SIDING AND TIE CAMP, 1914. Freight cars are parked at the siding, ready for loading from Ireland's tie camp. Towering above the siding are two of the Sangre de Cristo Mountains' "fourteeners," Mount Lindsey (14,042 feet) on the right and Blanca Peak (14,345 feet) on the left.

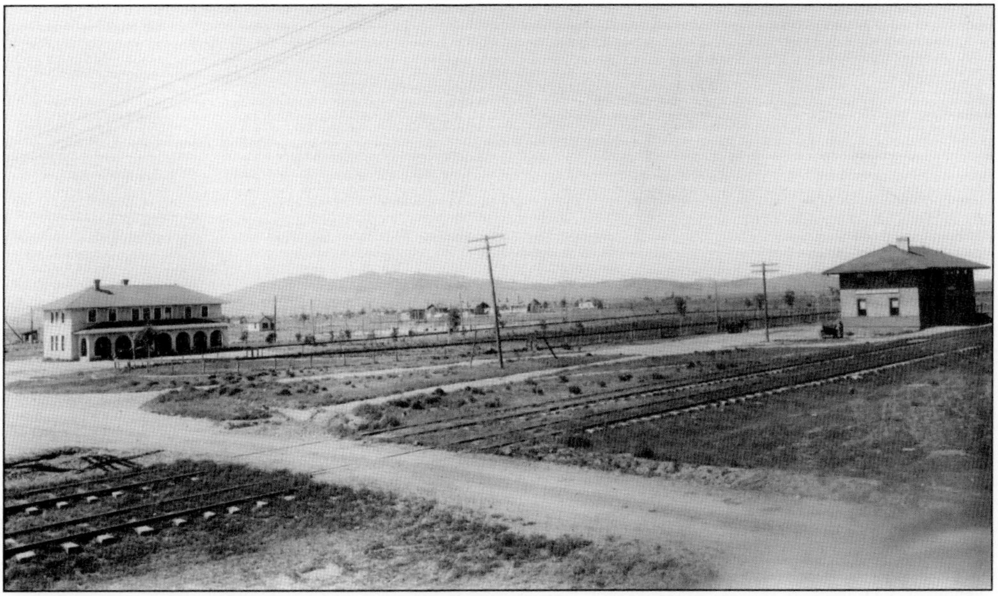

San Acacio, 1915. The Beaubien Hotel (left) and the San Acacio depot (right) were located 15.8 miles south of Blanca on the San Luis Southern Railroad. This independent line began operations in April 1910 on a 31-mile length of standard-gauge track from Blanca to the New Mexico border, serving farms and ranches in the area.

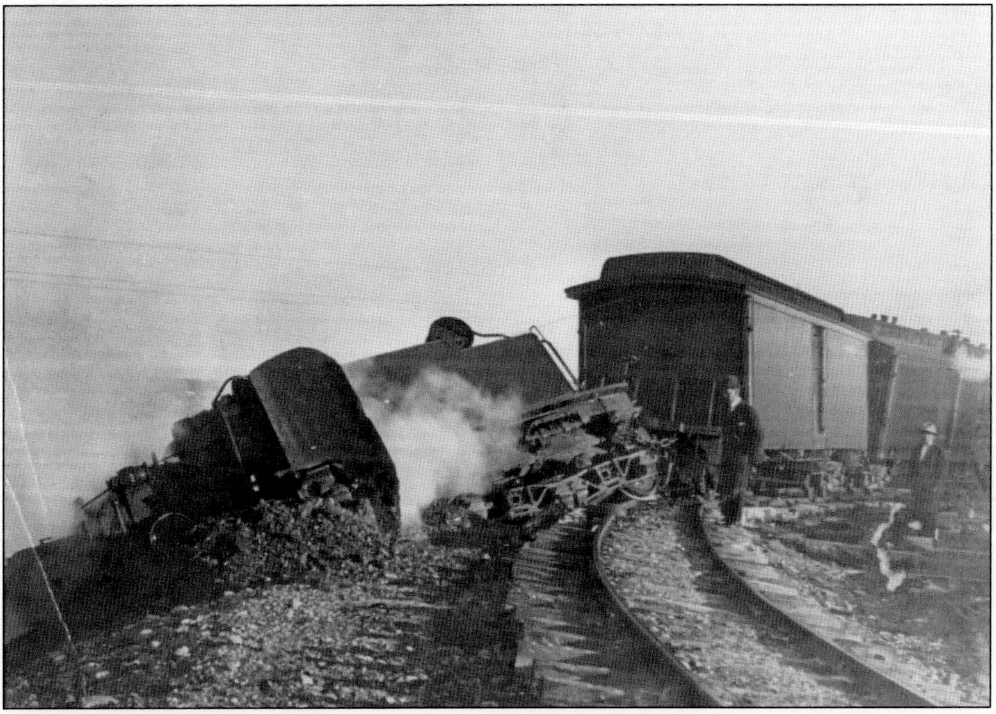

Cumbres Pass Wreck, c. 1910. Locomotive and tender have derailed to the left in this dramatic scene on Cumbres Pass. The D&RG completed its narrow-gauge line over Cumbres Pass (10,015 feet) from Antonito to Durango in 1881. This section of the line was never converted to standard gauge. *Cumbres* is Spanish for "summits."

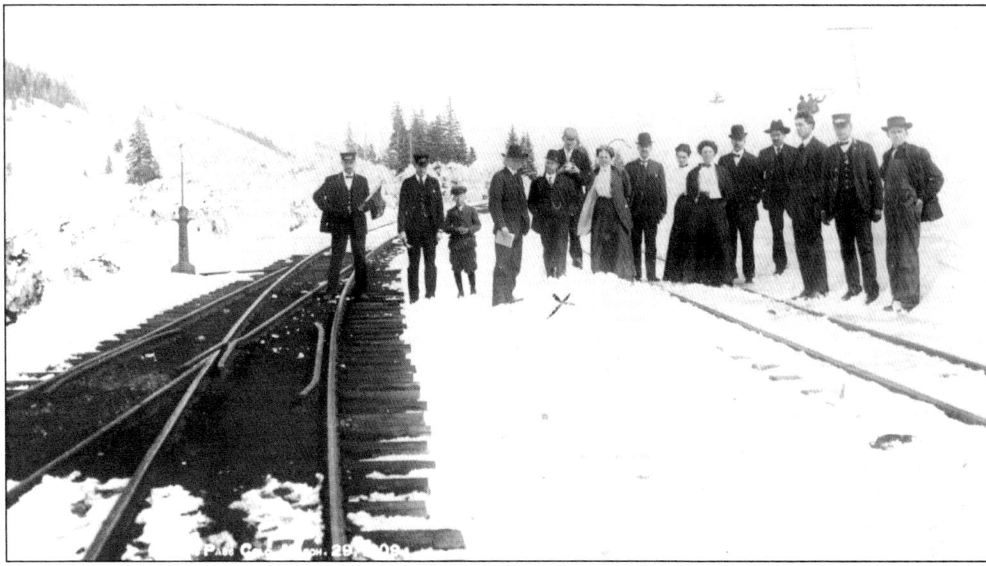

F.A. WADLEIGH GROUP, MARCH 28, 1909. O.T. Davis rode the D&RG narrow gauge to Cumbres Pass with this group on a snowy March day. Frank A. Wadleigh was a general passenger agent for the D&RG at the time. Passenger service continued over Cumbres Pass until 1951. Freight service, hauling lumber, sheep, cattle, and agricultural products, continued until 1968.

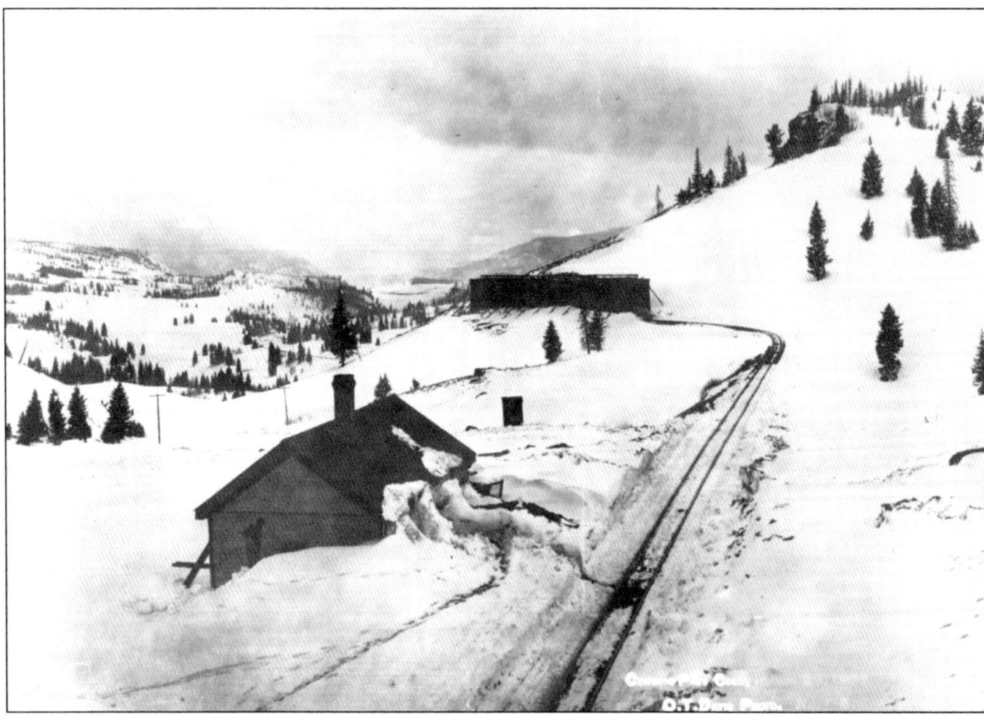

SNOWSHED ON CUMBRES PASS, MARCH 28, 1909. Note the pathways dug through the snow to the section house in the foreground. The D&RG ceased operations over Cumbres Pass in 1968, and, in 1970, it sold 64 miles of track between Antonito and Chama to preservation groups from Colorado and New Mexico for $547,120. Today, the two states jointly operate the line in summer months as the Cumbres & Toltec Scenic Railroad.

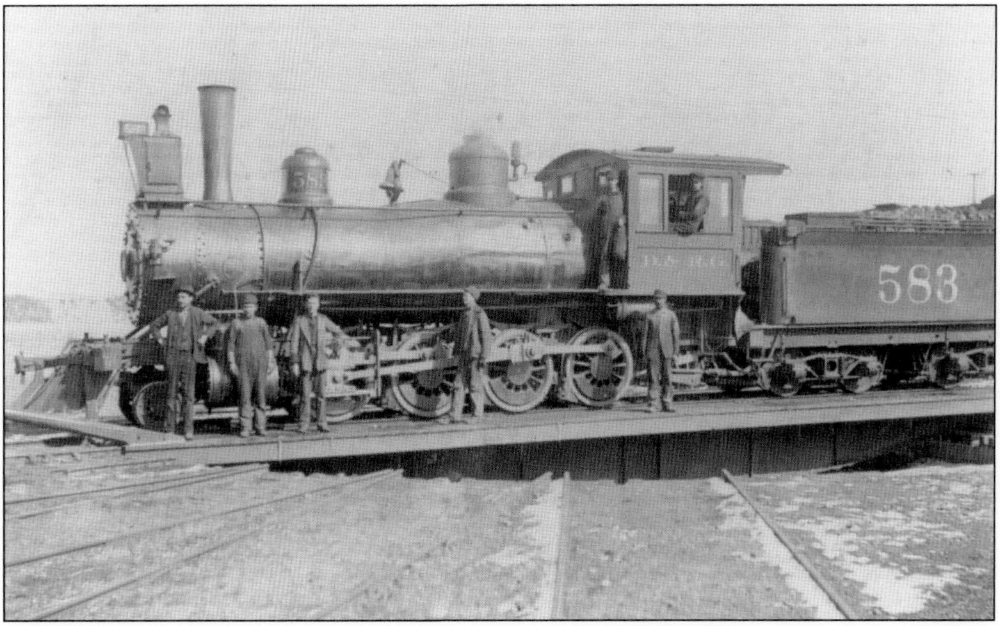

Turntable, c. 1900. D&RG standard-gauge engine No. 583, built by Baldwin in 1890, sits waiting for a turn on the Alamosa turntable. Turntables enabled engines to be moved in and out of bays in the roundhouse where repairs and maintenance were conducted.

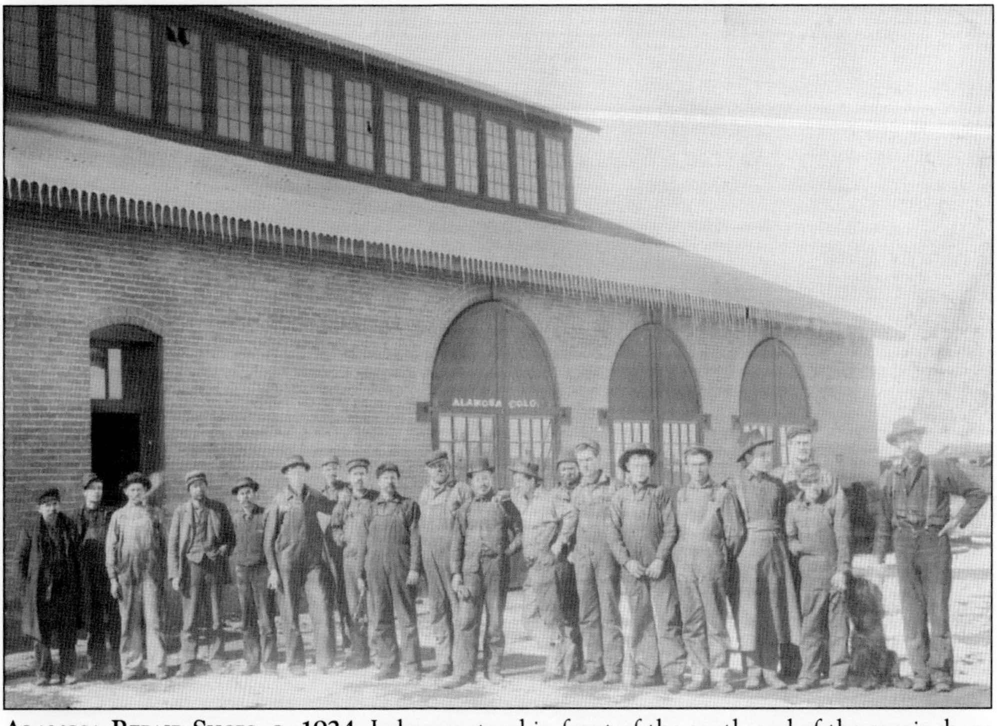

Alamosa Repair Shops, c. 1924. Laborers stand in front of the south end of the repair shops in Alamosa. This was a busy place because Alamosa was in the center of D&RG operations in the San Luis Valley. The large workforce here completely rebuilt hundreds of narrow-gauge stock cars and boxcars in the 1920s, converting them to standard gauge.

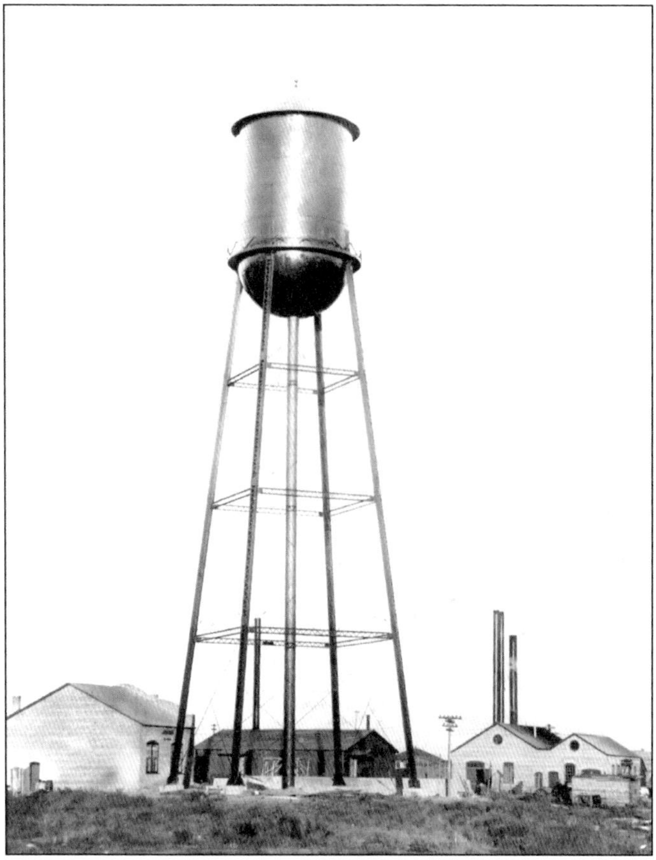

Alamosa Water Tower, c. 1925. This large water tower near the rail yards was fed by six artesian wells and supplied the city's water needs for many years. O.T. Davis climbed the tower on October 6, 1911, and took photographs of the rail yards, seen on page 32.

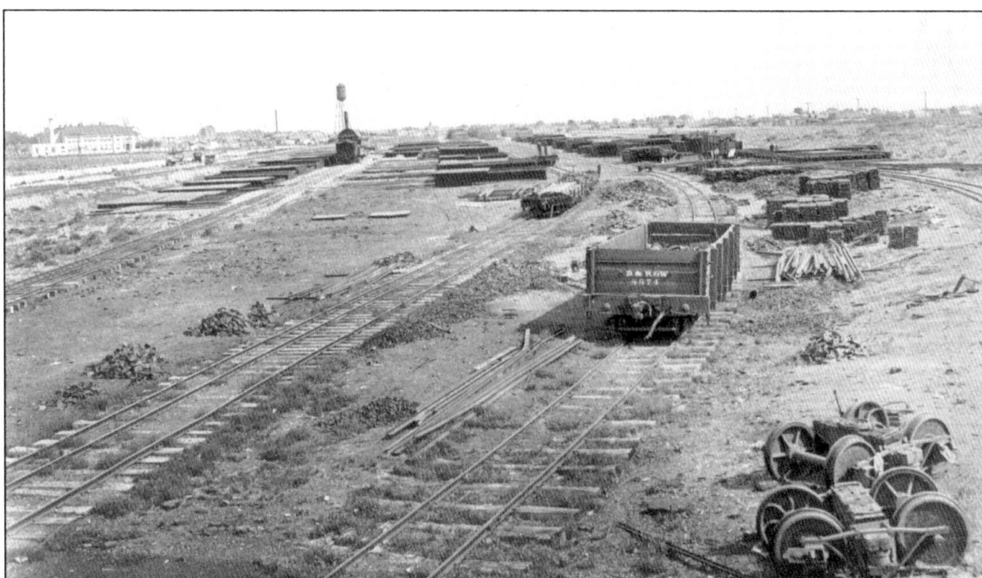

D&RG Rail Yards, Alamosa, c. 1920. The water tower can be seen rising above the rail yards just left of center. Note the tracks with three rails at the center and left, which could accommodate both narrow-gauge and standard-gauge trains.

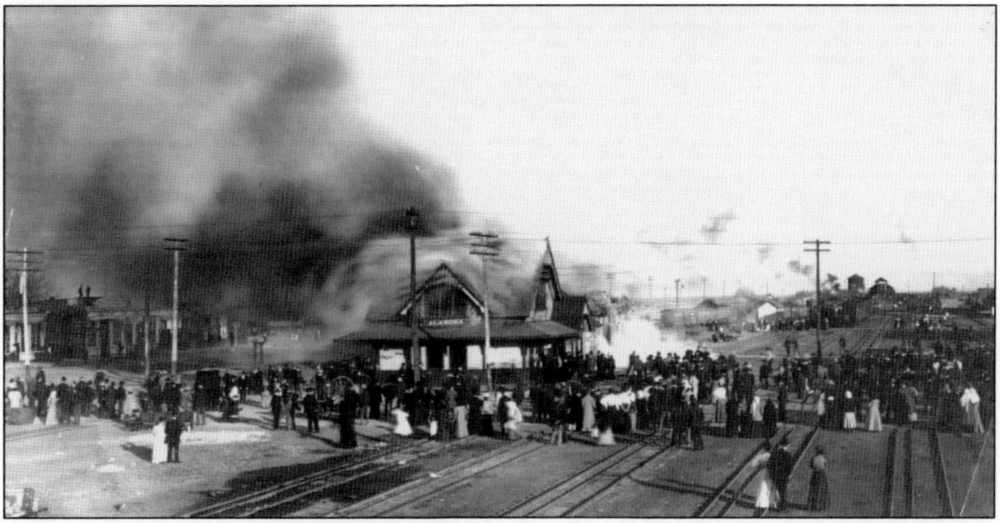

Alamosa Depot Fire, December 25, 1907. Disaster struck on Christmas Day, 1907, when the D&RG passenger depot, built in 1888, caught fire. Crowds gathered around hoping the volunteer fire department could put out the fire. But it was not to be—the building was a complete loss.

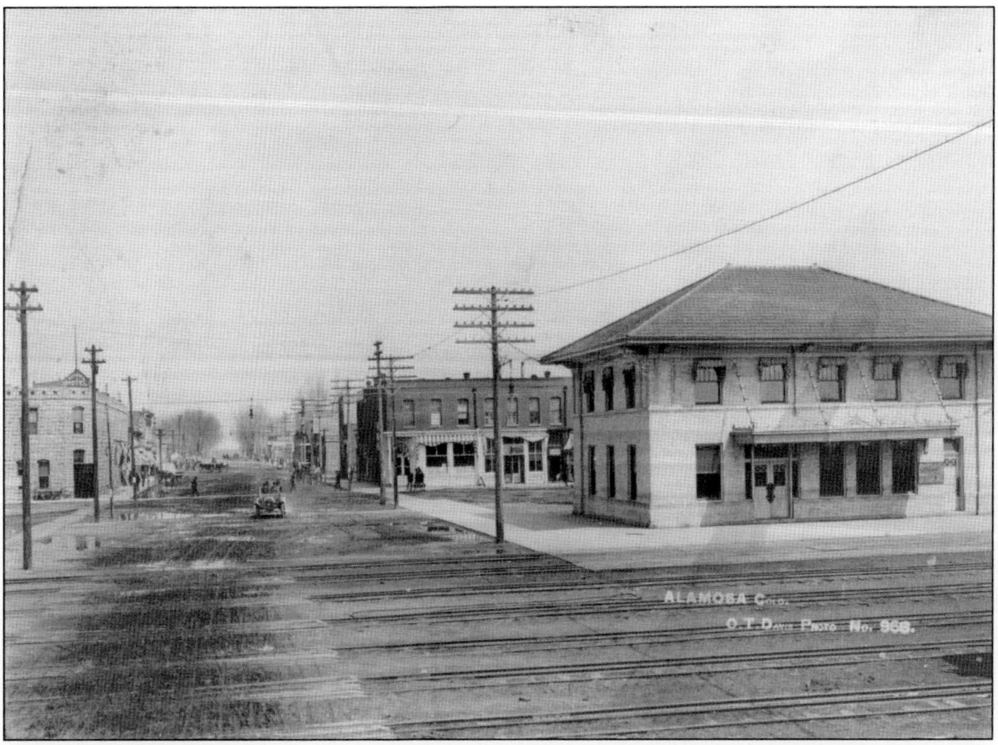

New Alamosa Depot, April 11, 1910. The new depot is the two-story brick structure on the right, built on the site of the old depot. Across the street on the left is the Victoria Hotel, famous for the breakfasts it served to passengers arriving on the overnight train from Denver.

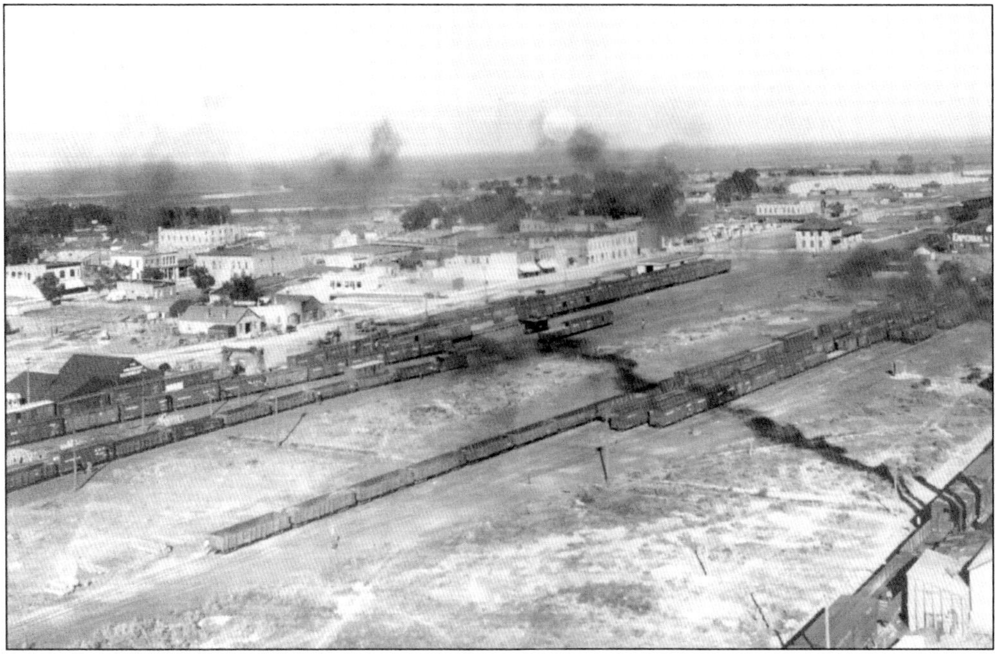

View of Alamosa, October 6, 1911. The view northeast from the water tower shows the new two-story brick depot at center right. The second story housed offices for D&RG officials, such as superintendents, dispatchers, and clerks. The depot still stands today, and part of it is used as the ticketing office of the Rio Grande Scenic Railroad, which runs passenger trains between Alamosa and La Veta.

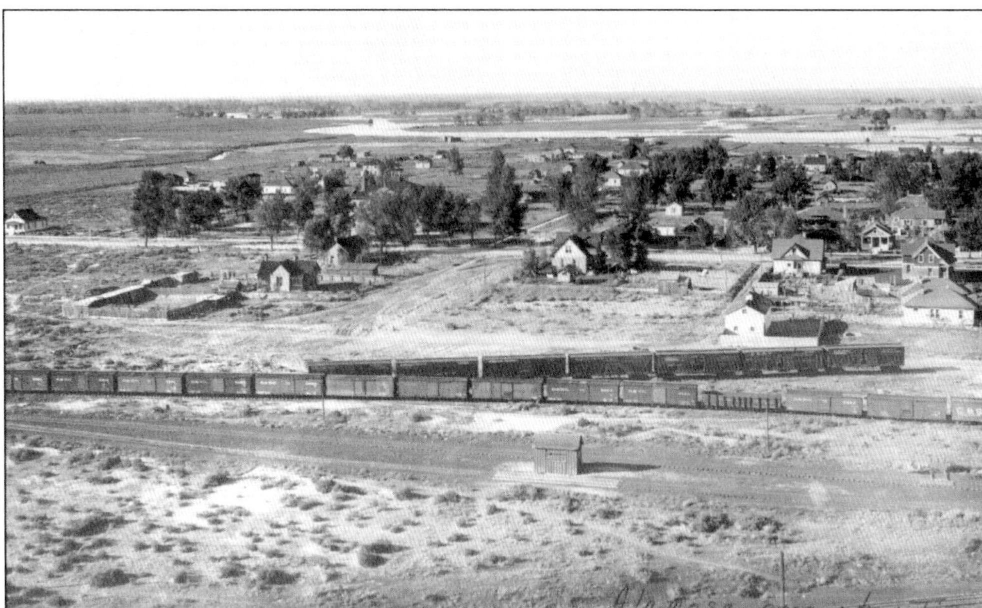

Alamosa Residential Area, October 6, 1911. This view north from the water tower shows homes built right up to the edge of the rail yards. In the distance, the Rio Grande is still at high water, showing the effects of the September flood. Usually, the river floods in the spring, but rare heavy September rains caused this flood.

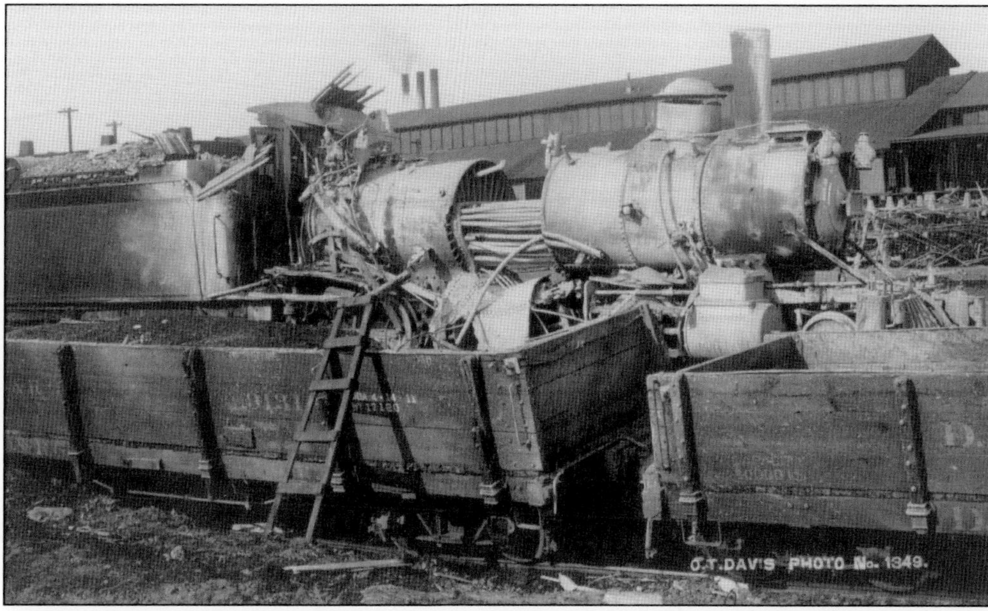

Alamosa Boiler Blowup, August 7, 1912. When a boiler blows up on a steam engine, the consequences are usually disastrous, with jagged metal sprayed in all directions. Here, the metal was shot into gondola cars sitting on the adjacent track, and the cab of the locomotive was destroyed.

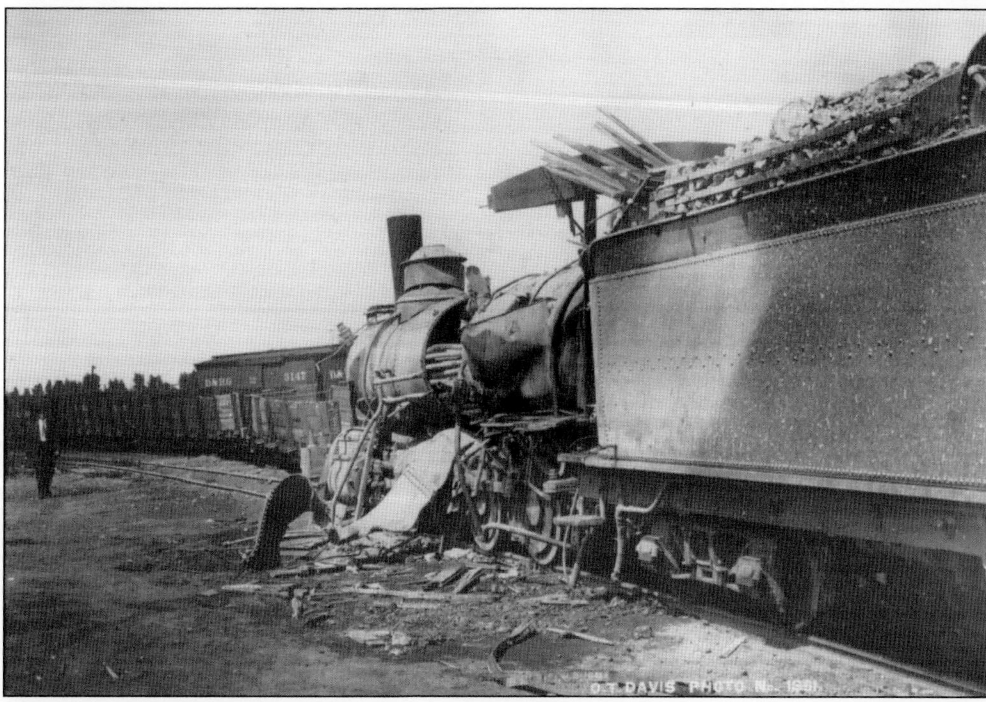

Boiler Blowup Aftermath, August 12, 1912. The Alamosa locomotive shops rebuilt many boilers of narrow-gauge engines between 1910 and 1920. The original wrought-iron boilers were replaced with steel ones. D&RG operations in Alamosa totaled some 600–700 workers in the 1920s.

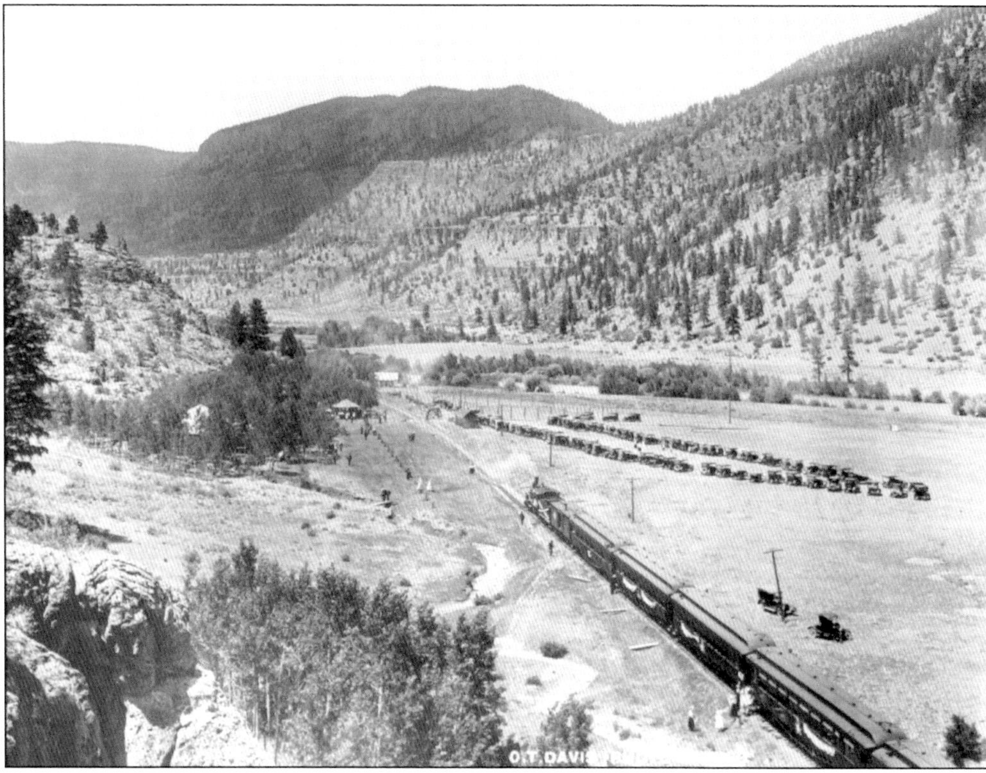

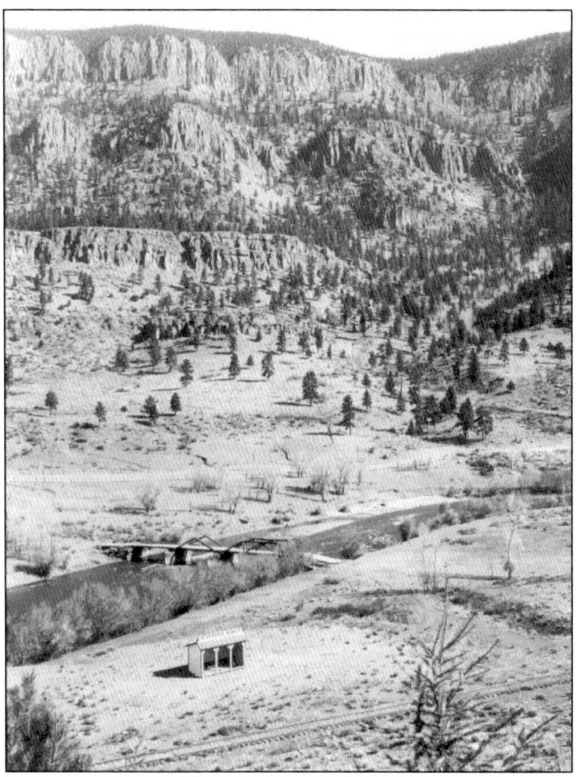

Masonic Park, June 25, 1917. Masonic Park was located four miles northwest of South Fork on the Rio Grande. In 1914, the San Luis Masonic Association purchased 166 acres of land here to serve as festival grounds for their annual St. John's Day celebration. The D&RG ran special excursion trains to the park, such as the one shown here with five passenger cars decorated for the occasion.

Riverside Ranch, 1915. Located north of Masonic Park, Riverside Ranch had its own train stop on the D&RG. The railroad built its narrow-gauge tracks north from South Fork, past the ranch, and on to Wagon Wheel Gap (a total of nine miles) in 1883. In this photograph, the bridge spanning the Rio Grande leads into the ranch (right) and out (left) to the primitive road to South Fork.

TRACKS TO WAGON WHEEL GAP, JUNE 1922. The hot springs at Wagon Wheel Gap prompted the D&RG to build this branch line in 1883. Wagon Wheel Gap was named after broken wagon wheels found there along the stage line on the road to the San Juan mines. The gap itself is the natural break formed by the Rio Grande between the mountains seen in the distant center of this photograph.

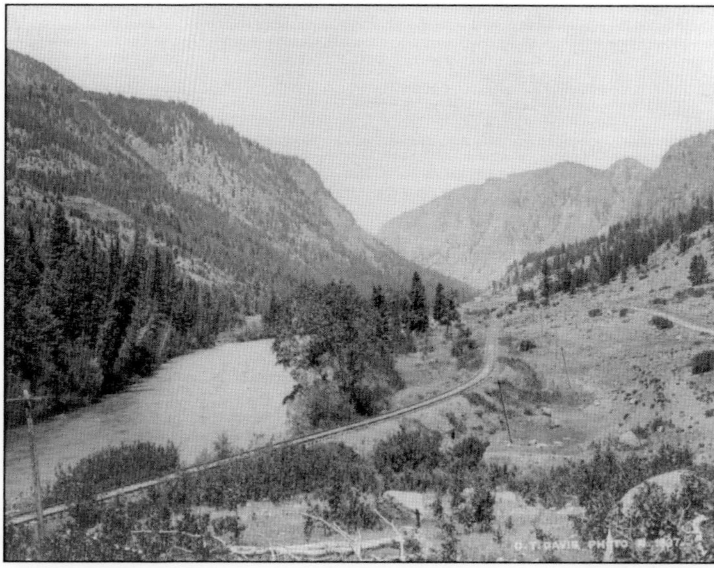

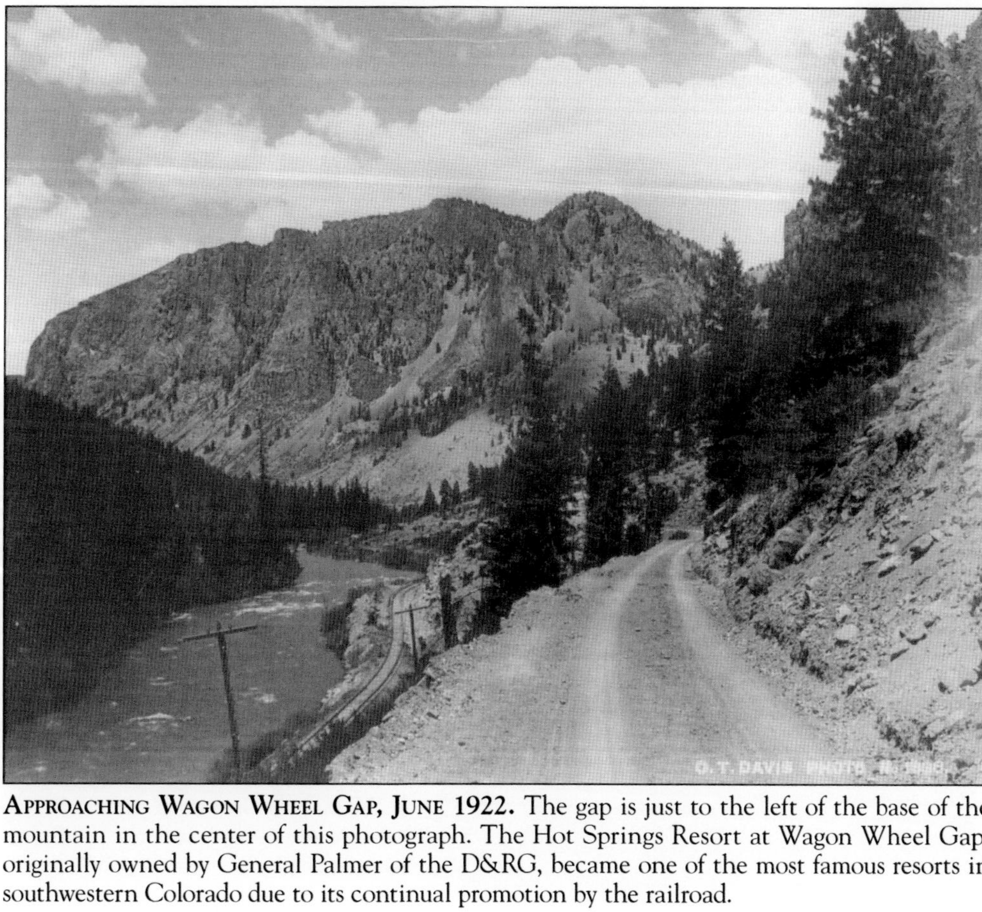

APPROACHING WAGON WHEEL GAP, JUNE 1922. The gap is just to the left of the base of the mountain in the center of this photograph. The Hot Springs Resort at Wagon Wheel Gap, originally owned by General Palmer of the D&RG, became one of the most famous resorts in southwestern Colorado due to its continual promotion by the railroad.

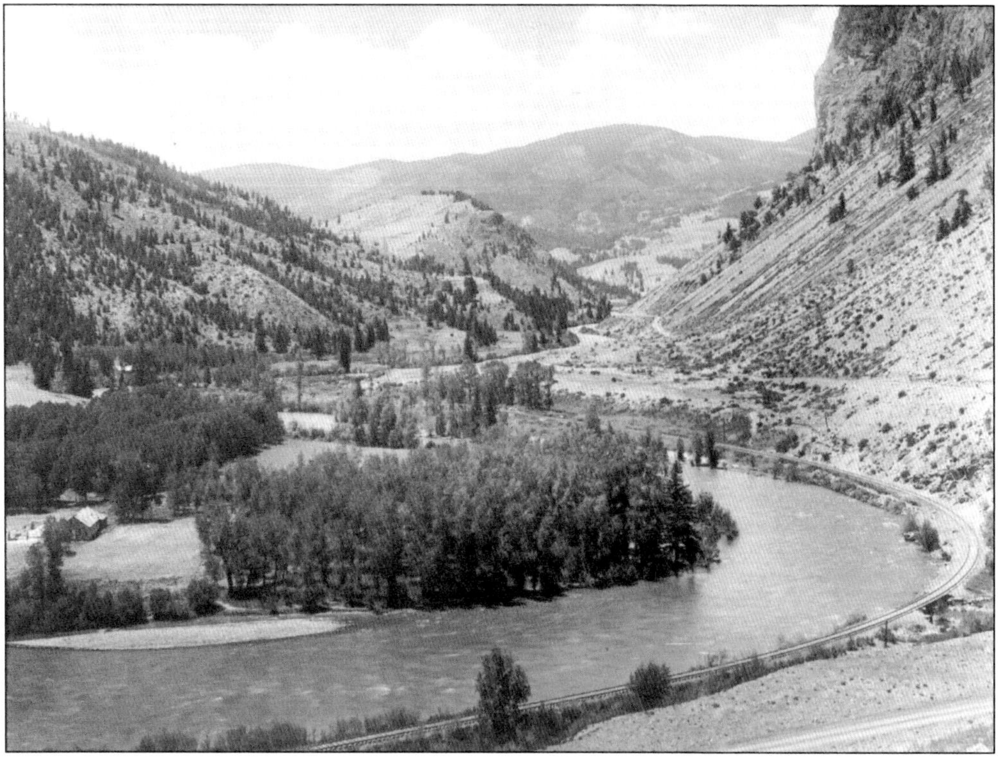

Wagon Wheel Gap, June 1922. The gap is in the direct center of this photograph. The D&RG line dead-ended here in 1883. Its completion farther north would have to wait until 1891, when silver discoveries at Creede prompted the railroad to build 9.7 more miles of track into the new mining town.

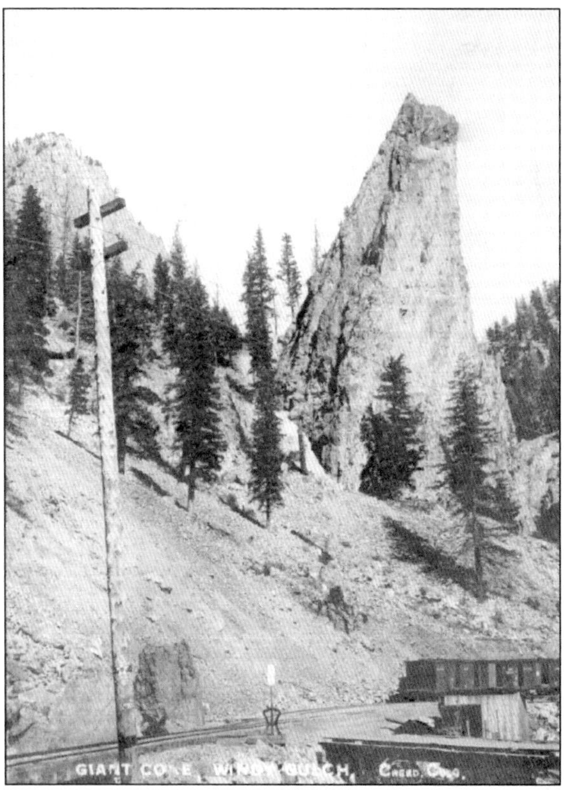

"Giant Cone," Windy Gulch, Creede, September 1896. With Nicholas Creede's discovery of silver ore at the Holy Moses Mine in 1889, thousands of prospectors rushed there. Overnight, the town of Creede was born, and the D&RG soon built tracks from Wagon Wheel Gap to Creede to serve the mines.

Three

MINING
"THERE IS NO NIGHT IN CREEDE"

After the Civil War ended in 1865, soldiers released from duty at Fort Garland soon flocked to the mountains in hopes of striking it rich in gold or silver. Just 15 miles northeast of Fort Garland, soldiers panned the streams for gold at Placer, and many were successful, leading to the establishment of a settlement there. Late in 1865, Capt. Charles Kerber, recently a member of the 1st Regiment of Colorado Volunteers at Fort Garland, led a group of settlers to the northern end of the San Luis Valley and established a settlement on Kerber Creek northwest of Villa Grove. In 1880, silver, lead, copper, and zinc were discovered at the Bonanza Mine on Kerber Creek. Just east of Villa Grove, extensive iron ore deposits were found at Orient, and the D&RG built a branch line there in 1881.

While the D&RG was also busy building the rail line to Silverton in 1881, many of the mining districts of southern Colorado were never served by the railroad. The fabulously rich Summitville gold mining district, 27 miles southwest of Del Norte at an elevation over 11,000 feet, was never reached by rail. Nor were nearby mines at Jasper or Platoro. Ore was shipped out by wagon on primitive roads to Del Norte or Antonito, where it was transferred to the D&RG lines. O.T. Davis worked at Jasper in 1903 and photographed the mines there, as well as others around the rim of the San Luis Valley.

Perhaps one of the most famous mining districts of southern Colorado visited by O.T. Davis was Creede. The silver boom there was met with construction of the D&RG line from Wagon Wheel Gap to Creede in 1891. Thousands of miners swarmed to Creede, and it seemed like there was activity around the clock. Creede was so busy that Cy Warman, editor of the *Creede Candle*, wrote a poem ending with the famous lines, "It's day all day in the daytime, and there is no night in Creede!"

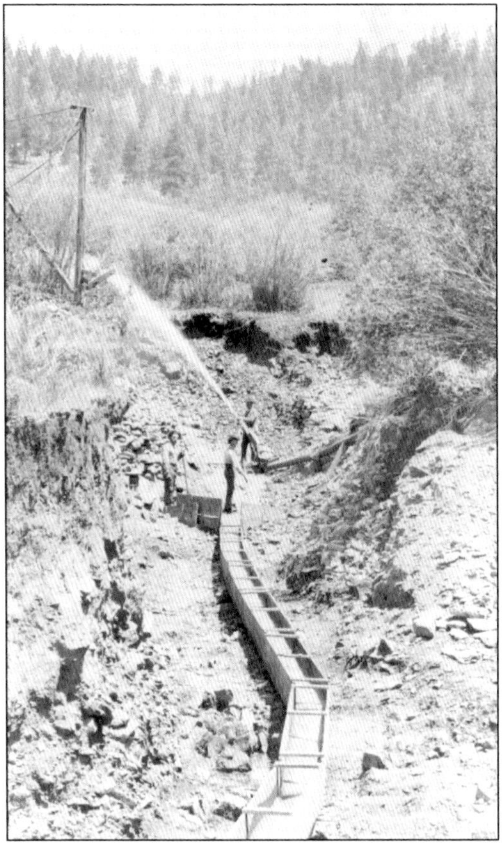

Spanish Gulch Placer, 1895. This placer operation was on the west side of Veta Pass, probably near the settlement of Placer. Placer is a Spanish word meaning "sand bank." Placer mining involves obtaining gold by washing the sand. In this case, sand was washed downhill into the row of sluice boxes, where the heavier gold particles settled on the bottom of the boxes.

Ebenezer Placer Pit at Russell, 1896. The settlement first named Placer by the D&RG was later renamed Russell in honor of the William Green Russell prospecting party of the 1870s. Here, a pit was dug in the sand and then flooded with water. The water runoff was then forced through the series of seven sluice boxes to the right.

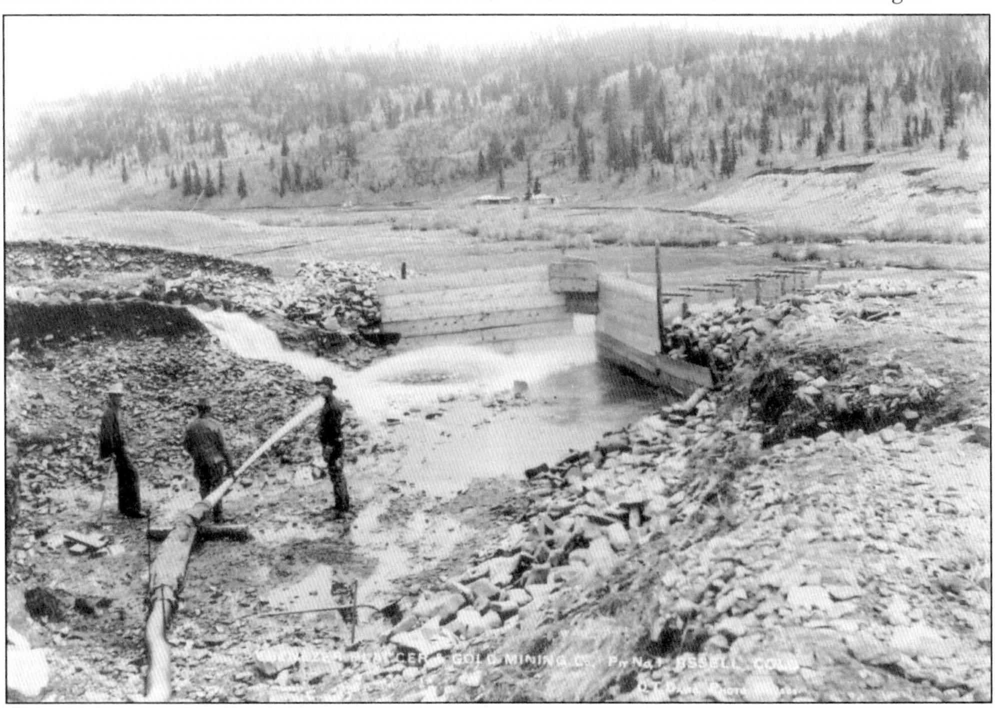

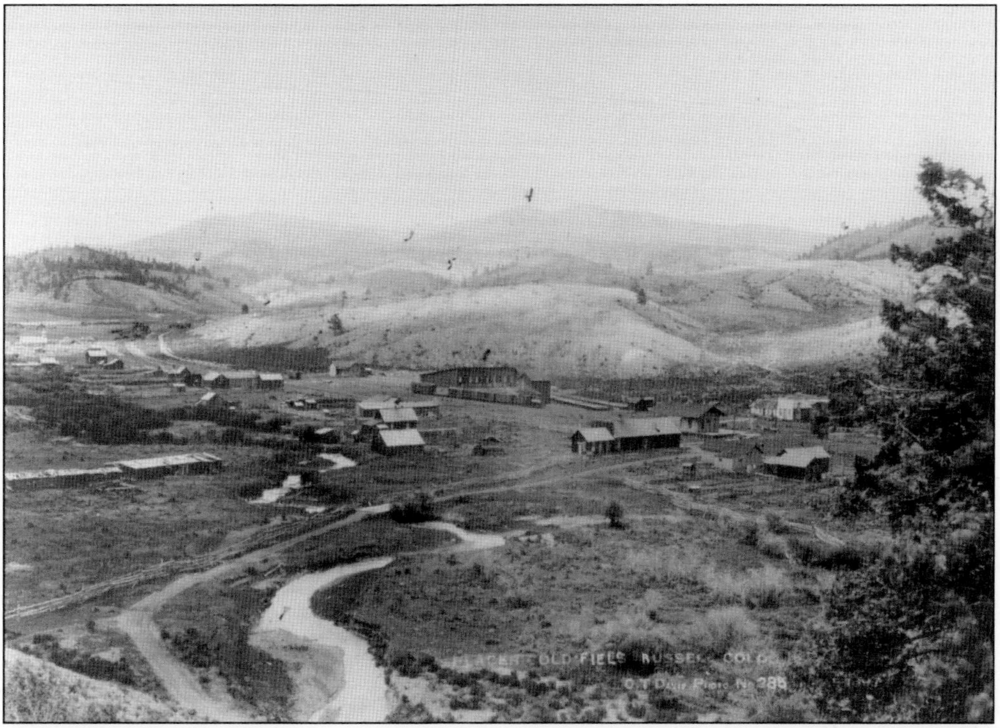

Placer/Russell Goldfields, 1897. O.T. Davis numbered the Placer goldfields 1–8 on this photograph. A train can be seen approaching the railroad depot toward the center right. Placer mining is very destructive to the environment, with gullies created by sand washing downstream and sandbars created from the outflow.

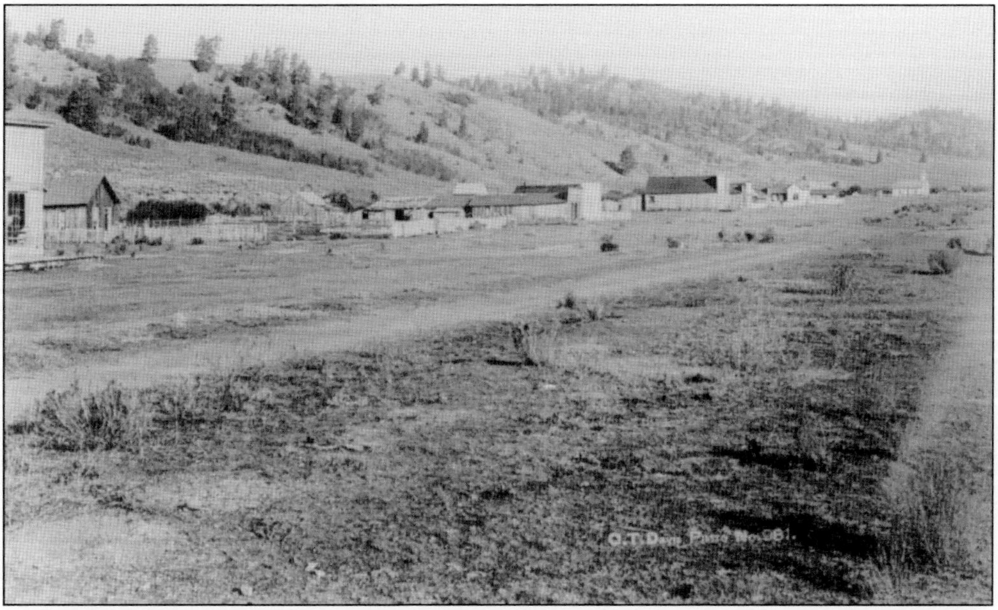

Placer/Russell, 1910. Gold mining operations were winding down by 1910, and much less activity is seen in the town. US Highway 160 now traverses the road in the center, where the scattered remains of Russell can still be seen today.

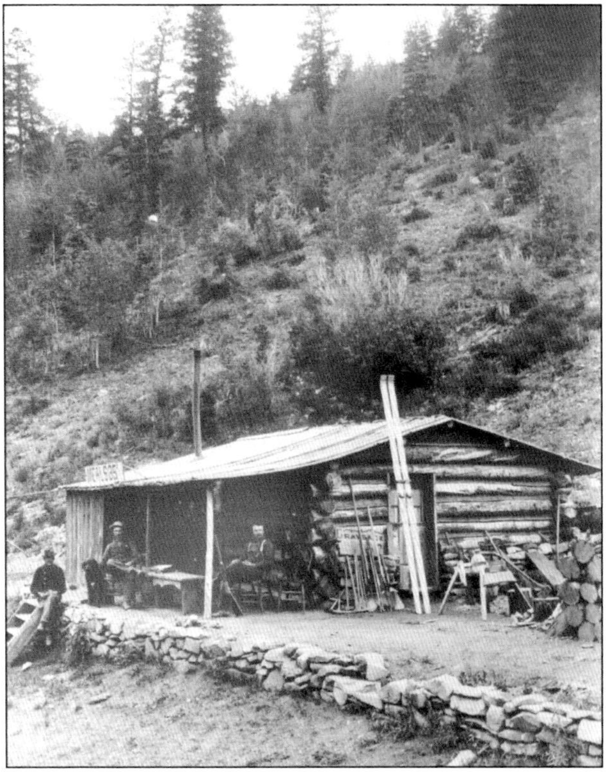

Johnson Cabin at Grayback, 1896. In 1881, the D&RG built a 2.1-mile narrow-gauge branch line from Placer northeast to the Grayback Mine. This mine had ore containing about 70-percent iron and 17-percent silver. Over 300 miners worked at the Grayback, and some obtained room and board in this cabin, where meals were 35¢.

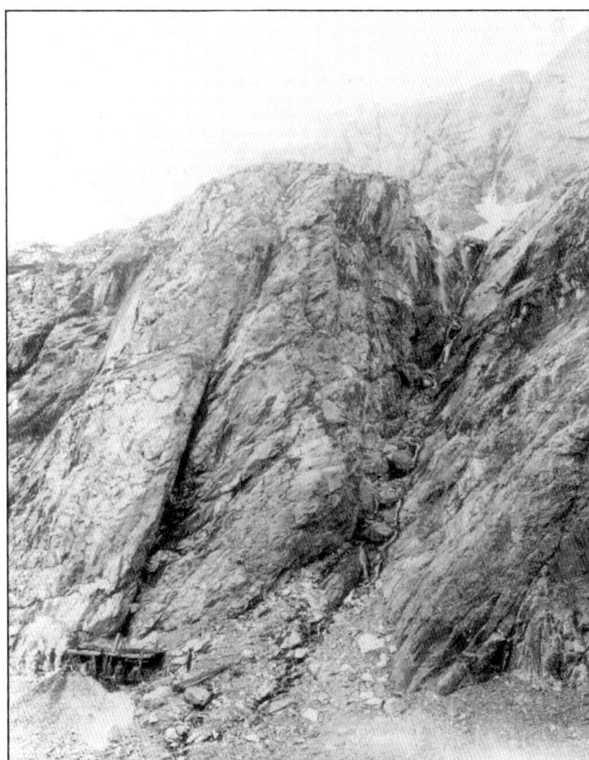

Hawkins Lode, August 10, 1899. O.T. Davis provided the location of this mine as "Sierra Blanco." It was on the north side of Blanca Peak and probably produced gold. Davis stated that there was a smelter for the Ohio Gold Mine, located on the nearby Huerfano River.

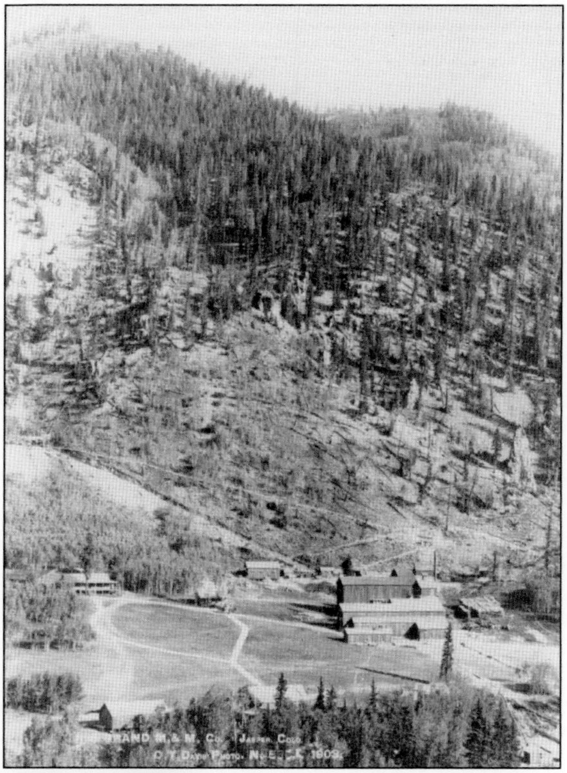

Rio Grande Mining & Milling Company at Jasper, 1903. Jasper was located just east of Summitville, but 2,000 feet lower, near the headwaters of the Alamosa River. The town sprang up in 1874, serving nearby gold and silver mines. The Miser was the principal gold-producing mine here.

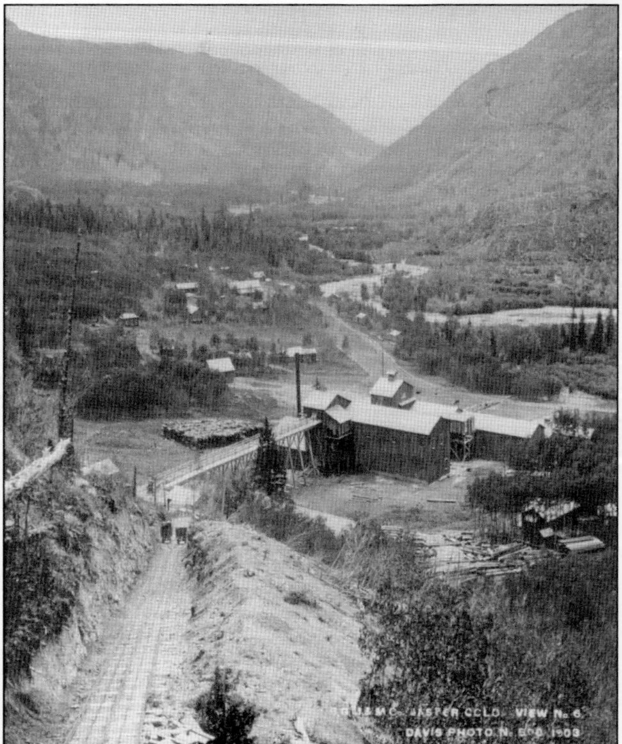

Ore Cart Tracks, Jasper, 1903. These tracks led from the mine down to the milling operations below. The stamp mill processed the gold and silver ore, which was then hauled out in wagons to Alamosa. The Alamosa River is seen winding through the middle of this photograph.

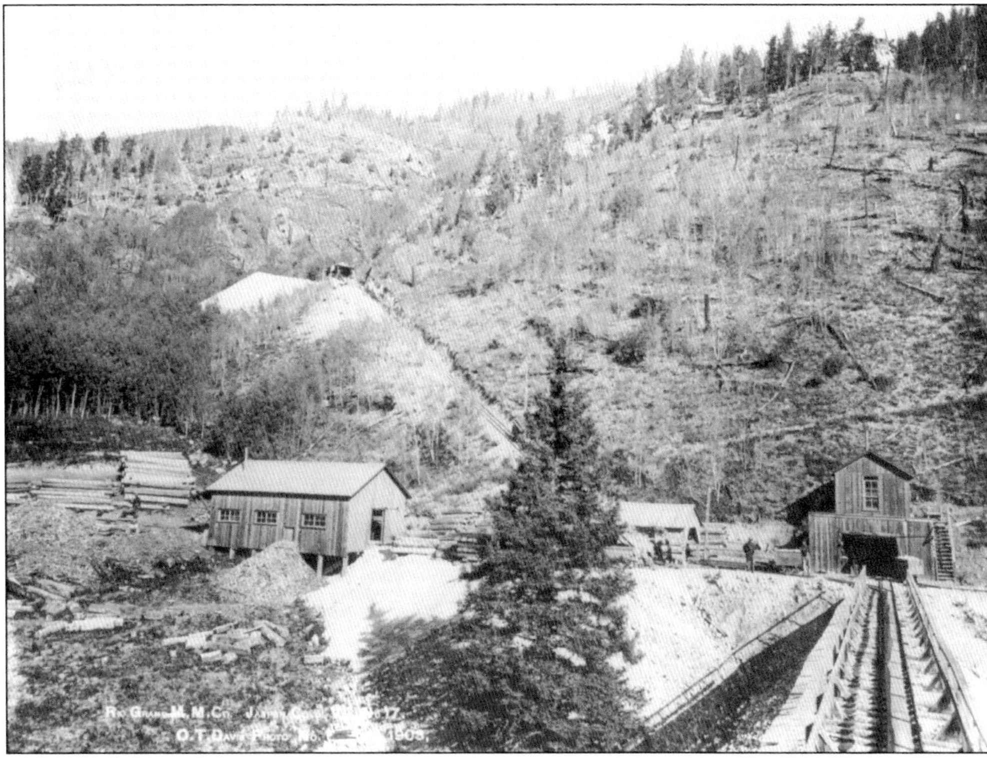

Jasper Mining Operations, 1903. The No. 1 tunnel to the mine is seen framed in the building at lower right. The ore tracks led up the hill toward another tunnel opening, seen to the left of center. Note the logs used for mine timbers piled next to the building on the left.

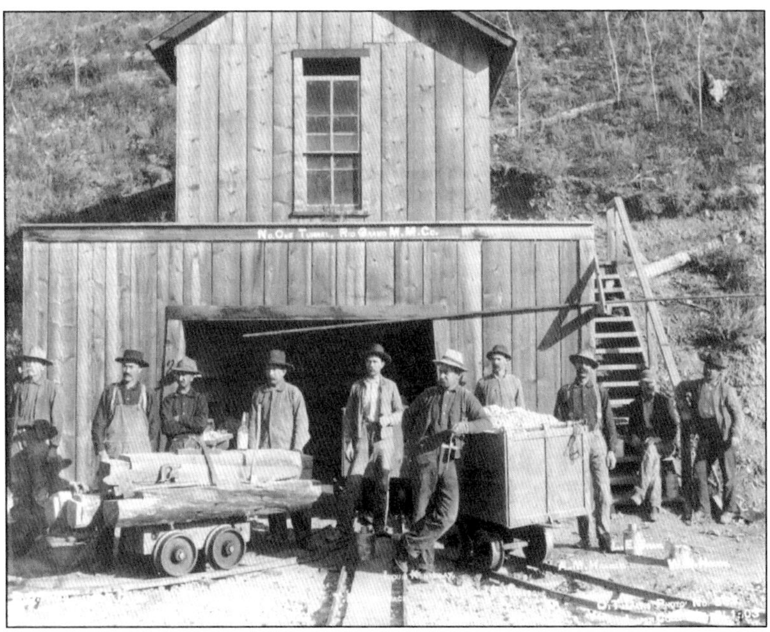

No. 1 Tunnel, Jasper, 1903. Pictured in front of the tunnel, from left to right, are miners Barney Allen, O.T. Davis, Bill ?, unidentified, T.B. Wack, Louie Kennedy, ? Henson, A.M. Hannen, L.E. Shaw, and W.B. Houck. The cart on the left hauled timbers into the tunnel for framing, and the cart on the right hauled out the mined ore.

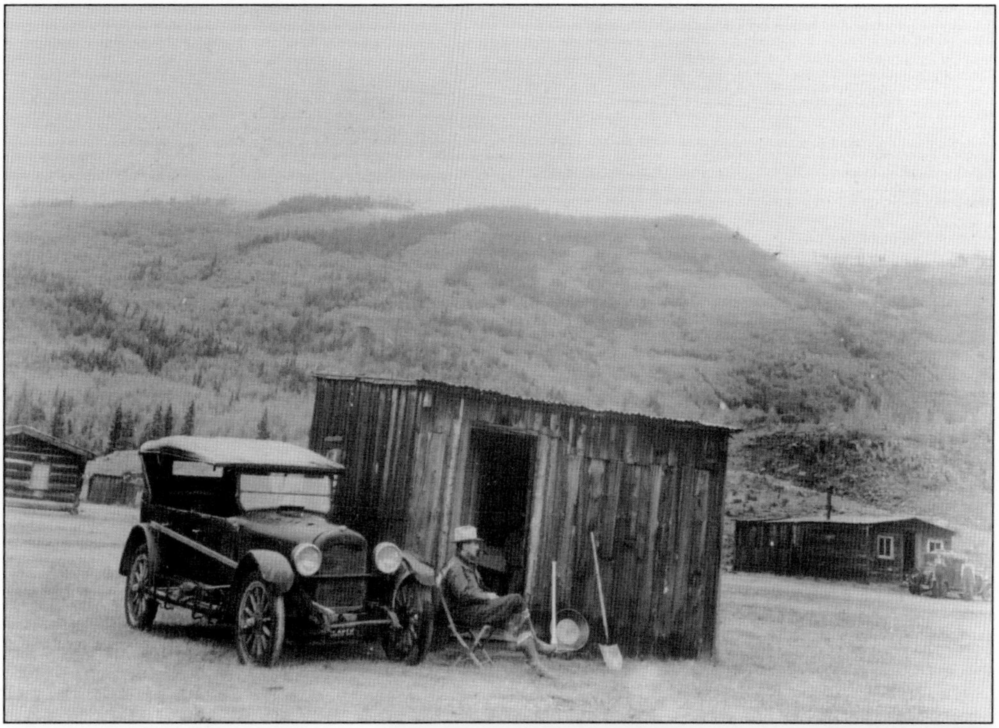

Miner's Shack at Platoro, 1934. Platoro is located on the Conejos River, just a few miles south of Jasper, at an elevation of 9,900 feet. There were large gold and silver mines here in the 1880s; thus, the town's name, Platoro: a combination of the Spanish words for silver (*plata*) and gold (*oro*). By 1934, most mining had ceased, and Platoro attracted fishermen and hunters.

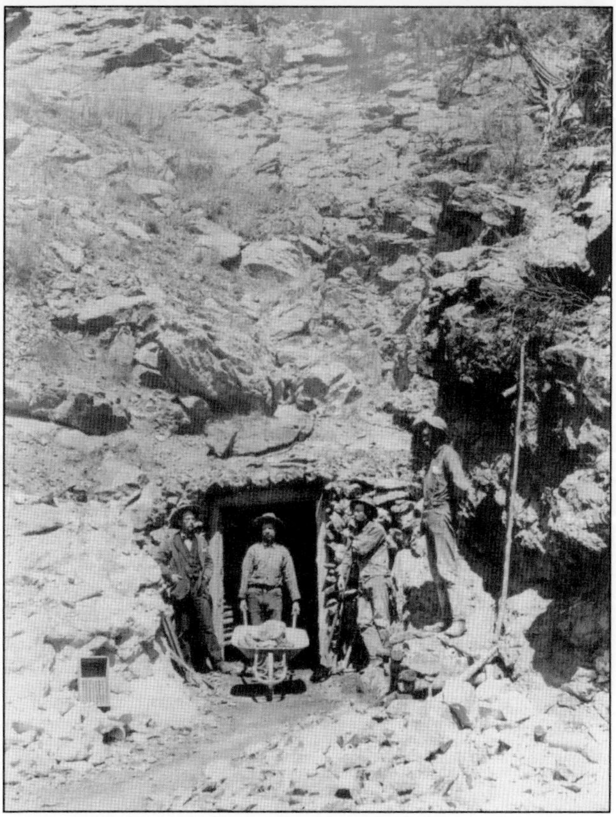

Plomo Mine near San Luis, 1894. San Luis, located in the southeastern part of the San Luis Valley, is Colorado's oldest town, having been founded in 1851. *Plomo* is the Spanish word for "lead," and that was the mineral produced at this mine.

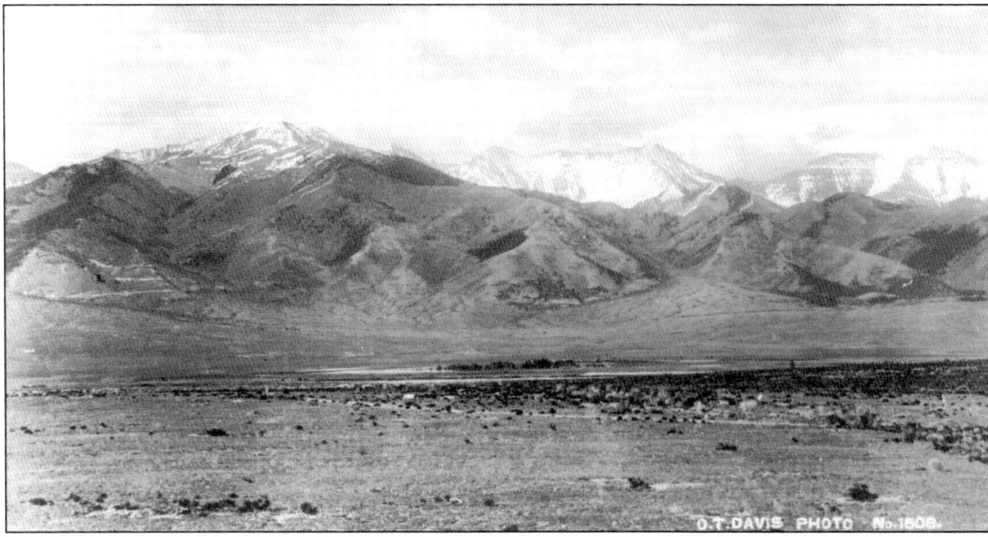

Orient Mine from Villa Grove, May 26, 1914. The D&RG extended the narrow-gauge line from Salida over Poncha Pass south to Villa Grove and the Orient Mine in 1881. Iron ore was produced in great quantities at the mine, and it was shipped out by rail to the steel mill in Pueblo. This view east shows the snow-capped Sangre de Cristo range, with the mine at center left.

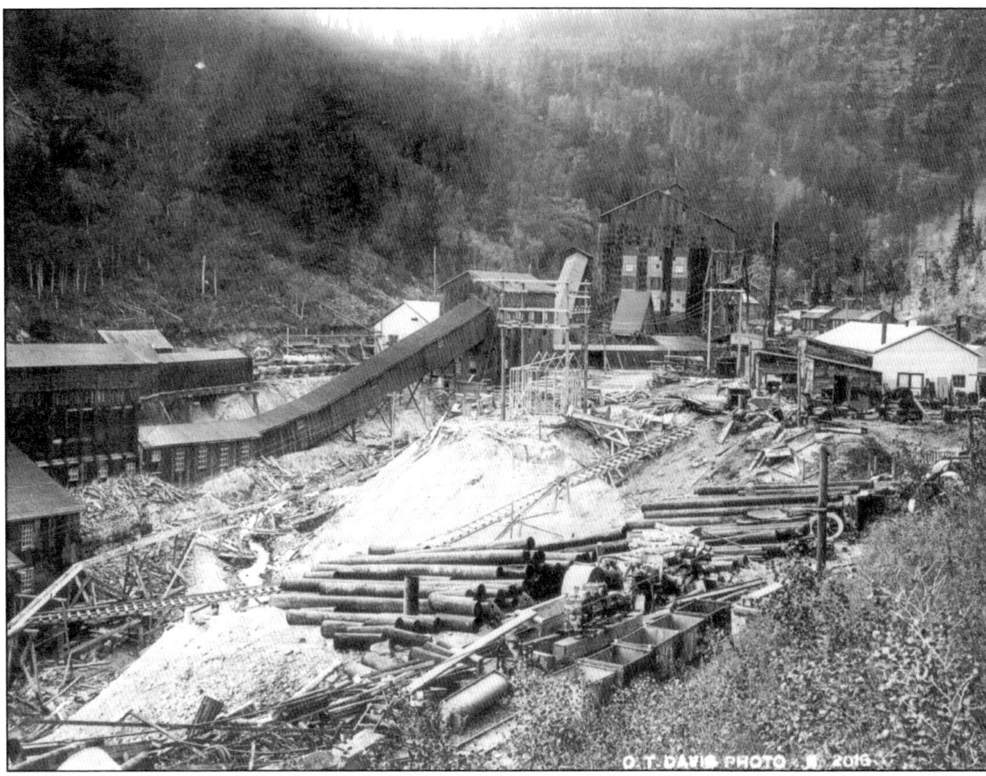

Rawley Mine at Bonanza, 1912. Bonanza, 16 miles northwest of Villa Grove, boomed in 1880 with the discovery of silver, lead, copper, and zinc. The Rawley Mine claim was filed on May 21, 1880, and the mine went into production in 1882. The nearby Bonanza Mine was staked on July 9, 1880. Ore from the mines was loaded into wagons for shipment to the D&RG at Villa Grove.

Four

Irrigation
"Less Rainfall than the Sahara Desert"

As Beryl McAdow noted in the book *From Crested Peaks: The Story of Adams State College of Colorado*, there is "less annual rainfall than the Sahara Desert" in the San Luis Valley, thus making ranching and farming a real challenge. The soil can be very productive, but it needs water to produce hay for cattle and food crops for people. Fortunately, the San Luis Valley is blessed with an abundance of underground water. Underneath the valley is an aquifer that collects snowmelt from the San Juan Mountains in the west. The underground aquifer slopes down from west to east, and an impervious layer of clay caps it. When a well is drilled through the clay into the aquifer, the downhill flow of the underground water creates pressure, which forces water up through the well pipe, creating an artesian well. The San Luis Valley is dotted with hundreds of artesian wells, and O.T. Davis photographed the dramatic effect of water spewing from the wellheads.

Another source of irrigation water for the San Luis Valley is diverting water from the Rio Grande and other flowing surface streams through ditches. The first ditch was probably dug by Hispanic settlers in San Luis in 1852, when they dug a ditch to draw water from the Culebra River. These irrigation ditches (*acequias* in Spanish) provided water to fields around small towns throughout the valley. Mechanized ditch digging arrived in the early 1900s with the arrival of steam-powered ditch diggers. O.T. Davis captured marvelous scenes of these behemoths as they tore into the San Luis Valley soil.

Hispanic settlers migrated north to southern Colorado from New Mexico to engage in irrigated farming and sheep ranching. However, the impetus for Anglo-American settlement in Colorado in the 19th century was mining, not farming. But hungry miners, pack mules, and horses quickly created a large market for food and feed. The farms and ranches of the San Luis Valley were able to meet this need thanks to artesian wells and surface irrigation.

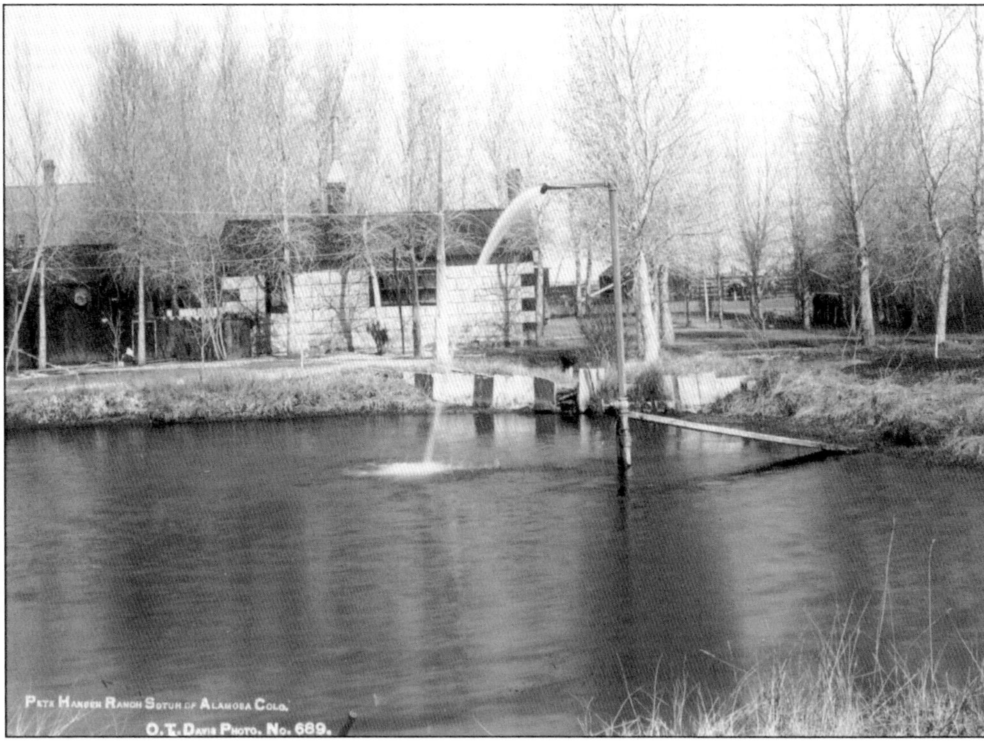

Artesian Well, Peter Hansen Ranch, 1908. Peter Hansen and his wife, Emma, owned this ranch located south of Alamosa. Here, the artesian well fills a small pond. Water is channeled out of the pond (through the opening in the small wall at the top center of the pond) into ditches carrying water to various fields at the ranch.

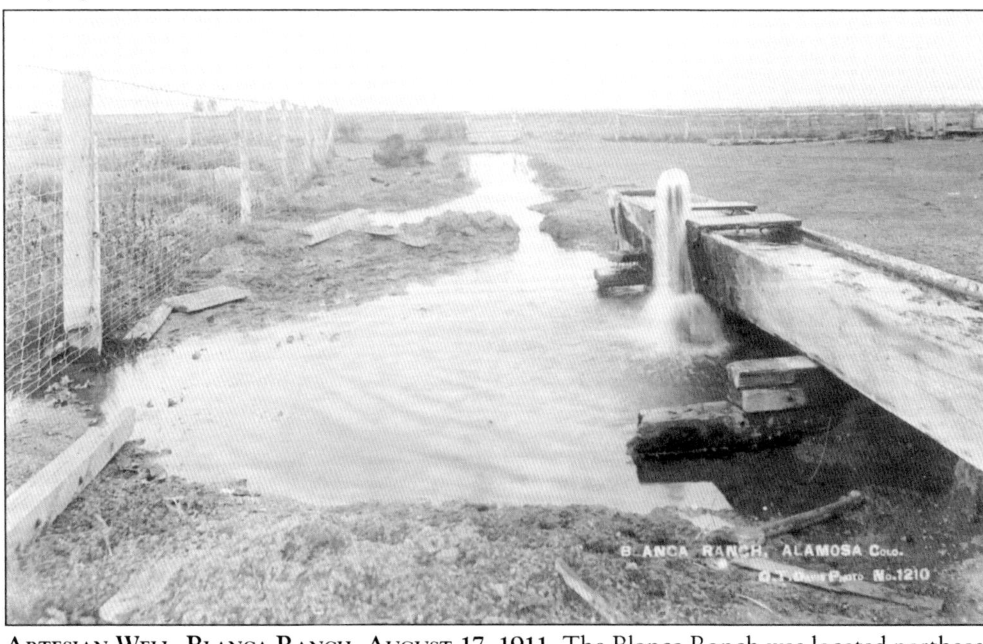

Artesian Well, Blanca Ranch, August 17, 1911. The Blanca Ranch was located northeast of Alamosa. Water flowed from the wellhead to the San Luis Canal.

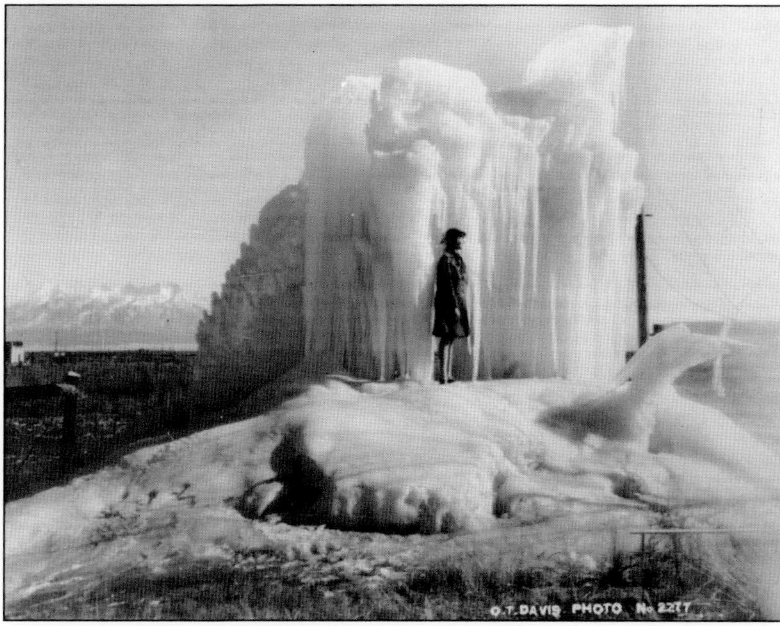

Artesian Well, Ray Curtis Ranch, 1935. If water is allowed to flow out the wellhead in winter, this is the result—massive icicles! This ranch was near Saguache. The Sangre de Cristo Mountains can be seen in the left background. Note the bare legs of the woman standing next to the ice.

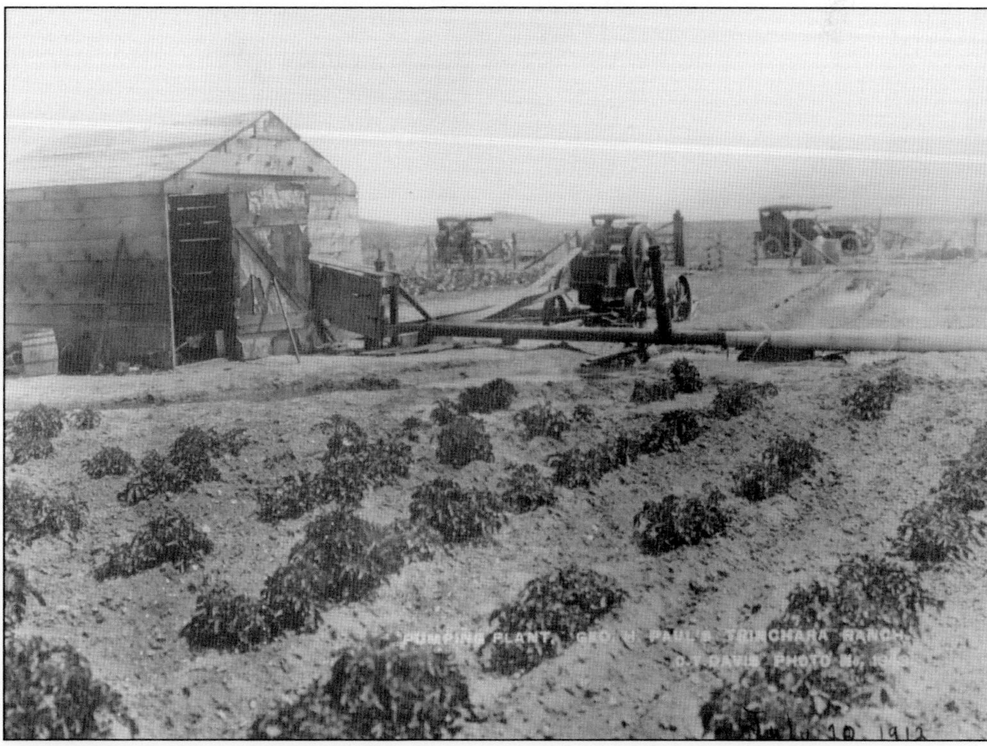

Pumping Plant, Trinchera Ranch, July 20, 1912. The Trinchera Ranch was near Fort Garland. Here, a steam tractor is equipped with a pulley belt that is attached to the well. Water is pumped to the pipe with holes in it, and it then flows down the rows of plants. This was an early precursor to today's massive center-pivot irrigation systems in the San Luis Valley.

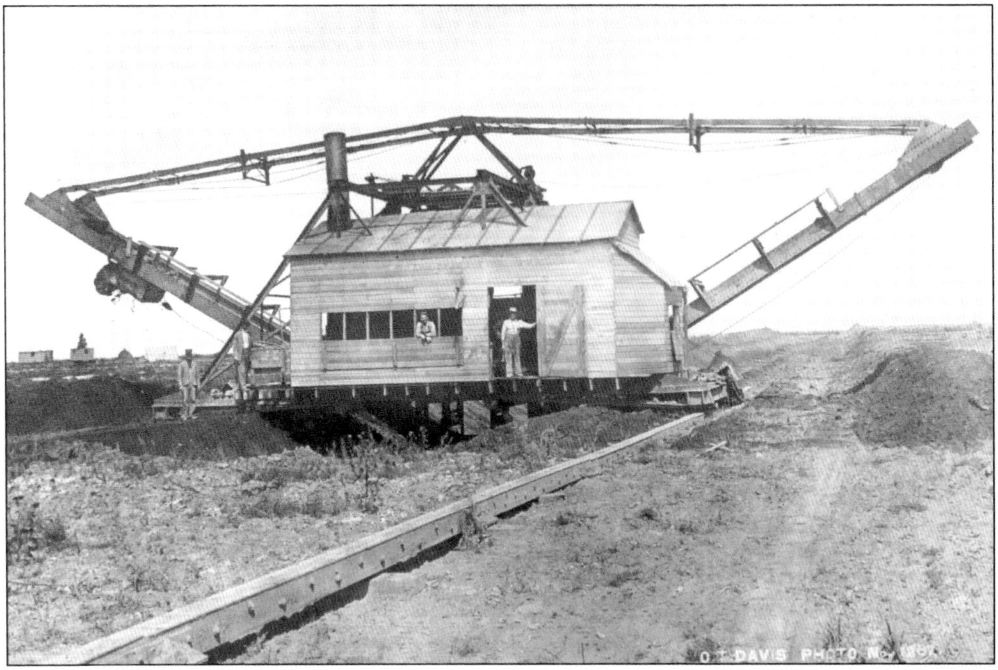

STEAM-POWERED IRRIGATION DITCH DIGGER, SEPTEMBER 24, 1911. This contraption, set up near Hooper, was able to dig wide, deep canals, such as the one pictured below. These canals could carry artesian or stream surface water for long distances to the thirsty fields.

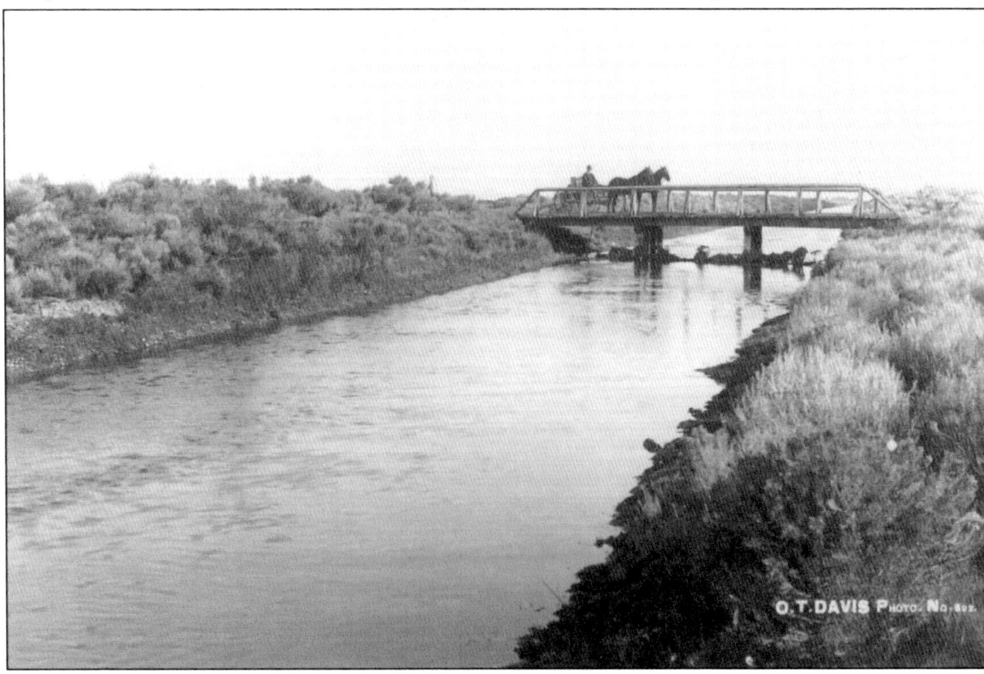

WAVERLY BRIDGE, 1907. Waverly was located southwest of Alamosa. This bridge carried horse-and-buggy traffic over the Empire Canal. A canal this wide and deep was dug by a steam-powered ditch digger, such as the one shown above. This canal is quite a contrast from the hand-dug ditches of early Hispanic settlers.

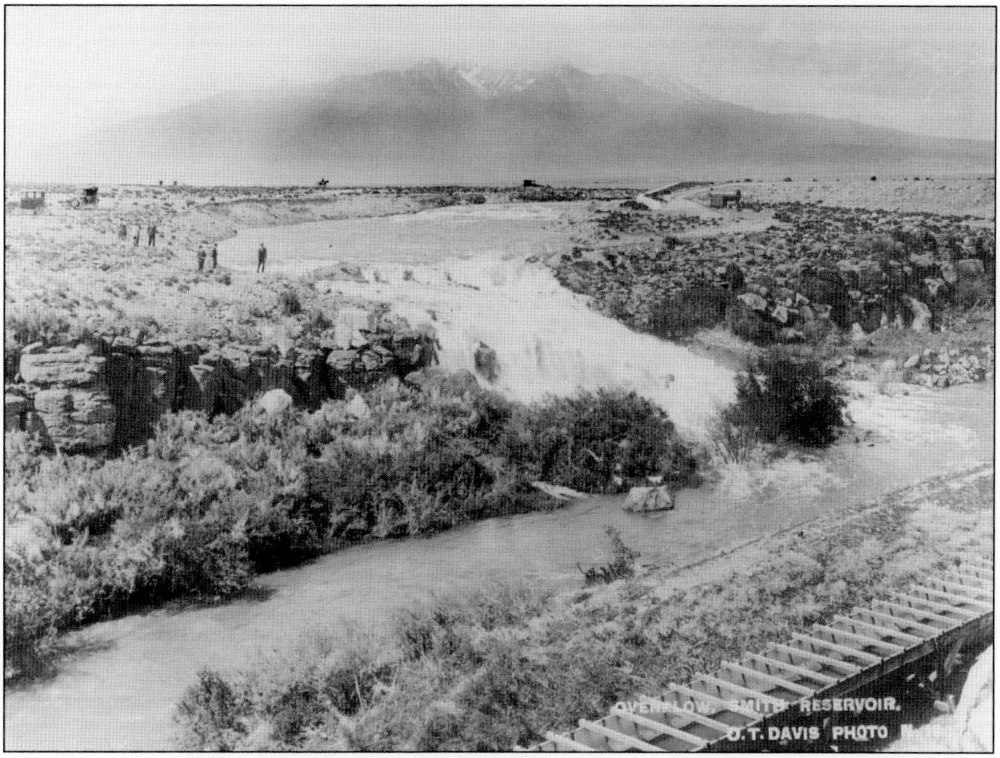

SMITH RESERVOIR, MAY 12, 1921. Named for resident engineer C.H.W. Smith, the reservoir was formed by damming Trinchera Creek four miles southwest of the town of Blanca. Blanca Peak dominates the skyline. The flume in the lower right carried irrigation water to the Trinchera Estate. The Trinchera Estate was formed when William Gilpin, the former governor of the Colorado Territory, purchased the Sangre de Cristo land grant from its heirs in 1863.

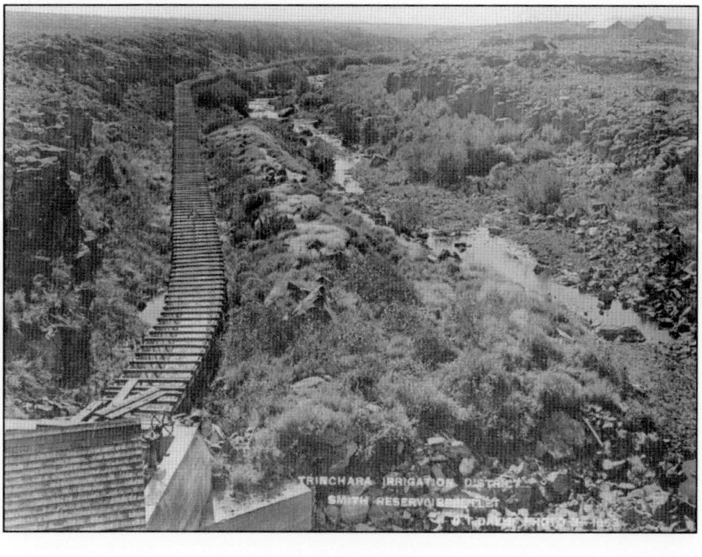

SMITH RESERVOIR OUTLET, SEPTEMBER 14, 1918. The flume carried water released from Smith Reservoir to the Trinchera Irrigation District. Originally one large estate created from the Sangre de Cristo land grant, the Trinchera has been continually subdivided into a number of smaller ranches. Today, those looking for a piece of land to own in the Wild West can purchase five-acre parcels of the former estate.

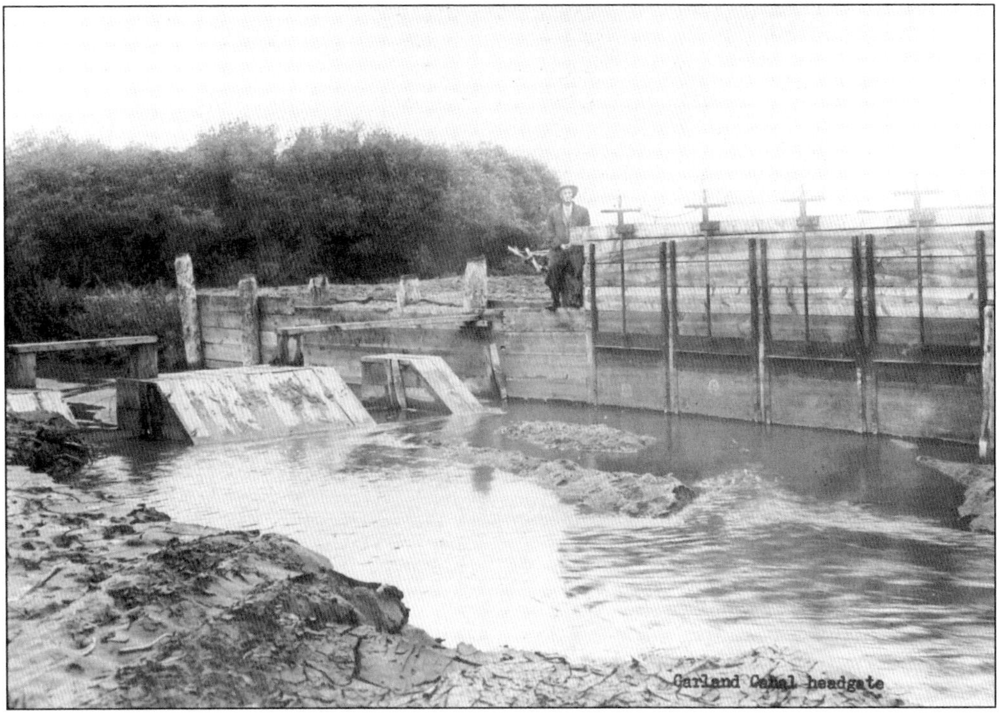

GARLAND CANAL, SEPTEMBER 5, 1909. This head gate of the Garland Canal was located in the vicinity of Fort Garland. Sangre de Cristo and Ute Creeks were the source of the water. Note the four wheels to the right of the gentleman—these were used to raise and lower the gates below, controlling the amount of water in the canal.

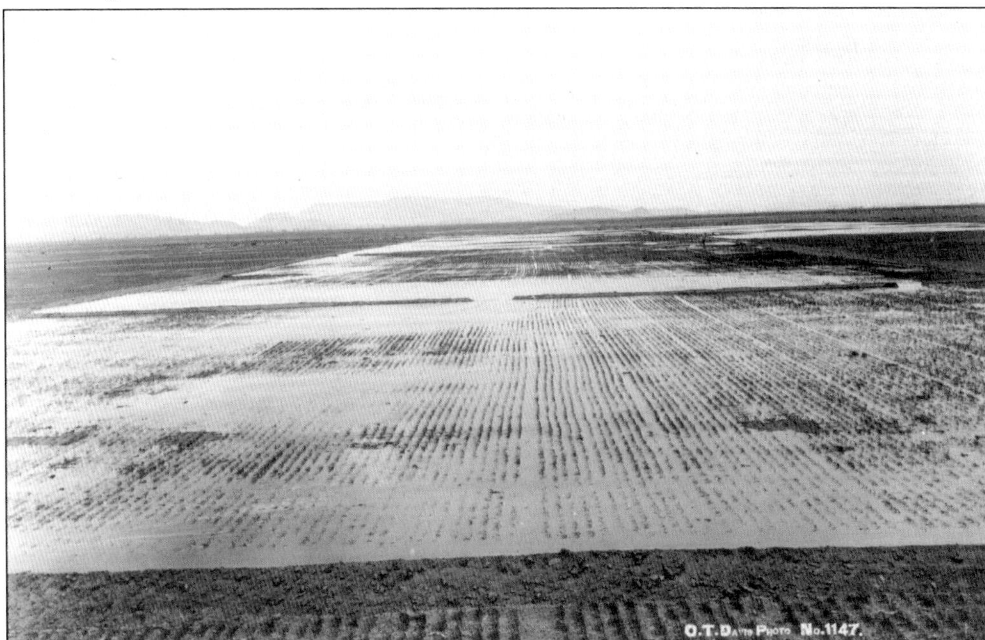

FLOOD IRRIGATION, 1907. At times, the irrigation canal gates were opened wide to allow water to completely flood the fields. This is a flooded field near Alamosa.

Five

Ranching
"The Stockman's Paradise"

An 1891 promotional booklet for the San Luis Valley bragged that the valley was "the stockman's paradise." But the booklet then went on to state that beyond the grasses growing in streambeds and mountain meadows, "on the plains or prairies there is no grass to speak of, and the natural production is grease wood and chico." A stockman's paradise indeed. To raise cattle in such a harsh environment generally required a larger allotment than the 160 acres given to homesteaders who filed a claim under the Homestead Act of 1862. Thus, consolidation of ranches into larger and larger units began in the San Luis Valley in the 1870s and 1880s, particularly after 1874, when Colorado's surveyor general invalidated Mexican land grants in the valley.

It was the Mexican land grants of the 1830s and 1840s that persuaded Hispanic ranchers from New Mexico to move north to Colorado's San Luis Valley, where they could raise sheep on the mountain and valley grasses. After 1874, stockmen in the San Luis Valley, often backed by wealthy Eastern investors, either bought out the small Hispanic sheep ranches or, in some cases, resorted to force to drive the sheepherders out. Conflicts between Hispanic sheepherders and Anglo cattlemen escalated throughout the 1800s, culminating in the cattlemen's burning of the ranch home of sheep raiser Teofilo Trujillo, located just west of the Great Sand Dunes, in 1902.

The consolidation of ranches resulted in some very large cattle ranches in the eastern section of the San Luis Valley. The Zapata Ranch, south of the Great Sand Dunes, and the Medano Ranch, west of the Dunes, were each over 30,000 acres in size. To the north of the Dunes, the corporate owners of the former Baca grant controlled over 100,000 acres for their cattle operation. (For photographs of these ranches, see the author's book Images of America: *Great Sand Dunes National Park.*) Later, the introduction of irrigation allowed for smaller ranch sizes, as hay crops could be grown for cattle feed and large grass grazing areas were no longer as necessary.

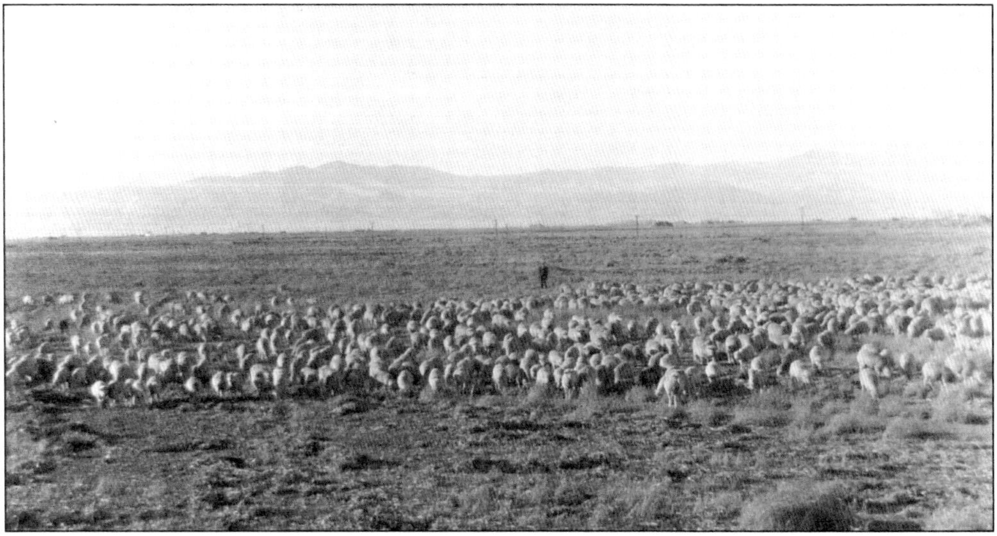

San Luis Valley Sheep, 1911. The earliest Hispanic settlers brought sheep to the San Luis Valley in the 1850s. The sheep were descended from original Spanish stock, and, over the years in the New World, they had become well adapted to harsh conditions and sparse vegetation. They could survive just about anywhere.

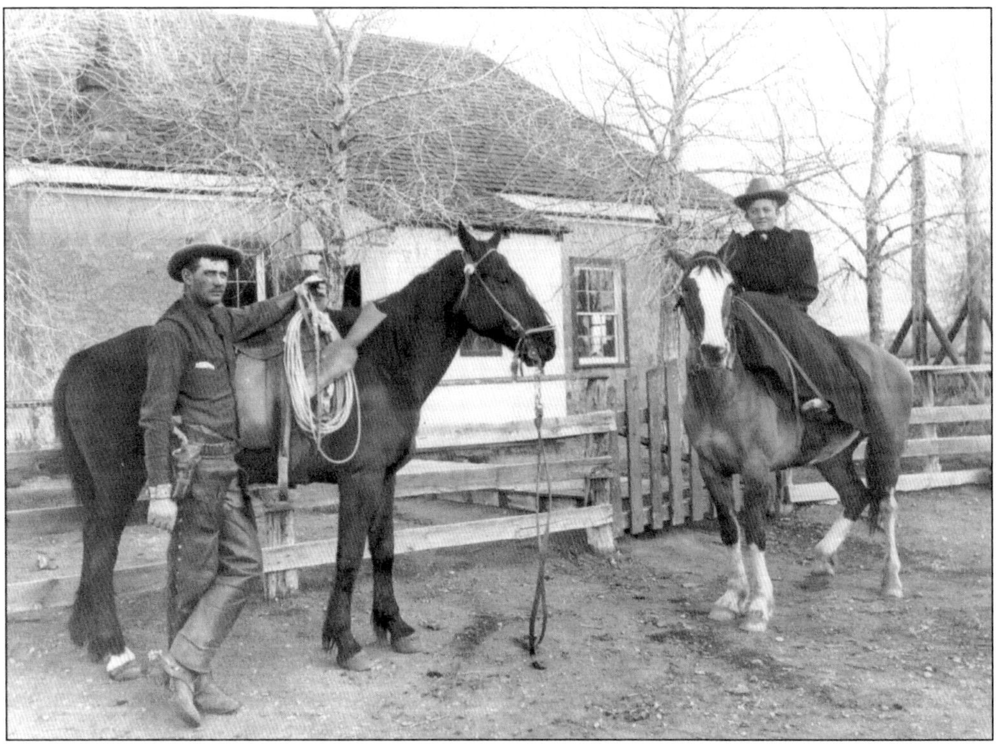

Hansen Ranch, April 28, 1889. In 1889, William M. Hansen, son of Peter Hansen (see page 46), still felt the necessity of protective weapons on his ranch near Fort Garland. He is prepared with a pistol on his hip and a rifle in the scabbard on his horse. Rustlers and outlaws still threatened isolated ranches. Note Mrs. Hansen riding sidesaddle.

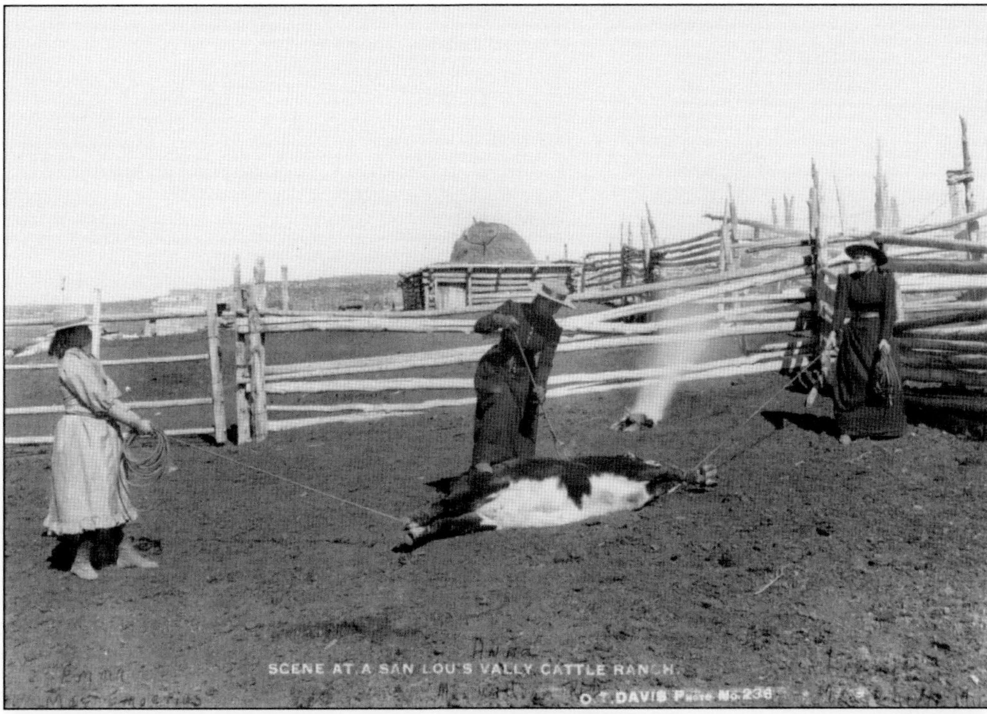

BRANDING CATTLE, OCTOBER 9, 1894. Three daughters of cattleman Harry Becker help out with the branding. The Becker ranch was 14 miles southeast of Alamosa. O.T. Davis identified the three daughters as Emma, Anna, and Lizzie.

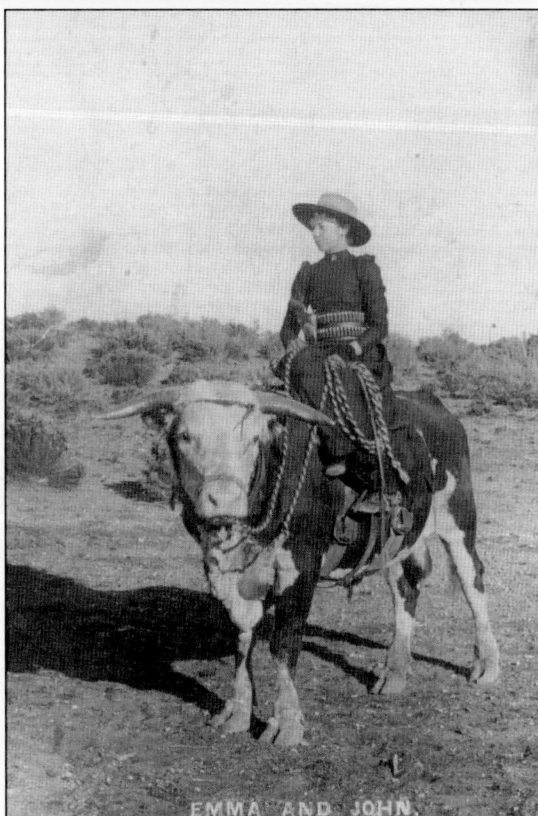

EMMA AND JOHN, OCTOBER 9, 1894. Emma Becker was riding sidesaddle on John the bull on this day at the Becker ranch. Emma is dressed up for the photograph with her gun and bullet belts.

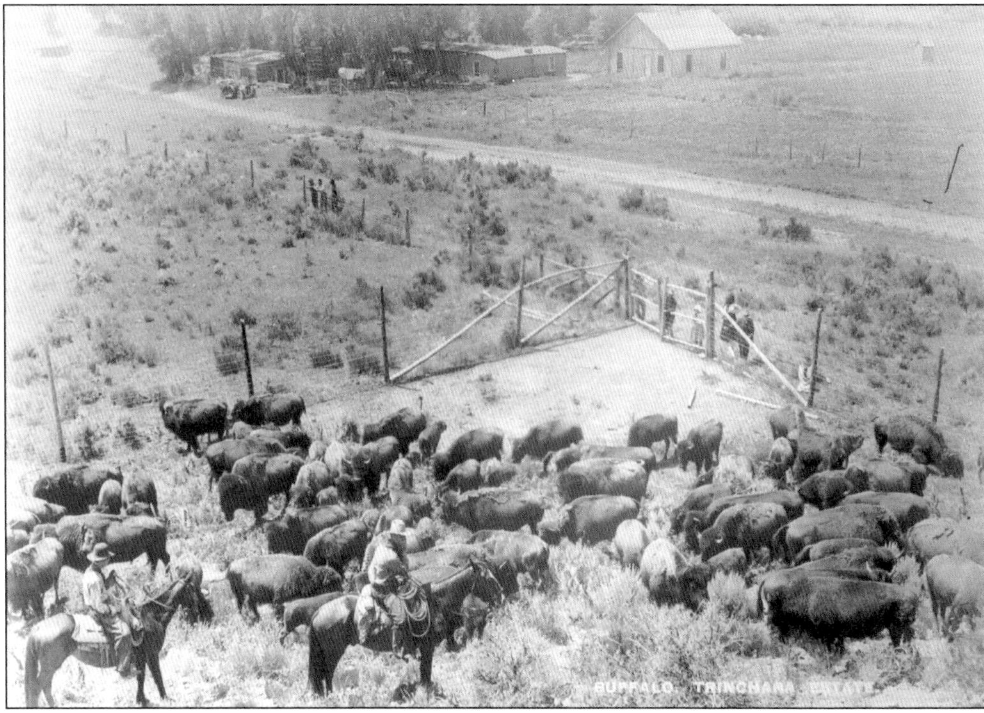

BUFFALO, TRINCHERA ESTATE, JULY 20, 1912. On this date, 83 head of buffalo valued at $25,000 were herded 275 miles from Dalhart, Texas, to their new home on the Trinchera Estate. The estate, near Fort Garland, was the northern half of the old Sangre de Cristo Mexican land grant, with the Costilla Estate forming the southern half.

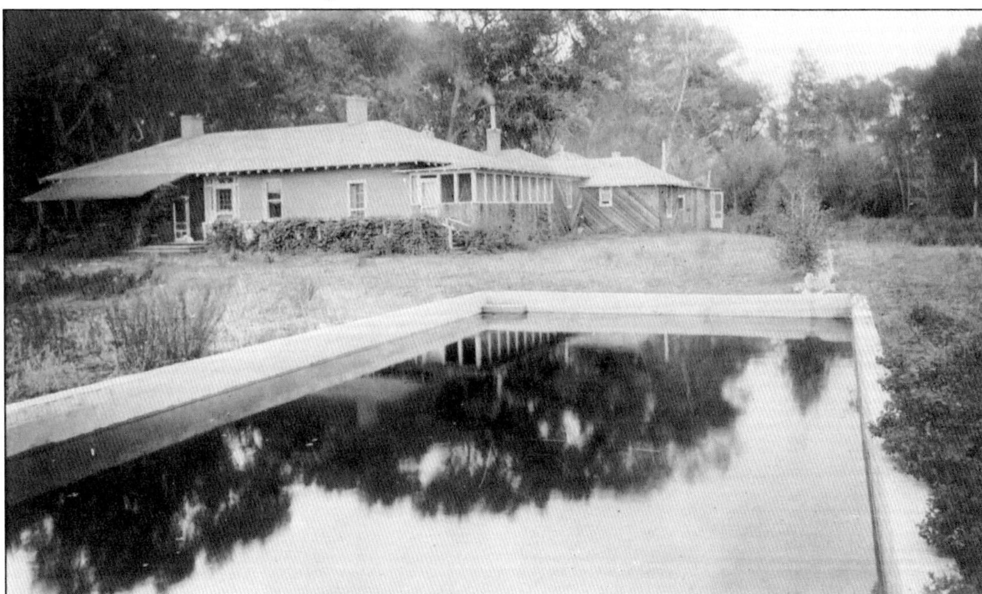

TRINCHERA ESTATE RANCH AND POOL, JULY 1926. Before being broken up into smaller parcels by its later owners the Forbes family, the estate was very large and prosperous. In 1937, Ruth McCormick Simms of Santa Fe purchased the 420,000-acre estate for a price of $500,000.

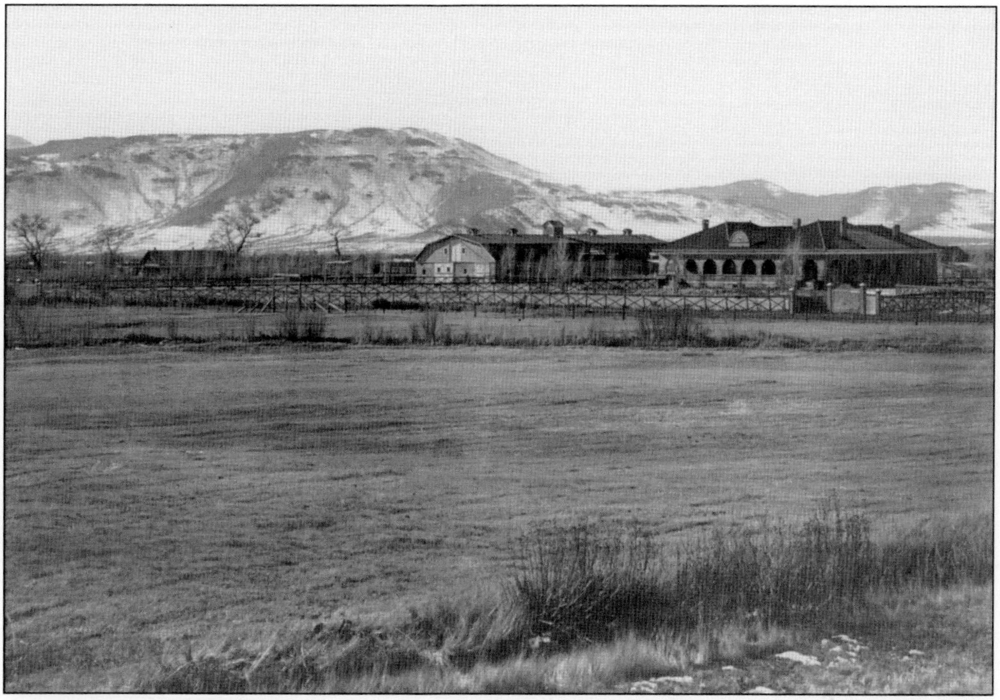

Austin Ranch on the Conejos River, 1907. The Conejos (Spanish for "rabbits") River rises in the San Juan Mountains and flows east to join the Rio Grande. Bob Austin was a Denver saloon owner and gambler. It was said that he built this beautiful ranch home for his wife using $60,000 won in a single night's game.

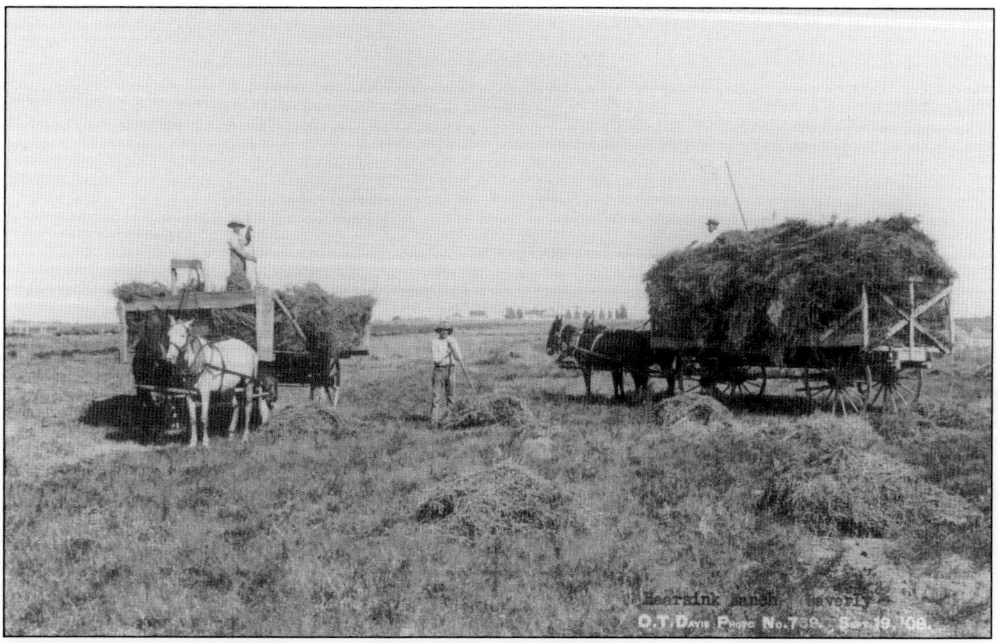

Heersink Ranch near Waverly, September 19, 1908. In the early 1900s, once the hay was cut, it was gathered by hand raking and tossed into wagons. Horse teams then pulled the wagons to a central unloading point for later distribution to cattle on the ranch.

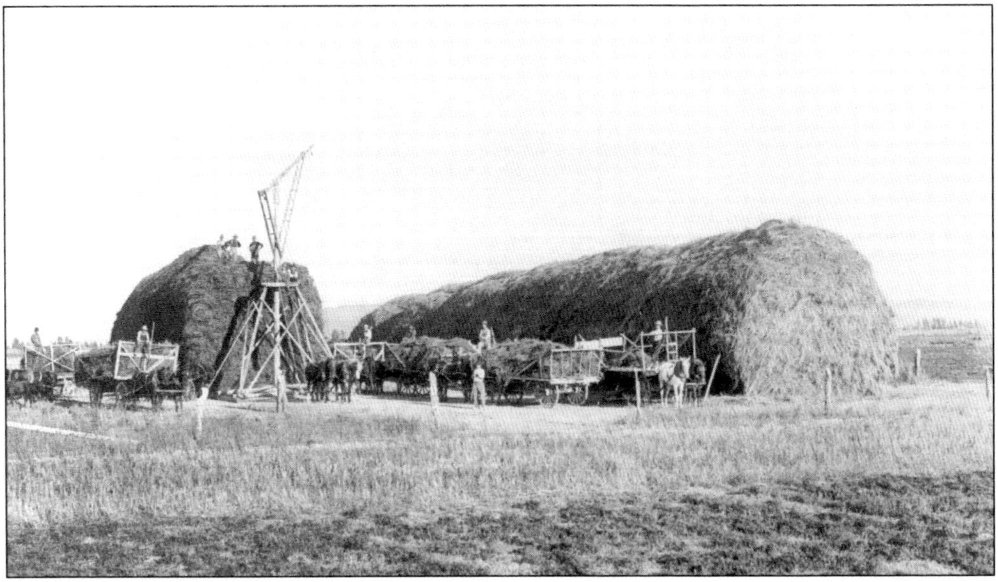

Unloading Hay, September 1911. When the cut hay was brought by horse-drawn wagons to a central location, it was unloaded, creating large stacks for later use in feeding cattle. This was the C.E. Hansen ranch, south of Alamosa.

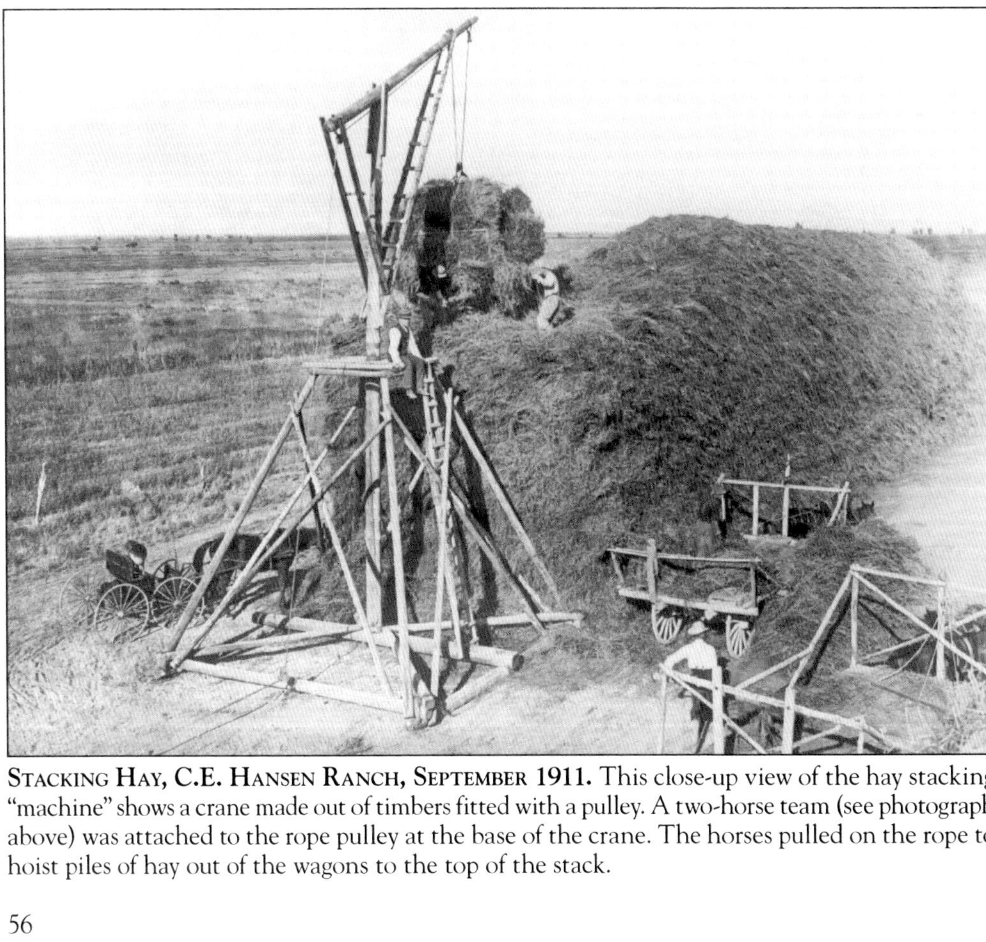

Stacking Hay, C.E. Hansen Ranch, September 1911. This close-up view of the hay stacking "machine" shows a crane made out of timbers fitted with a pulley. A two-horse team (see photograph above) was attached to the rope pulley at the base of the crane. The horses pulled on the rope to hoist piles of hay out of the wagons to the top of the stack.

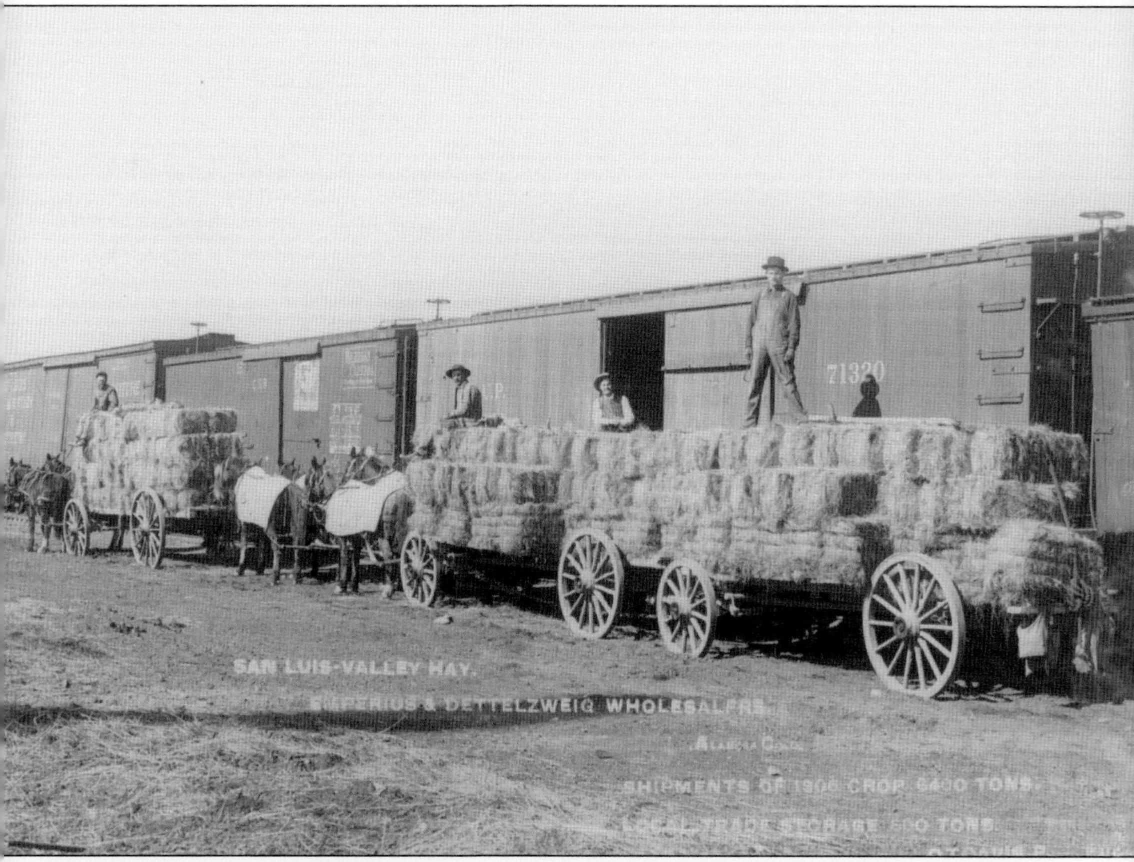

HAY SHIPMENT ON THE D&RG, 1906. Not all hay was used on the ranches where it was grown. Excess hay could be sold to wholesalers, such as the firm of Emperius & Dettelzweig in Alamosa. Its large warehouse was located just a block south of the D&RG depot in Alamosa. The hay was often shipped to the mining camps, where hungry mules and horses awaited its delivery. Of the 1906 hay crop from the San Luis Valley, O.T. Davis noted that Emperius & Dettelzweig shipped 6,400 tons.

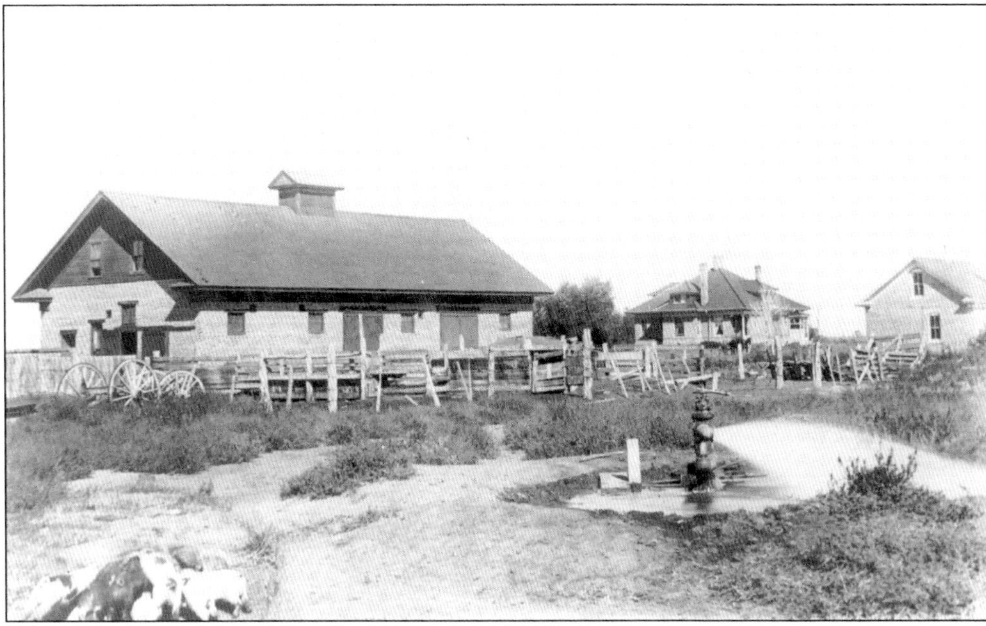

Ranch Home of Oscar Wilkins, 1899. This brick ranch home and barn was south of Alamosa near the Rio Grande. Note the artesian well. The Wilkins ranch was a major hay producer, and the 1891 *San Luis Valley Illustrated* booklet proclaimed, "Oscar Wilkins has thousands of tons of hay which find market of merit in the home trade and the big demand of the mining camps."

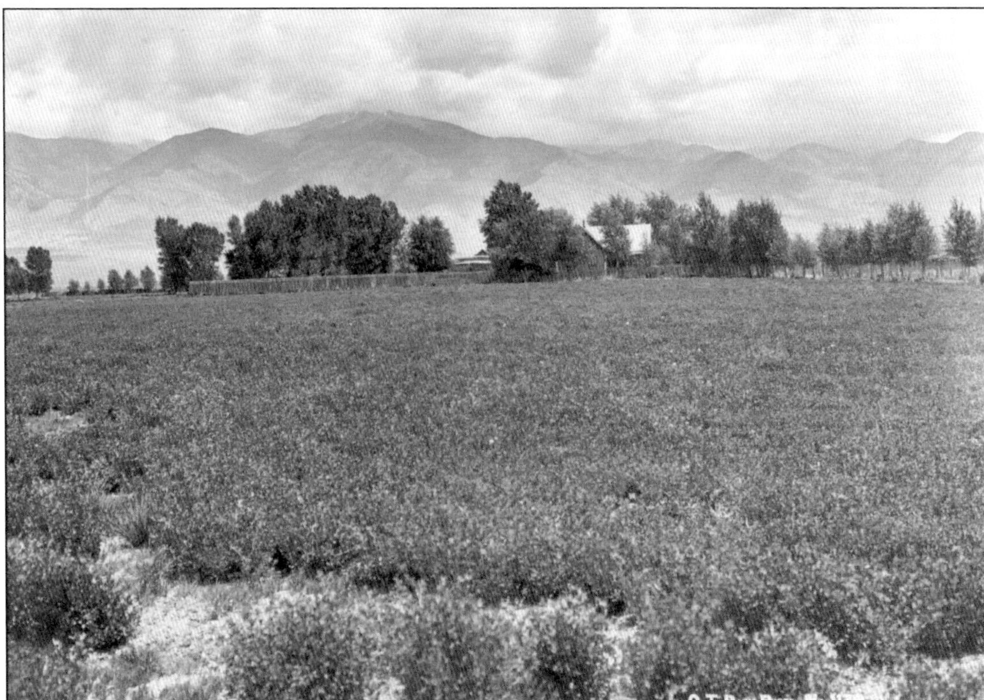

Rominger Ranch, August 2, 1911. This ranch was northeast of Moffat. O.T. Davis did not identify the crop growing in the foreground. The Sangre de Cristo (Spanish for "blood of Christ") Mountains tower in the background.

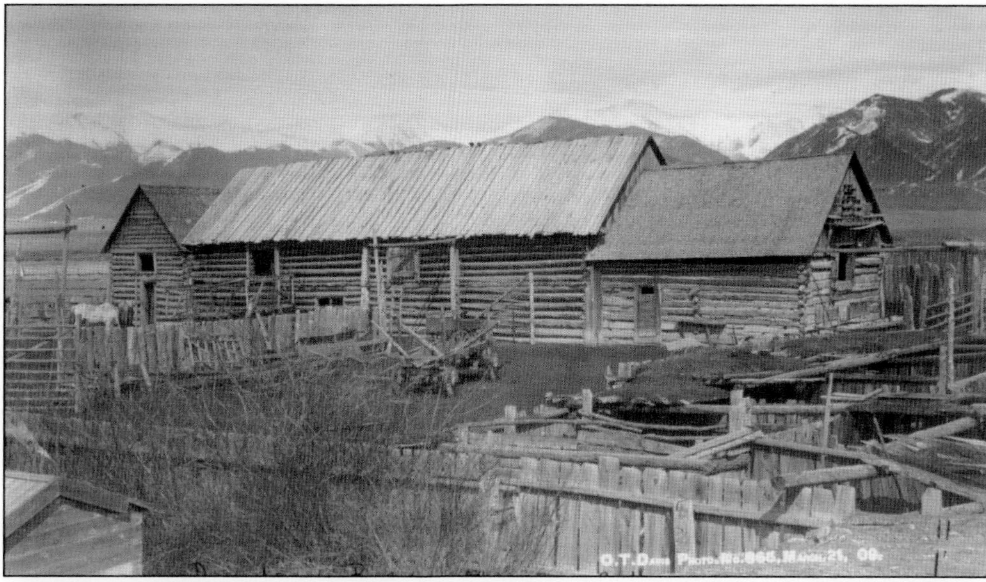

LOG BARN NEAR VILLA GROVE, MARCH 21, 1909. This log barn was on the W.D. Davidson ranch. Note the two horses at the left and the snow-capped Sangre de Cristo Mountains in the background. Villa Grove, at the north end of the San Luis Valley, served as a stage stop in the 1870s. It was originally called Norton Villa, named after Frank Norton, the stage station operator.

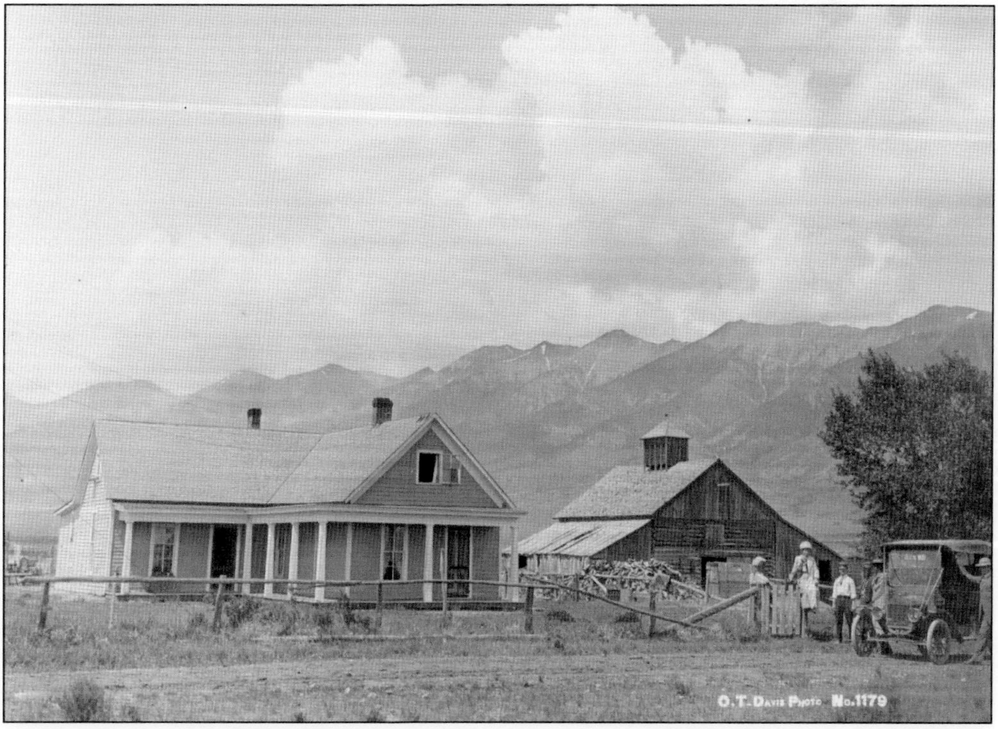

SHIPPEY RANCH NEAR VILLA GROVE, AUGUST 2, 1911. This ranch, two miles east of Villa Grove, belonged to Dr. Orland P. Shippey, a physician and surgeon with an office in Saguache. The D&RG built a narrow-gauge line over Poncha Pass to Villa Grove in 1881, and the town prospered as a supply base for mining camps to the northwest (Bonanza) and southeast (Orient).

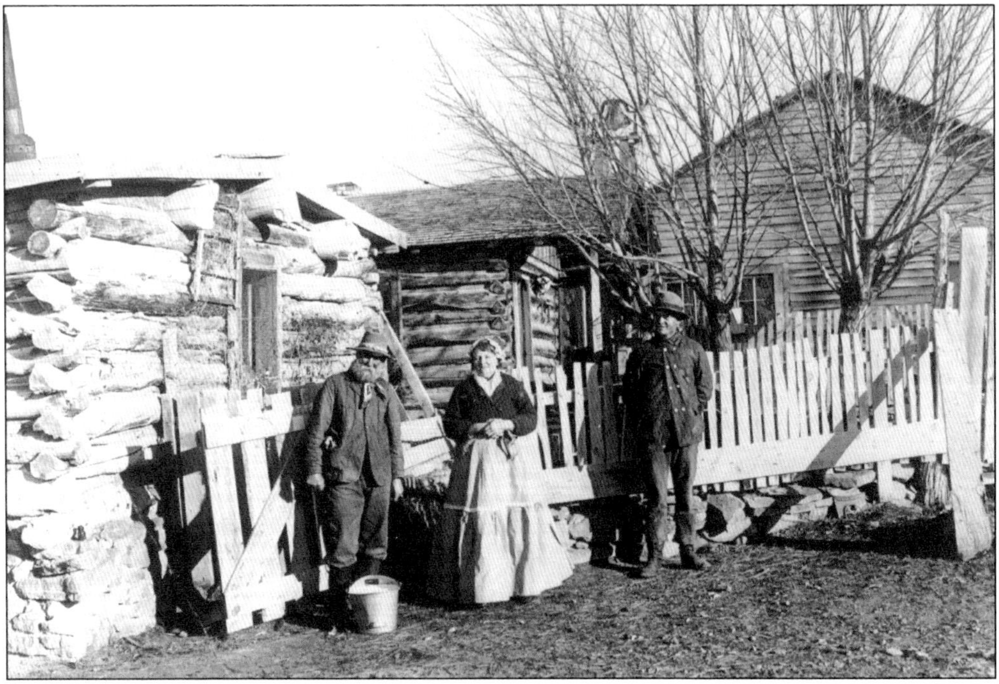

John Davey Ranch near Saguache, February 5, 1909. In the photograph, from left to right, are John "Rawhide Jack" Davey; his second wife, Mary Rees Davey; and her son Tom Rees. *Saguache* is a Ute Indian word meaning "blue earth." The Los Pinos Ute Agency was located near Saguache. John Davey, a blacksmith by trade, made horseshoes for Ute Indian ponies.

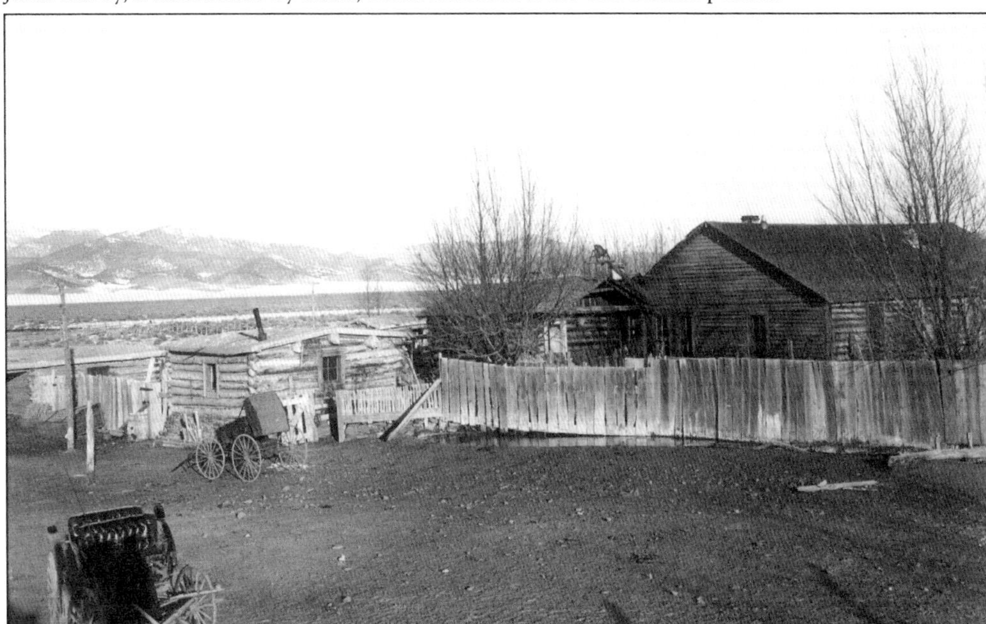

Davey Ranch, February 5, 1909. Here is another view of the Davey ranch buildings. The ranch was about eight miles south of Saguache. The town never had a railroad, so cattle and crops had to be shipped 18 miles east to the D&RG railhead at Villa Grove.

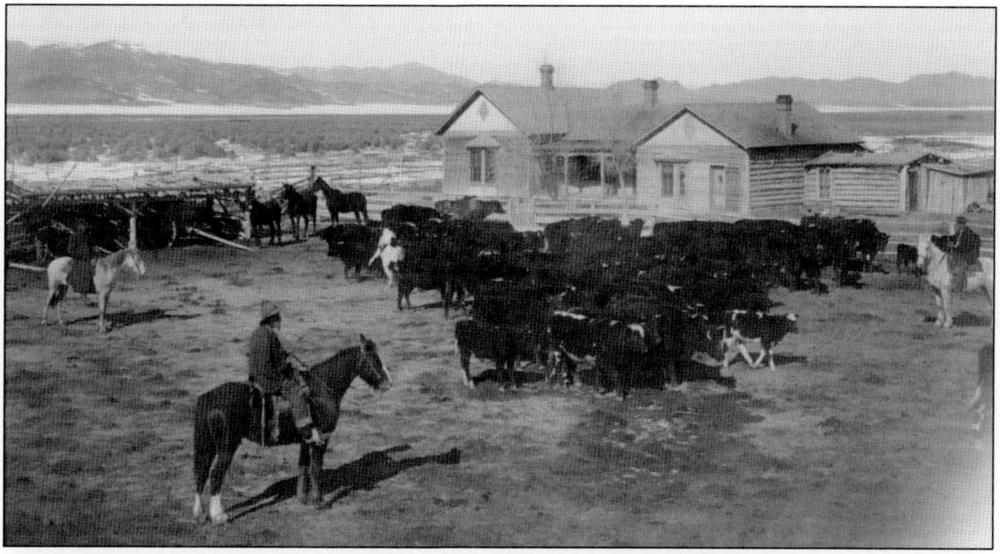

Trite's Ranch near Saguache, February 5, 1909. Ranchers did not mind having a herd of cattle in their front yard when it was roundup time. When the cattle were sufficiently fattened on mountain grasses and ranch hay, they were driven by cowboys on horseback to the D&RG railheads in Villa Grove or Moffat.

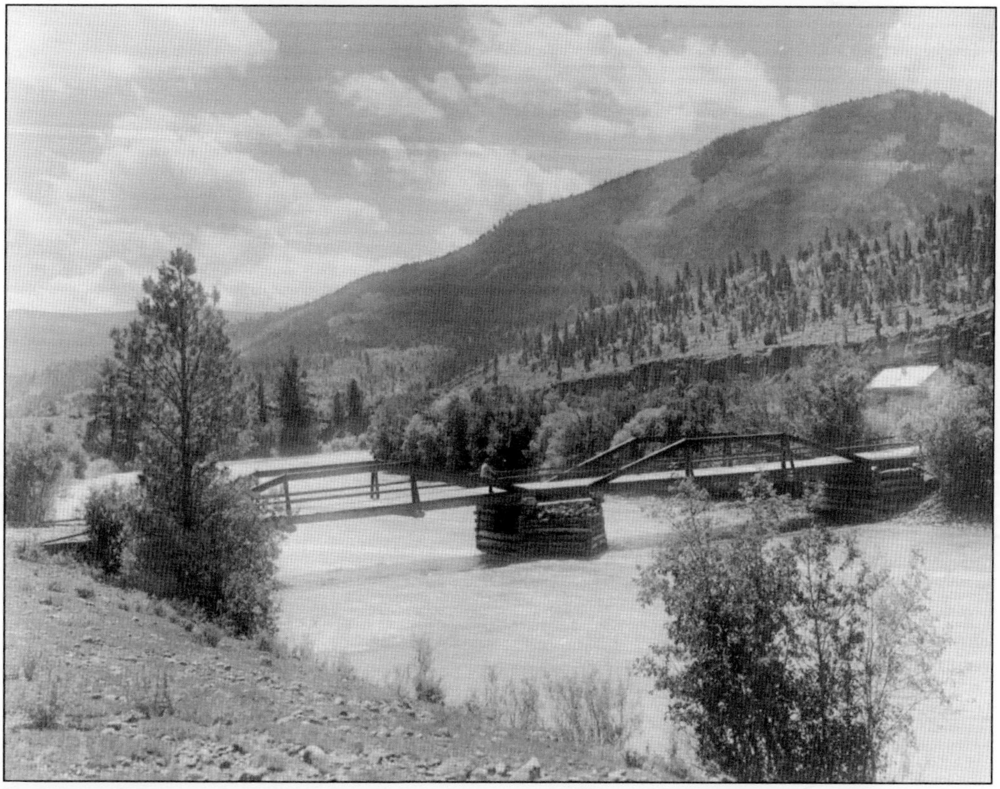

Riverside Ranch on the Rio Grande, 1915. Located between South Fork and Wagon Wheel Gap, the ranch raised cattle for local markets, particularly the mining town of Creede, just to the north. Note the person sitting on the rail near the center of the bridge.

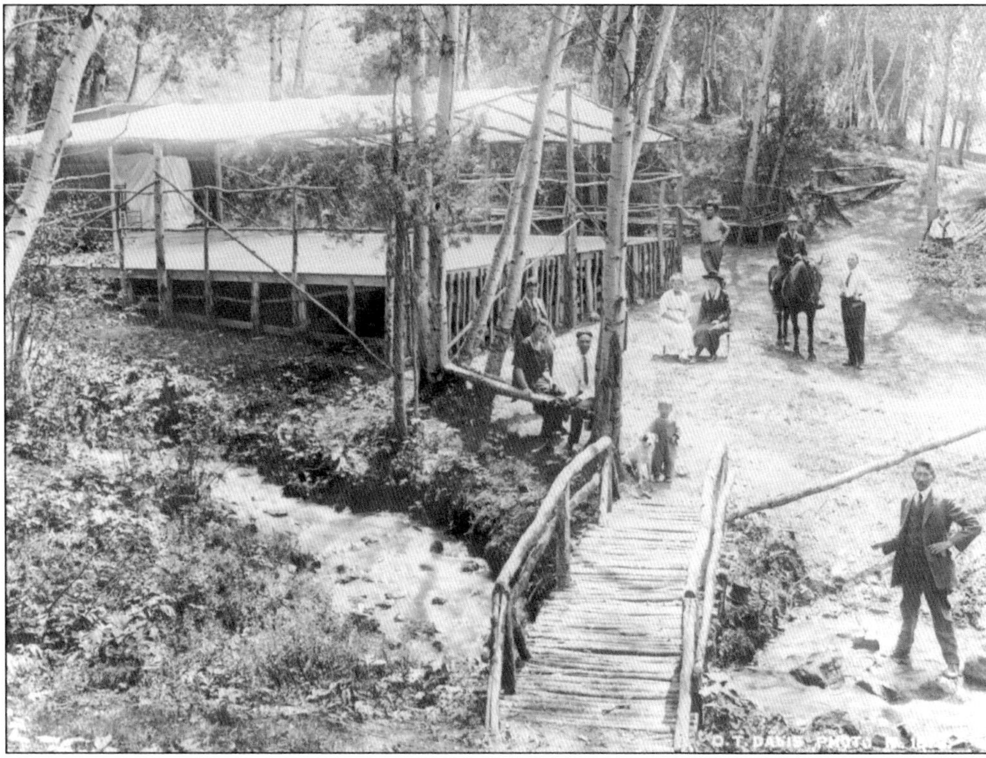

DANCING PAVILION AT ARROWHEAD RANCH, 1922. The Arrowhead Ranch was six miles north of Blanca in the foothills of the Sangre de Cristo Mountains. Recreational facilities for ranch families were limited, and this dance floor attracted folks from a wide area. The gentleman standing in the creek is identified as Bill Wilde.

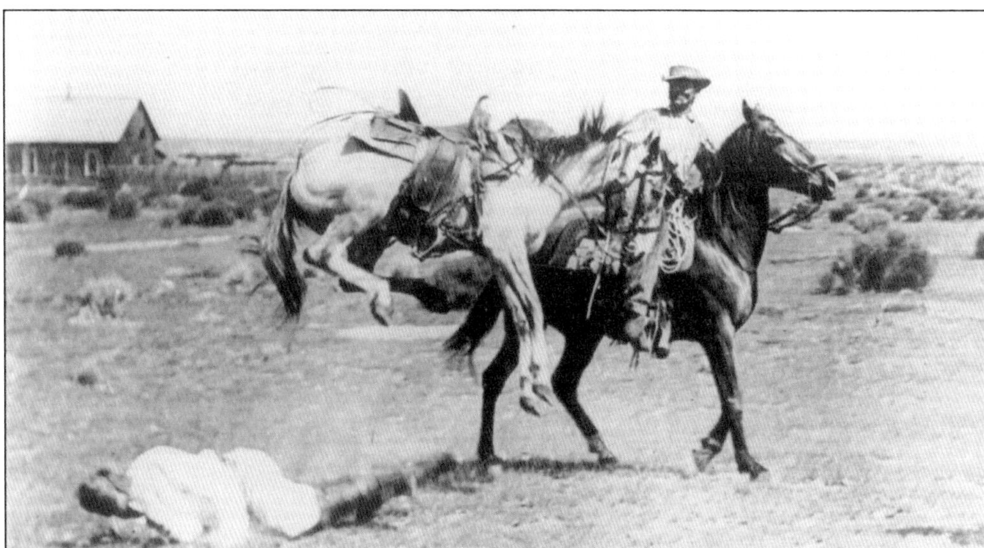

BUCKING HORSE, 1934. O.T. Davis was on hand to capture this action-packed scene north of Alamosa. Ranch life was always difficult, and being bucked off a horse was just one of the hardships associated with everyday life.

Six

Farming
"Peas, Pigs, and Prosperity"

For purposes of grouping photographs, this book was divided into separate chapters on ranching and farming. In reality, of course, the two activities are seldom mutually exclusive. Cattle ranches often grow food crops, such as wheat and vegetables, and farmers sometimes have a few head of cattle, chickens, and pigs in addition to their mainstay of food crops. In the San Luis Valley, peas could be grown in the fields and pigs were fattened off the peas. The practice was so common that author Leland Feitz, in his book *Alamosa: A Quick History*, noted that the phrase "Peas, Pigs, and Prosperity" became a rallying cry for the valley.

Particularly affecting farming in the southern San Luis Valley in the late 1930s was a division of the US Department of Agriculture known as the Farm Security Administration (FSA). Created in 1937 as an agency to deal with the Great Depression in rural areas, the FSA was instrumental in assisting farmers driven off the southeastern Colorado plains by the dust bowl effects of 1938–1940. The small town of Waverly, 11 miles southwest of Alamosa, with its school and Christian Reformed Church, formed the nucleus of an FSA project known as San Luis Valley Farms. There were 86 dispersed farm sites selected by the FSA, each either an 80-acre or 160-acre parcel. The land was leased to the displaced dust bowl farmers, and each family received a house with electricity and water, as well as a barn, chicken house, and hog house. O.T. Davis's photographs of "Waverly wheat" in the early 1900s testify to the productivity of this irrigated area, which was never affected by the dust bowl effects seen in southeastern Colorado.

A wide variety of crops, including wheat, oats, hay, barley, sugar beets, peas, cabbage, lettuce, cauliflower, and, of course, the mainstay of the valley, potatoes, has always been grown in the San Luis Valley. Even during the Great Depression, in 1930, San Luis Valley crops were bountiful, with 11,000 railcars of potatoes shipped out that year, as well as 2,200 carloads of other vegetables, including 700 carloads of lettuce.

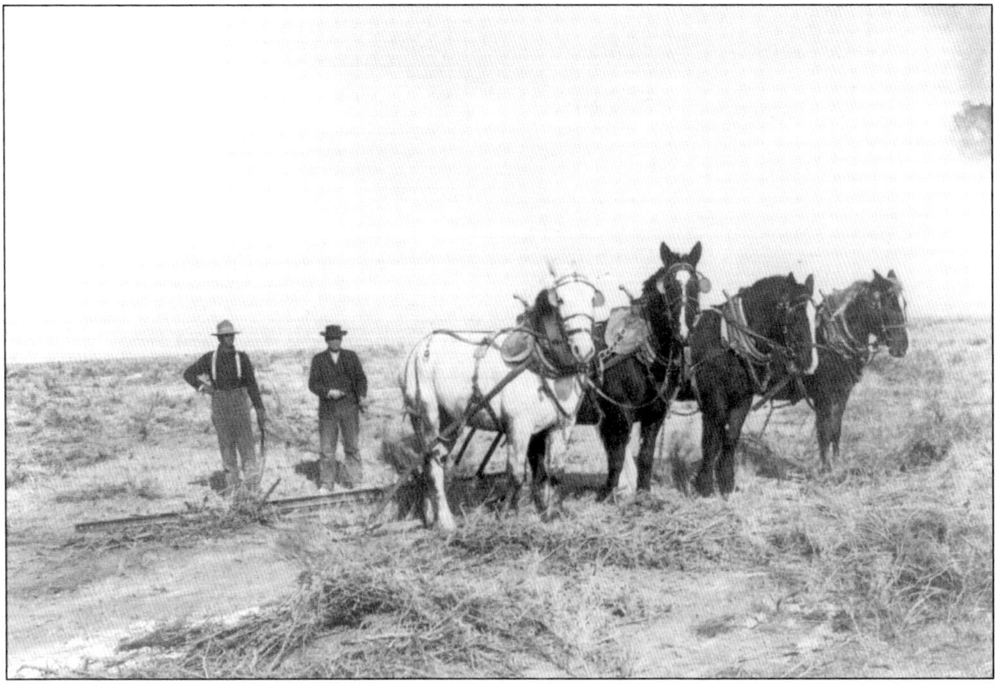

Breaking Brush near Mosca, 1907. Before San Luis Valley fields could be sown with seed and irrigated, they first had to be cleared of native arid-climate plants, such as sagebrush, chico, and greasewood. In this instance, a four-horse team was hitched to several iron rails that were pulled across the brush, breaking it down and clearing it away.

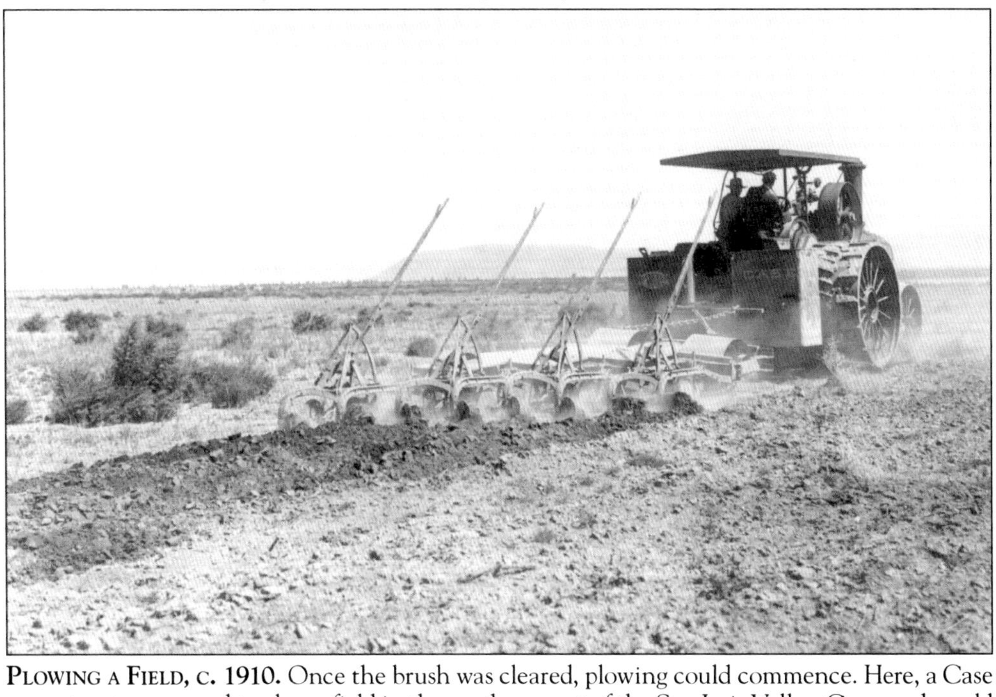

Plowing a Field, c. 1910. Once the brush was cleared, plowing could commence. Here, a Case steam tractor was used to plow a field in the southern part of the San Luis Valley. Crop seed would then be planted in the furrows opened up by the plow.

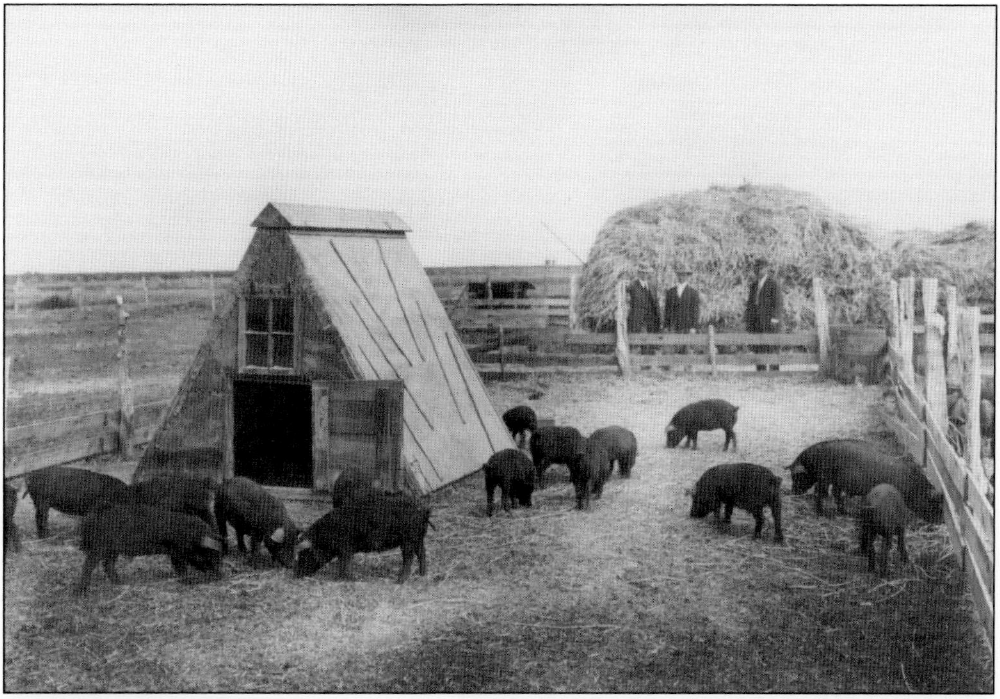

PALMER RANCH NEAR ALAMOSA, 1912. The prize hogs in this corral appear to be feeding on hay supplied from the haystack in the background. Peas were also grown for hog feed in the San Luis Valley. The men are unidentified.

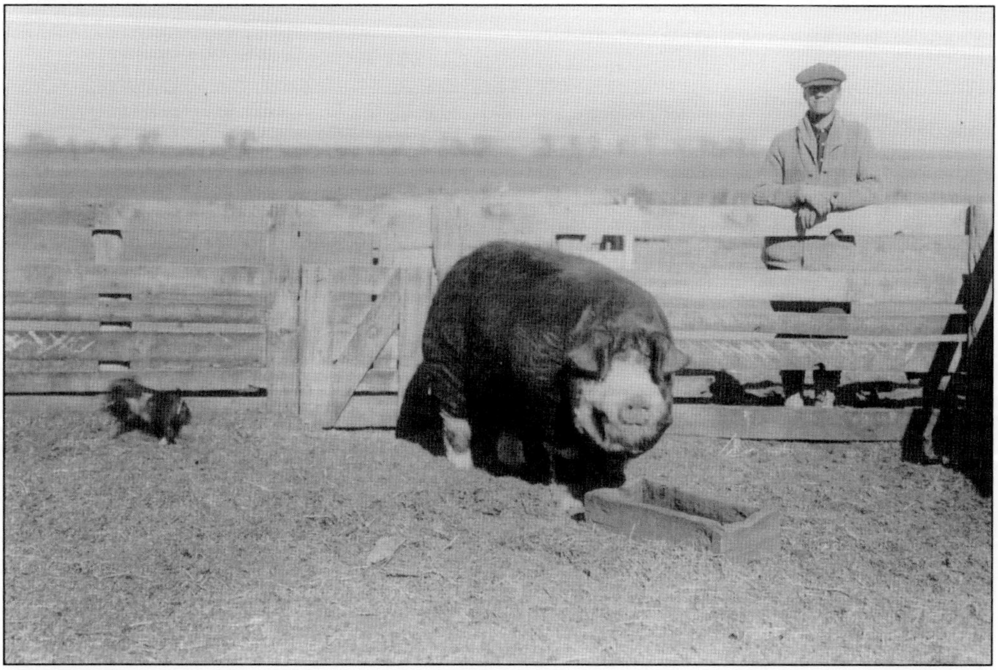

UTE MOUNTAIN RANCH, 1915. This was a prizewinning hog on the Ute Mountain Ranch, in the south San Luis Valley. The man is not identified. In 1930, a total of 110 train carloads of hogs were shipped out of Alamosa.

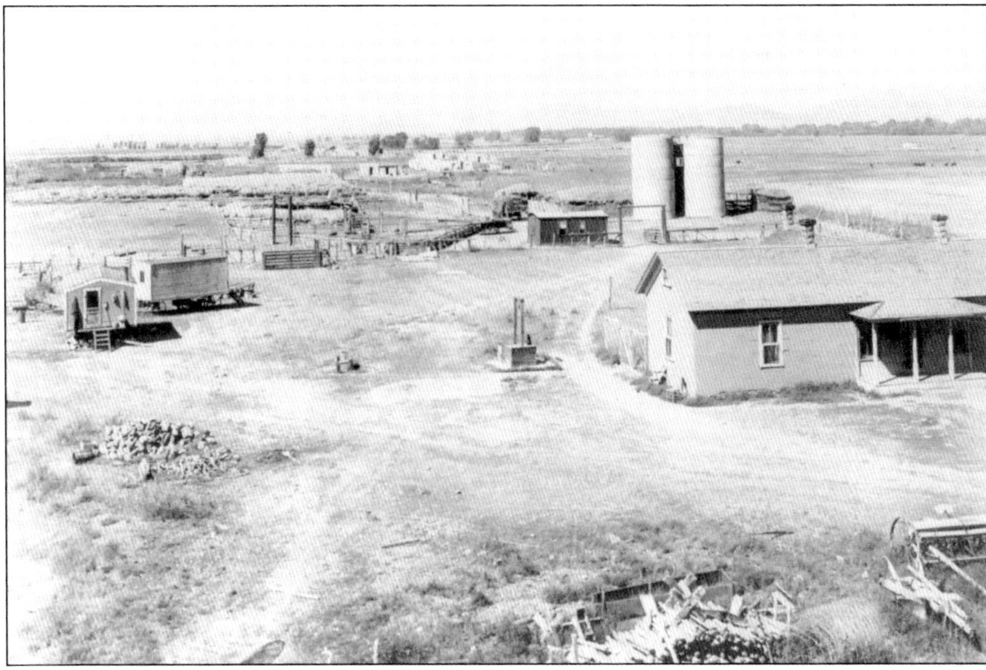

HOMES ON THE UTE MOUNTAIN RANCH, 1915. In addition to hogs, the Ute Mountain Ranch raised sheep, as witnessed by the two sheepherder wagons to the left and the sheep inside the fenced corral in the left background. The main ranch house, in the right foreground, was built with adobe bricks, as were the worker homes in the center background.

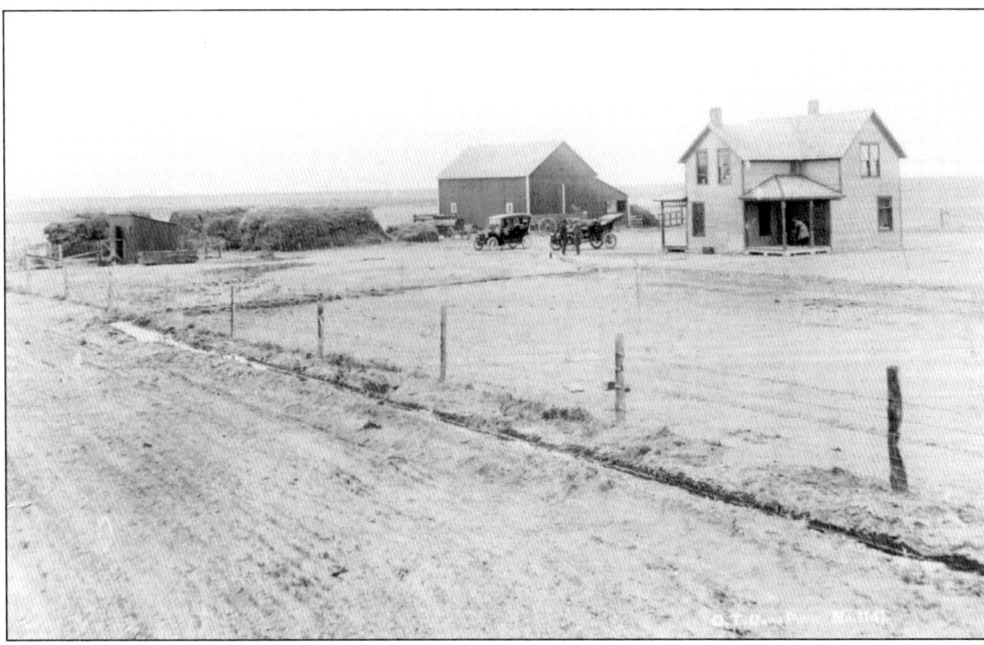

A.O. NORTON RANCH, MAY 12, 1911. This ranch was southeast of Alamosa. A variety of crops were grown on the ranch, including hay (note the haystacks to the left of the barn), oats, and wheat. The automobile had a huge impact on the isolated San Luis Valley farms, as trips to town for supplies could be made much more quickly and easily.

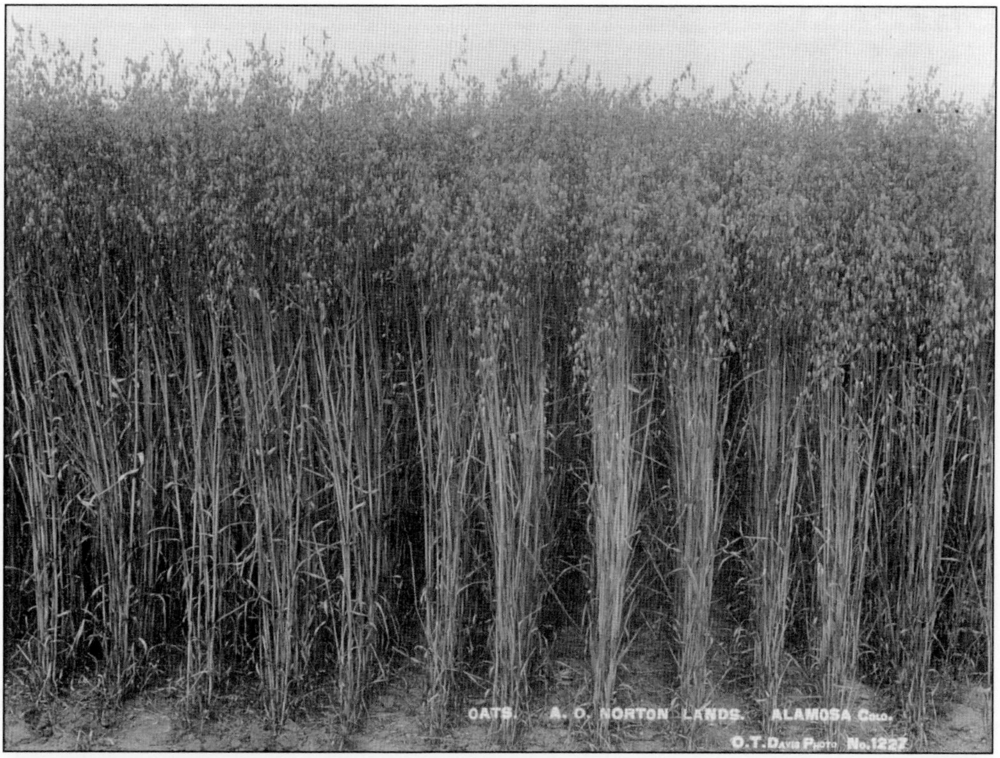

FIELD OF OATS, 1911. This healthy field of oats on the A.O. Norton farm gives testimony to the life-giving irrigation water of the San Luis Valley. Oats were raised as feed for horses as well as for human consumption.

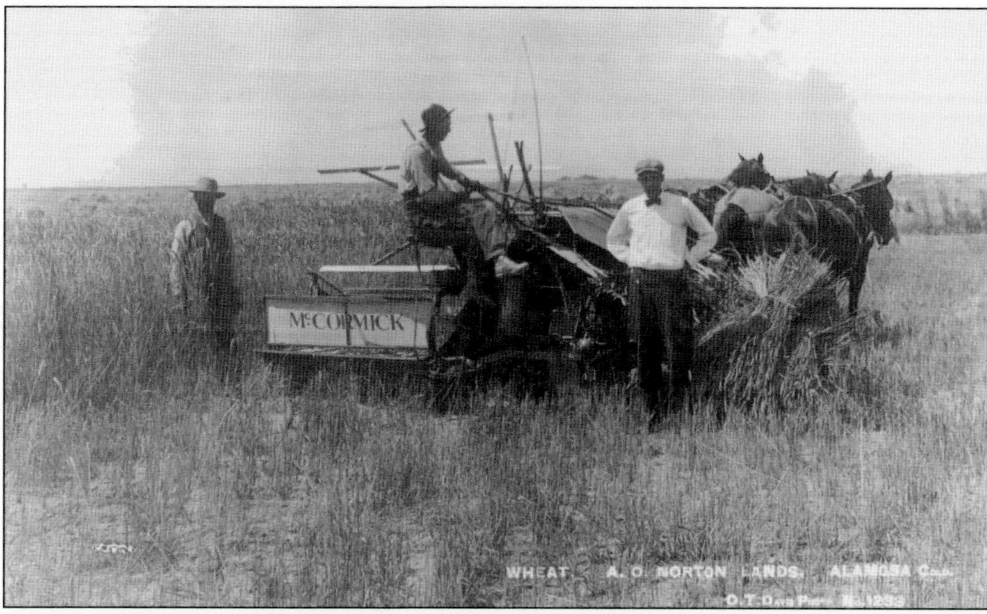

CUTTING WHEAT, AUGUST 30, 1911. On the A.O. Norton farm, a horse-drawn McCormick binder was used to cut and bind the shocks of wheat. The bound shocks were then left in the fields to dry. The men are not identified.

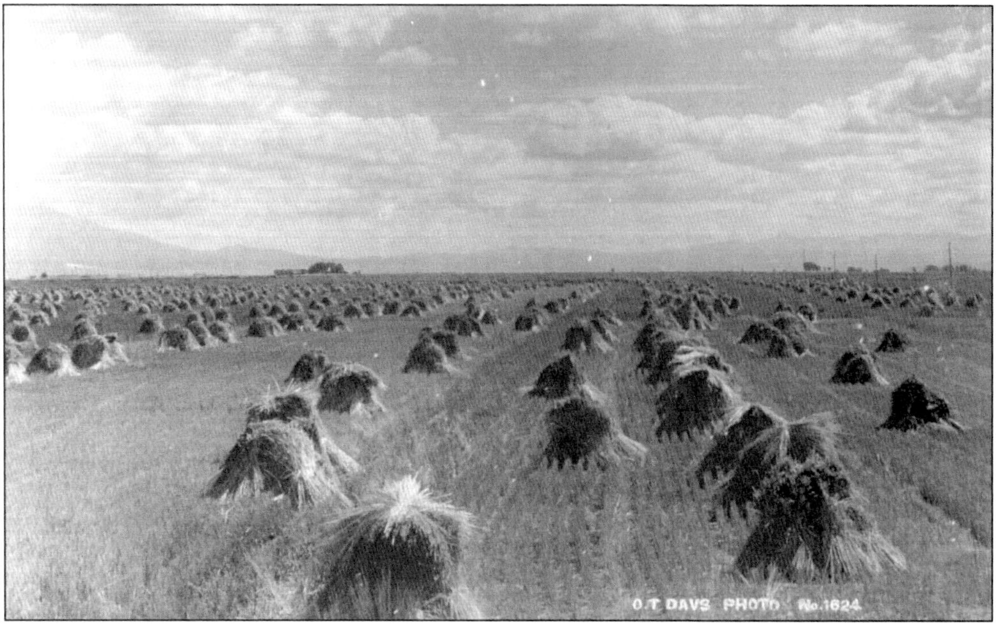

SAN LUIS VALLEY WHEAT HARVEST, 1916. After the wheat was cut and bound into shocks, it was left to dry in the fields. After drying, men would pitch the shocks into horse-drawn wagons, which would transport the wheat to a central location for threshing.

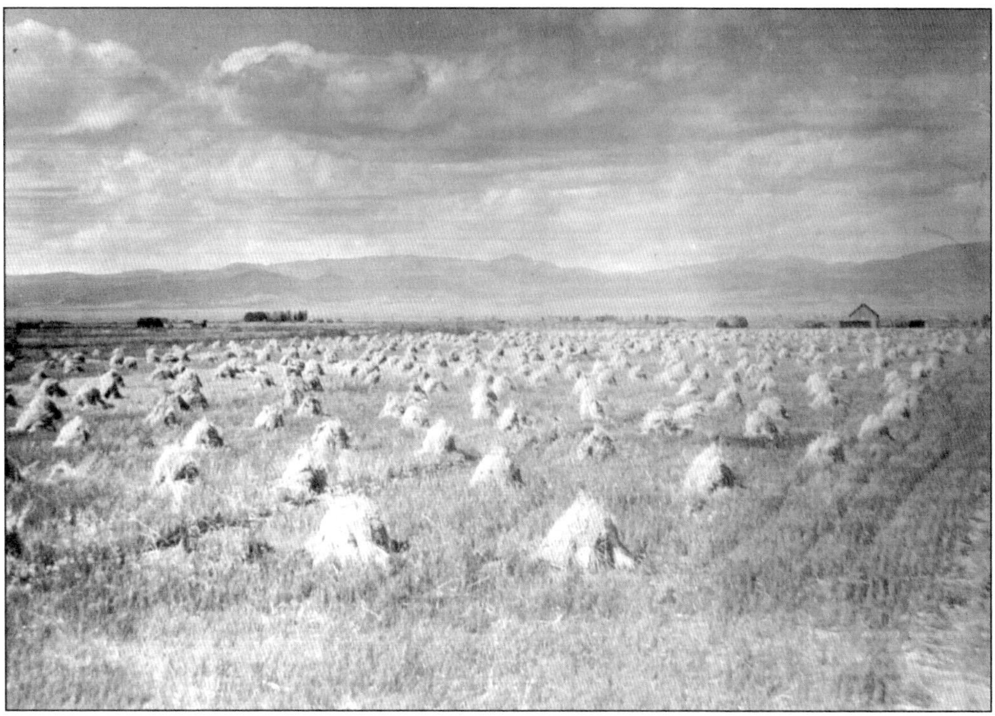

WAVERLY WHEAT, C. 1910. Shocks of wheat are ready for gathering and threshing in this field near Waverly. Waverly was the site for resettlement of dust bowl–stricken farmers from southeastern Colorado from 1938 to 1940. The Farm Security Administration set up viable 160-acre farms for the incoming settlers to lease.

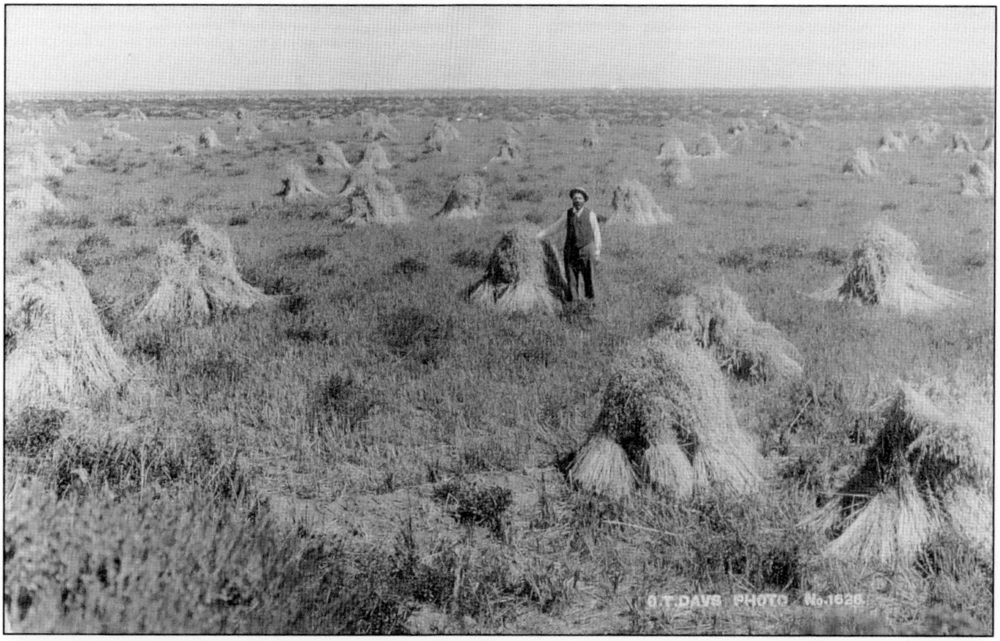

SHOCKS OF WHEAT, C. 1916. The size of the wheat shocks is shown here, reaching nearly waist high on the man in the field. Large flour mills in the San Luis Valley at Mosca, Alamosa, Monte Vista, and other locations would grind the wheat into flour, which was then shipped out on the D&RG Railroad.

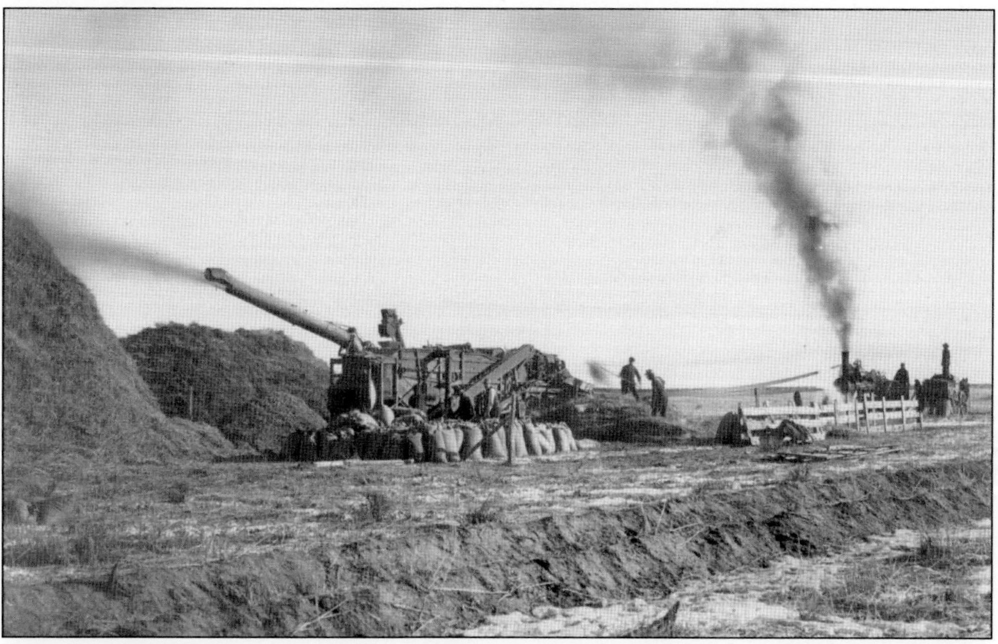

THRESHING MACHINE NEAR ALAMOSA, 1907. M.D. Blakley owned this steam-driven threshing machine. The conveyor belt from the steam engine was attached to drive the parts of the thresher. Men using pitchforks threw the shocks of wheat into the thresher, which beat the wheat grain from the stalks. The chaff was shot out to the left, and the wheat grains were bagged at the front of the thresher.

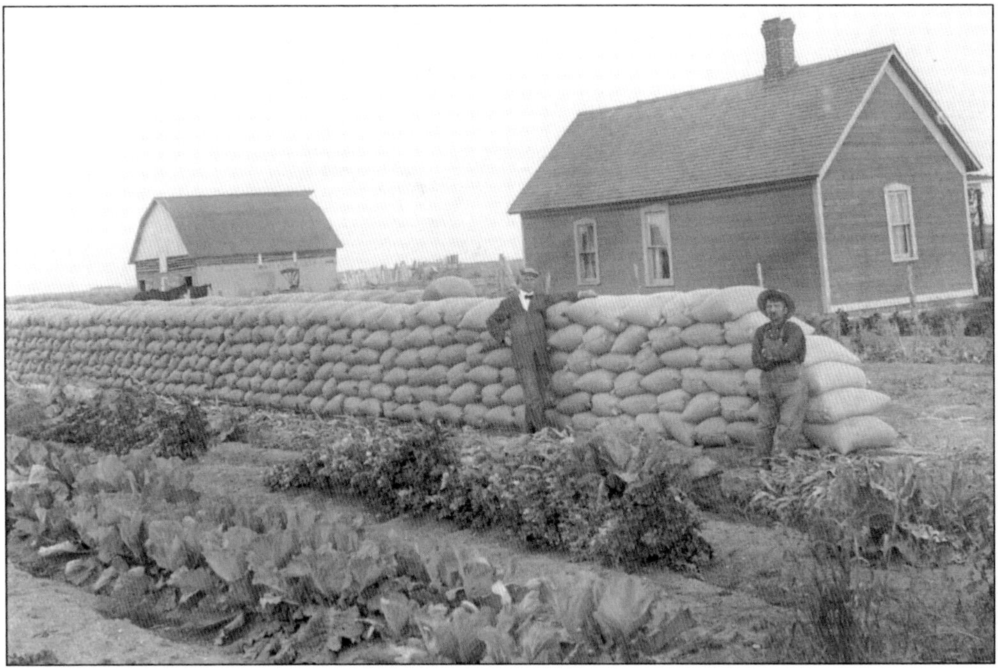

Farmhouse East of Center, September 1911. Sacks of grain (probably wheat) are stacked ready for shipping from this farm near Center. The town of Center was founded in 1898 to serve the prosperous farms of this part of the San Luis Valley. In 1913, the San Luis Central Railroad was built from Monte Vista north 12 miles to Center to serve this thriving market.

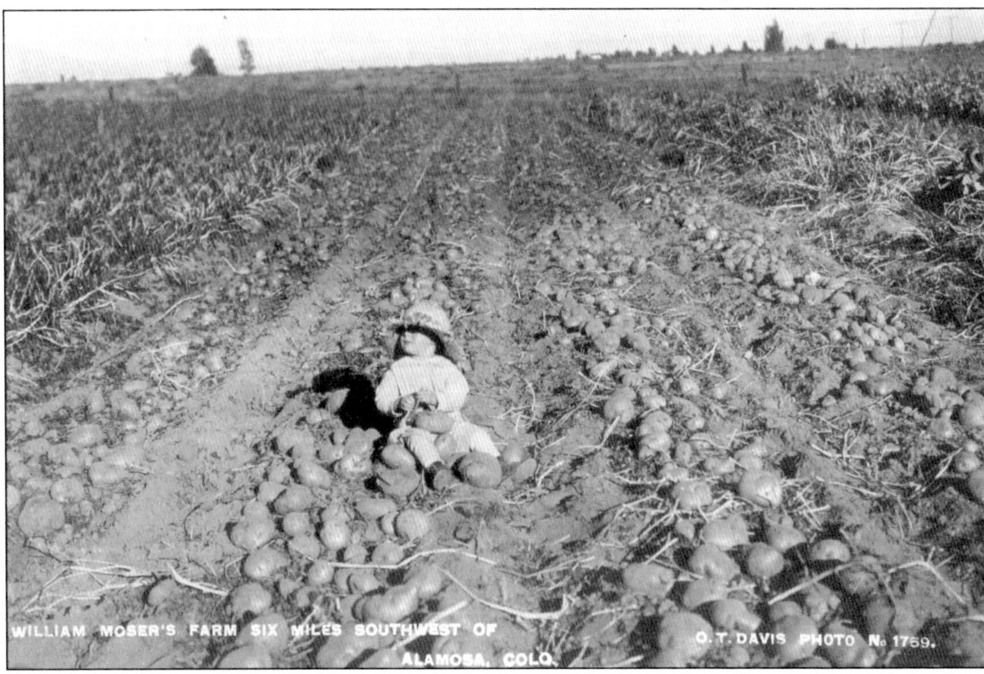

Potato Harvest, 1910. This was the bountiful potato harvest from the William Moser farm, six miles southwest of Alamosa. Potatoes have always been the main crop of the San Luis Valley. In 1930, a total of 11,000 train carloads of potatoes were shipped from the valley.

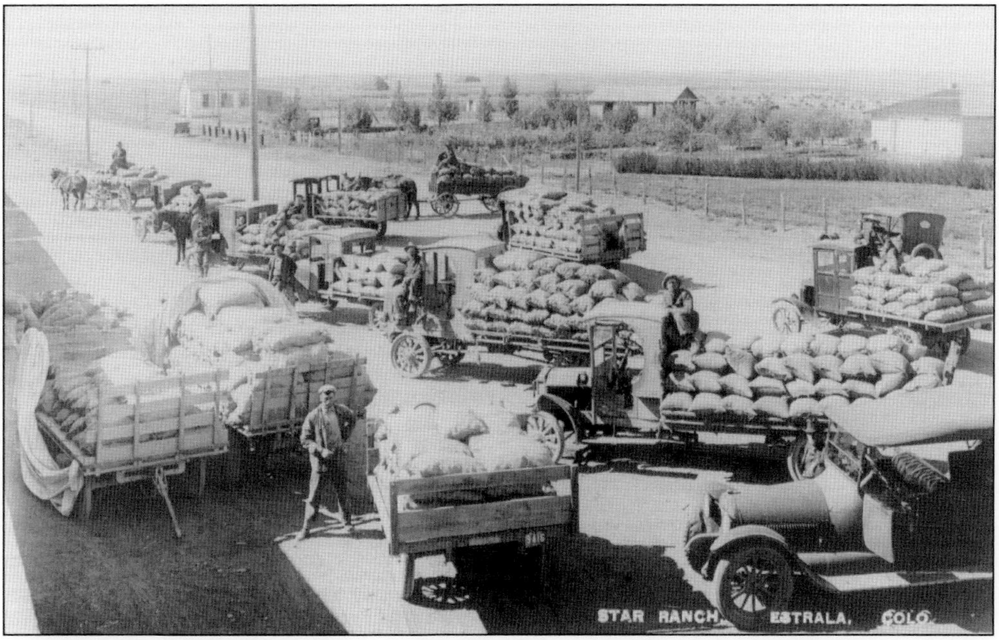

Star Ranch at Estrella, 1921. Estrella (Spanish for "star") was located between Alamosa and La Jara, just north of the Conejos County line. The Star Ranch produced these wagonloads and truckloads of potatoes and grain. Here, they are gathered waiting to be shipped out on the D&RG Railroad. In 1880, the D&RG built south from Alamosa 28.7 miles, connecting Estrella, La Jara, and Romeo to Antonito. In 1881, the line was extended west from Antonito to Cumbres Pass, Chama, and Durango.

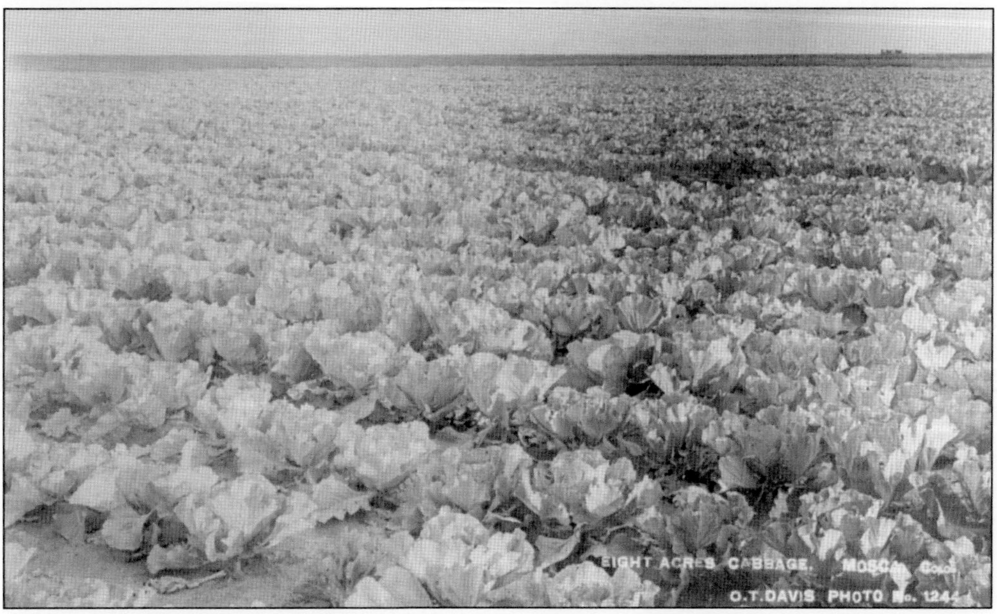

Cabbage Field, September 1911. Eight acres of cabbage are shown on the Charles Push farm near Mosca. Irrigation made possible the production of a variety of vegetable crops in the San Luis Valley, including cabbage, lettuce, broccoli, cauliflower, and spinach. In 1930, a total of 2,200 train carloads of vegetables were shipped out of the valley.

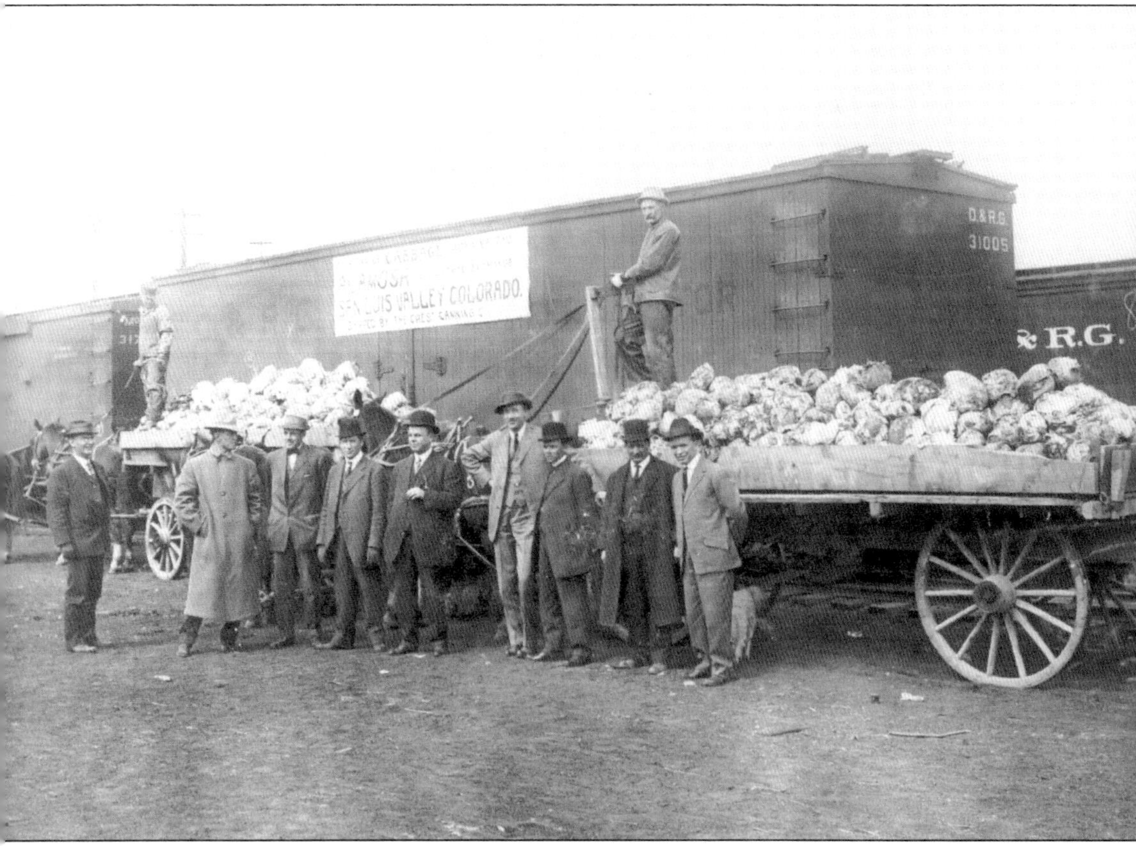

WAGONLOADS OF CABBAGE, 1911. These wagonloads of cabbage are ready to be loaded onto the D&RG at Alamosa. The sign on the boxcar reads, "This car of cabbage grown by the Alamosa Real Estate Exchange, San Luis Valley Colorado. Shipped by the Crest Canning Company."

Seven

Towns and Villages
"People Voted as They Pleased"

A glance at the map on page 10 reveals an axis of towns and villages on intersecting east–west and north–south lines largely following the route of the Denver & Rio Grande Railroad. From east to west are Walsenburg, La Veta, Fort Garland, Blanca, Alamosa, Monte Vista, Del Norte, and South Fork. From north to south are Villa Grove, Moffat, Hooper, Mosca, Alamosa, La Jara, Romeo, and Antonito. Some towns and villages were created by the D&RG, while others existed prior to the coming of the railroad. Walsenburg (as La Plaza de Los Leones, 1858) and La Veta (as Francisco Plaza, 1862) were founded well before the arrival of the railroad. A number of towns, such as Del Norte, South Fork, Wagon Wheel Gap, and Villa Grove, were stage stop towns before the railroad arrived. And some towns, such as Moffat, Hooper, Mosca, and Antonito, were created by the railroad. When the railroad arrived, most towns along its route prospered and came to rely on it heavily.

A few towns suffered and withered, however, as a result of the railroad. Conejos was bypassed by the railroad, as the D&RG built its own town at Antonito. Though only a mile apart, Conejos today is the smaller of the two towns, even though it is still the county seat. Some towns, such as Garland City, disappeared completely when they were no longer the end of track. In fact, Garland City's buildings were loaded onto railcars and moved to the new town of Alamosa.

Small towns in the region always seemed to have problems with elections. In Saguache, the town was said to have won the county seat away from Milton by a margin of six votes, which were suspected of having been cast by the oxen of a local Saguache farmer. In Bonanza, toll road builder Otto Mears, who plied the voters with wagons loaded with whiskey, ham, bacon, and other goodies, swayed townsfolk to vote a certain way. Nevertheless, as Helen Kempner noted in her book *Bonanza! A Pictorial History of Colorado's Kerber Creek Country*, "The people voted as they pleased!"

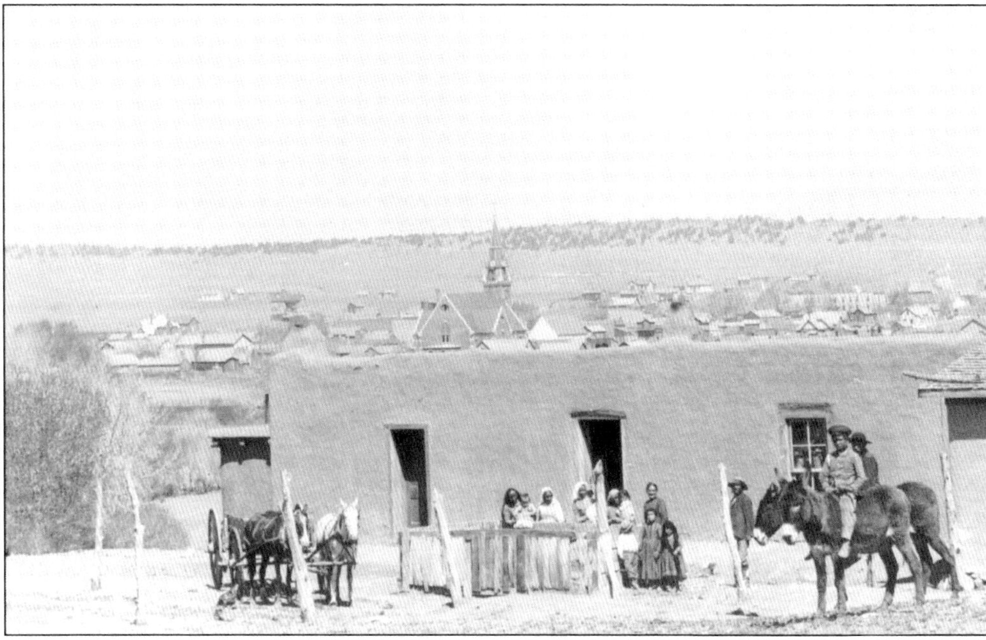

WALSENBURG, C. 1890s. This adobe home in Walsenburg reflects the heritage of Hispanics from New Mexico who settled there at La Plaza de Los Leones (Spanish for "Plaza of the Lions"), on the banks of the Cucharas River, in 1858. The church in the center is St. Mary's Catholic Church.

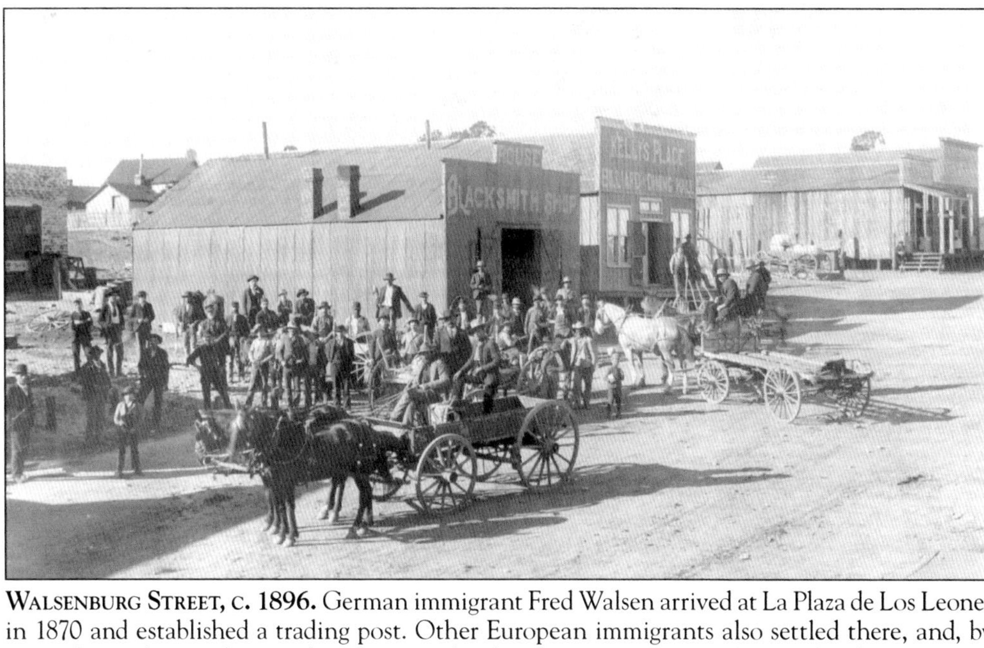

WALSENBURG STREET, C. 1896. German immigrant Fred Walsen arrived at La Plaza de Los Leones in 1870 and established a trading post. Other European immigrants also settled there, and, by 1872, the settlement became known as Walsenburg. O.T. Davis moved to Walsenburg in 1893. Later, he captured this scene with a large crowd gathered outside the blacksmith shop and Kelly's Place Billiard and Dining Hall.

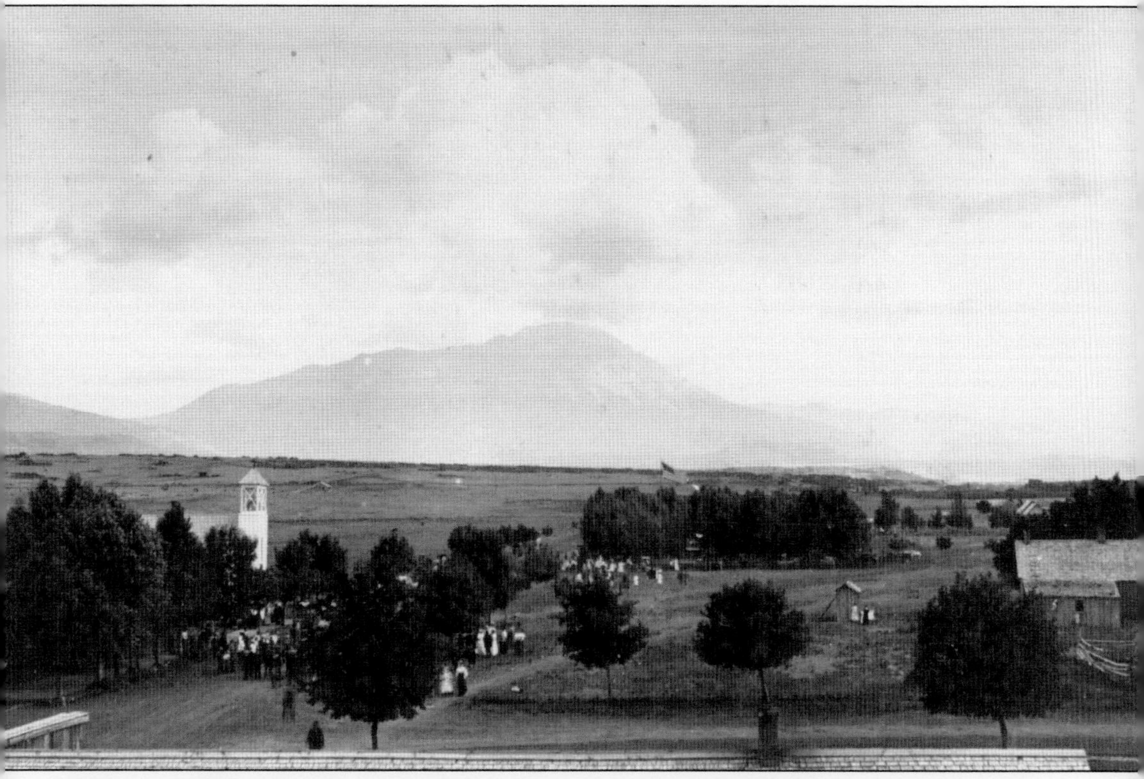

La Veta, c. 1890s. The West Spanish Peak dominates the view south from La Veta. The white church steeple belongs to the First Baptist Church, built in 1877 and still standing today. La Veta began in 1862 when rancher John Francisco built a protective fort against raiding Ute Indians. Known as Francisco Plaza and later as Francisco Fort, the fort was never defended by US soldiers, just by Francisco and his ranch hands and friends. The fort attracted other ranchers, and a settlement grew up around it. When the D&RG Railroad reached the settlement in 1876, tracks were laid right in front of the fort, and one of the fort's buildings served as the first railroad depot. A post office, named Spanish Peaks, had been established in the fort in 1871, but the D&RG soon moved their depot out of the fort and renamed the town La Veta (Spanish for "the vein"), possibly referring to a nearby mineral vein.

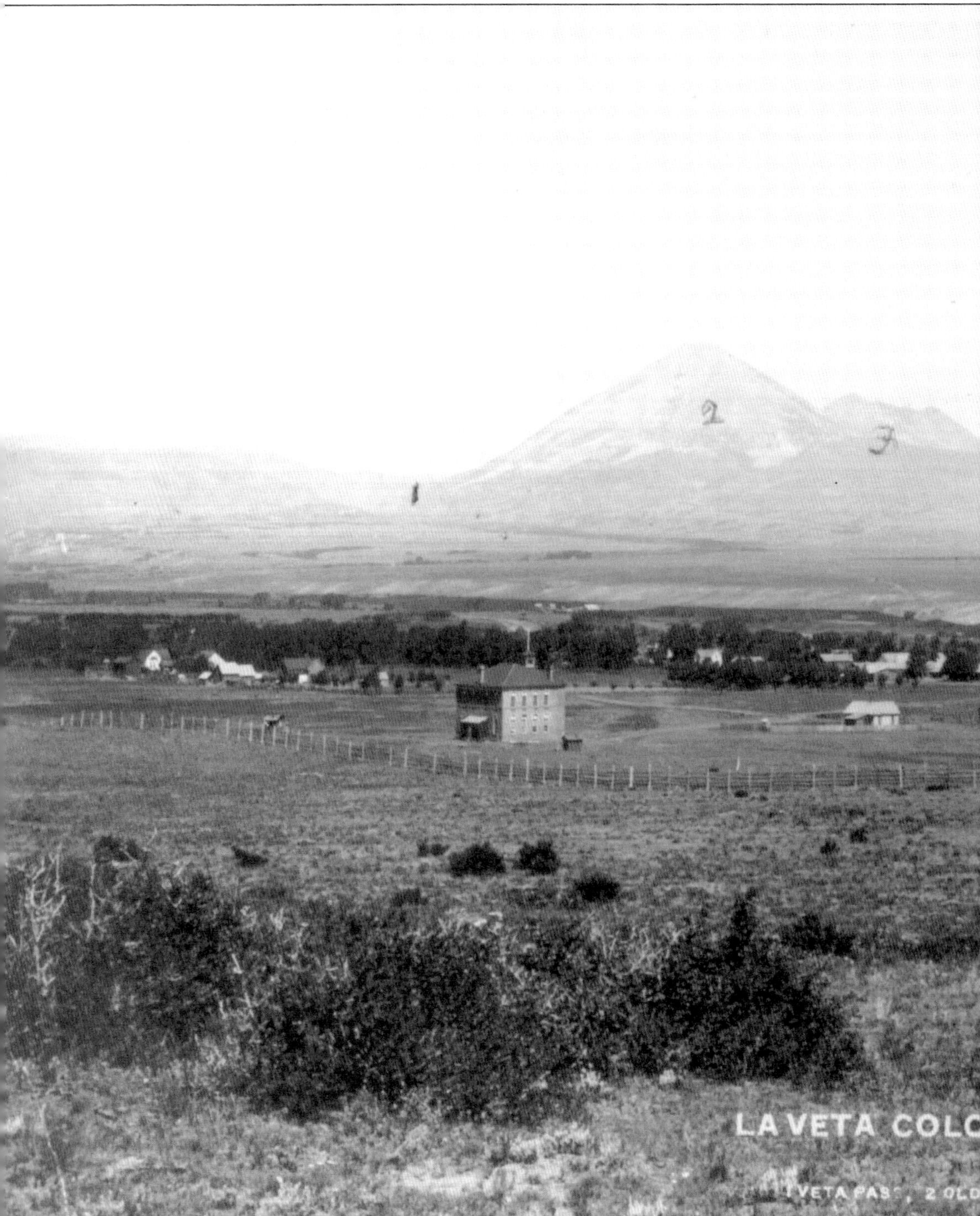

La Veta, June 17, 1894. Headquartered in Walsenburg and La Veta, O.T. Davis took spectacular photographs of the region. Here, his camera is pointed northwest with the following numbers referring to certain locations: 1. Veta Pass, 2. "Old Baldy" (now Mount Mestas), 3. Rough Mountain, and 4. Silver Mountain. The two-story building at the left is a brick schoolhouse constructed in

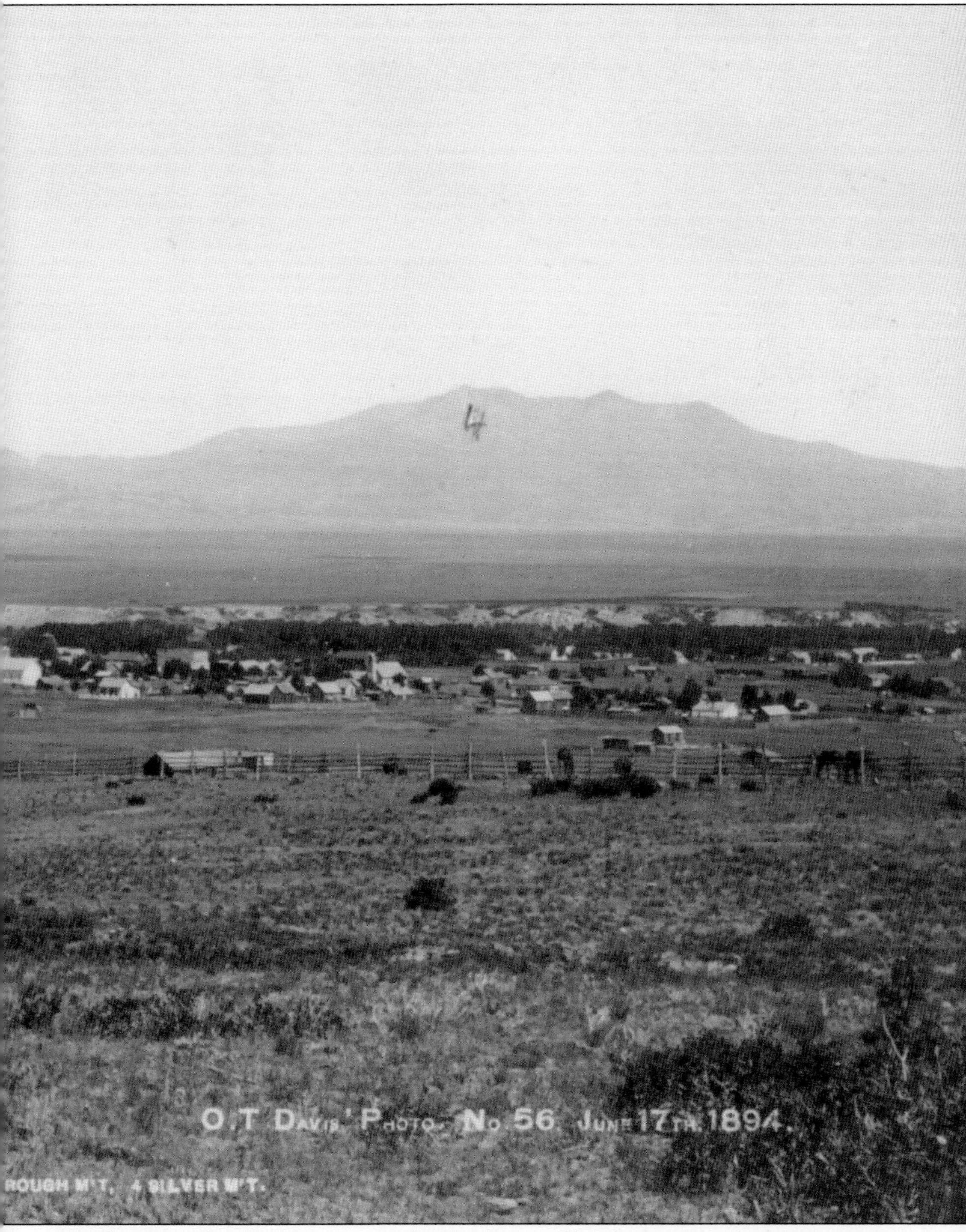

1887. The white church in the center is the First Baptist Church, shown on the previous page. Directly west across the street from the church was the location of Francisco Fort. In 1958, Francisco Fort was restored and opened to the public as a history museum for La Veta.

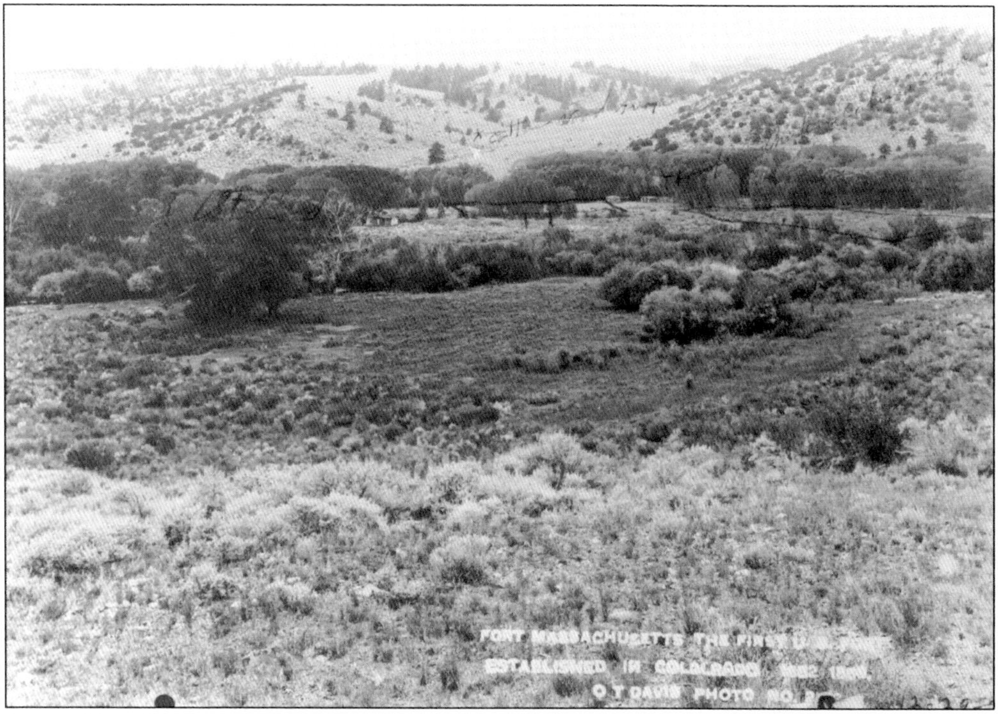

SITE OF FORT MASSACHUSETTS, DECEMBER 29, 1927. The fort was built on this site in 1852, a few miles north of present-day Fort Garland. It was the first US fort built in Colorado. Its purpose was to protect settlers and travelers from raids by Ute and Apache Indians. This fort was abandoned in 1858 and replaced by Fort Garland.

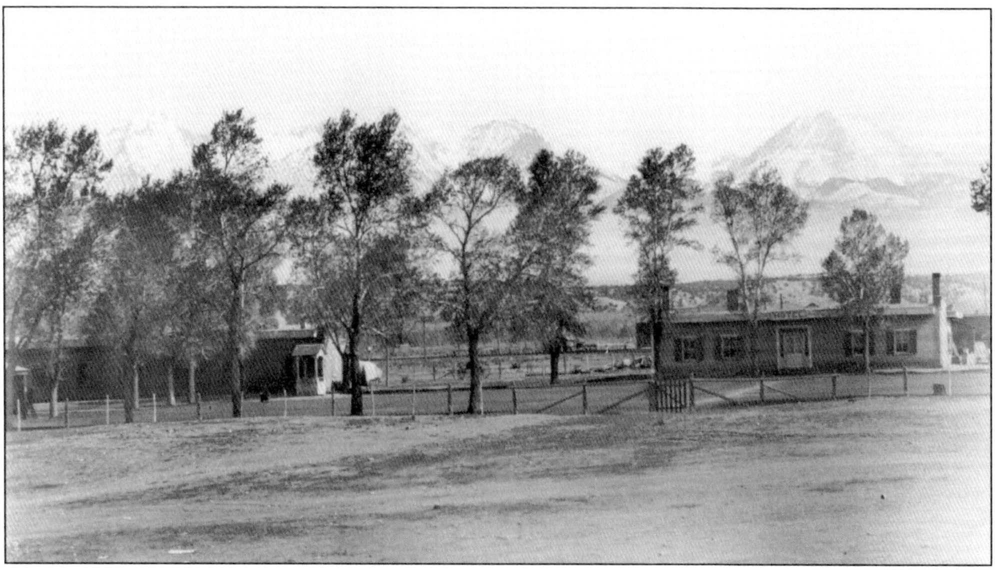

FORT GARLAND SITE, MAY 24, 1907. North of the fort, Blanca Peak (left) and Mount Lindsey (right) are clearly visible. Fort Garland served as a US military fort from 1858 to 1883, with Kit Carson as commander from 1866 to 1867. By the time of this photograph, the former officers' quarters, on the left, was being used as a private residence, and the building on the right served as a hotel.

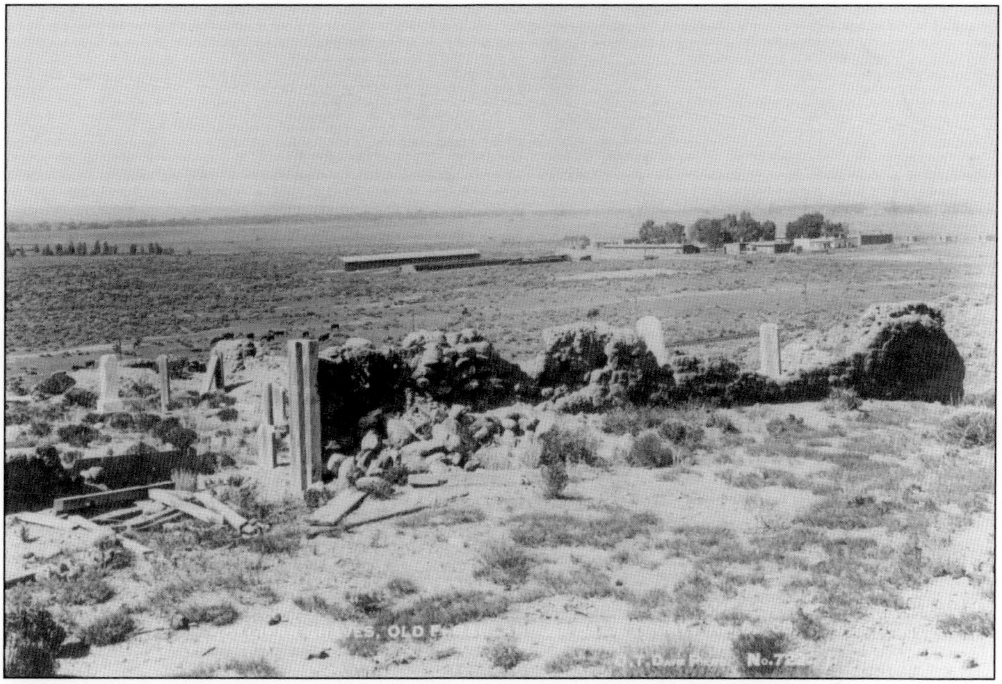

Fort Garland Cemetery Remains, August 6, 1908. This view looks southwest toward the fort with the cemetery remains in the foreground. Fort Garland, with its location on the plains, was much better situated for defense than its predecessor Fort Massachusetts in the hills. Fort Garland takes its name from Brig. Gen. John Garland, who commanded the Department of the Army of New Mexico in 1858.

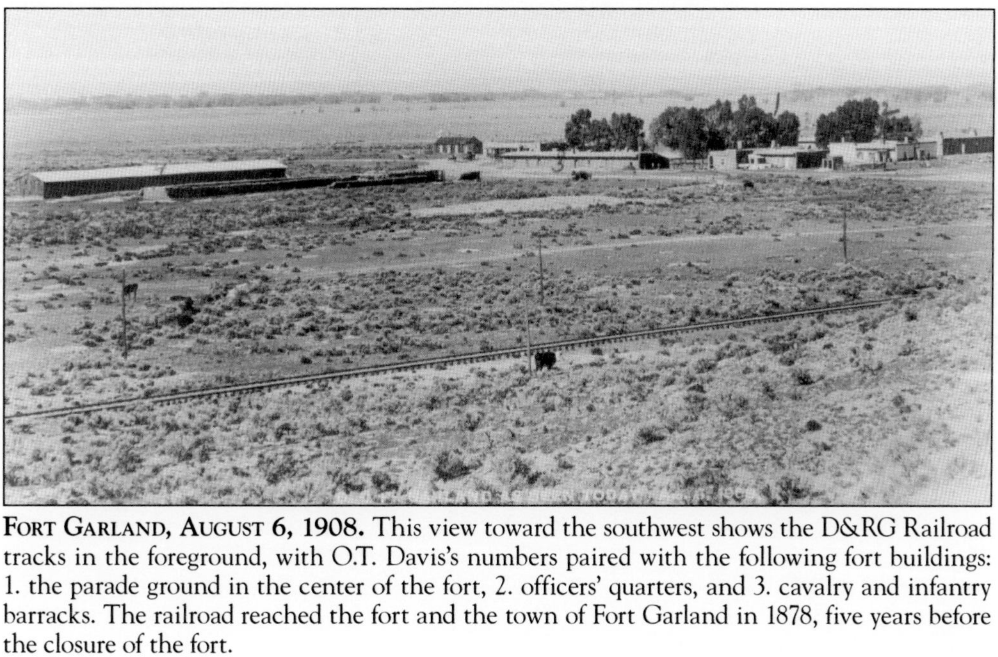

Fort Garland, August 6, 1908. This view toward the southwest shows the D&RG Railroad tracks in the foreground, with O.T. Davis's numbers paired with the following fort buildings: 1. the parade ground in the center of the fort, 2. officers' quarters, and 3. cavalry and infantry barracks. The railroad reached the fort and the town of Fort Garland in 1878, five years before the closure of the fort.

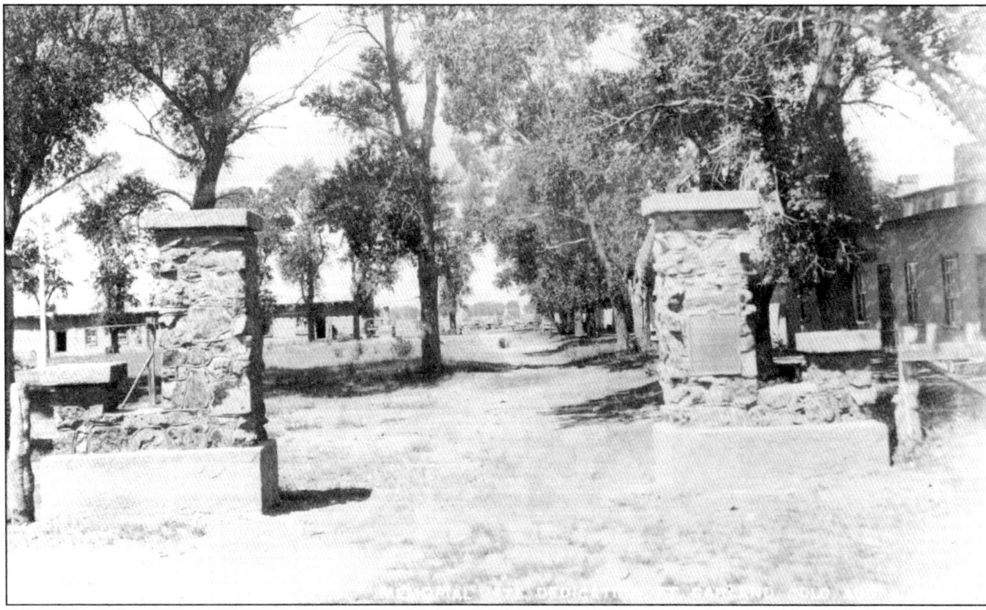

Memorial Gate Dedication, August 2, 1931. This memorial gate on the east side of Fort Garland was built to honor the soldiers who served there. Officers' quarters are on the right, and enlisted men's barracks are on the left. Kit Carson recommended enlarging and strengthening the fort in 1866, as there were still 800 Ute Indians and 250 Jicarilla Apaches raiding across the San Luis Valley.

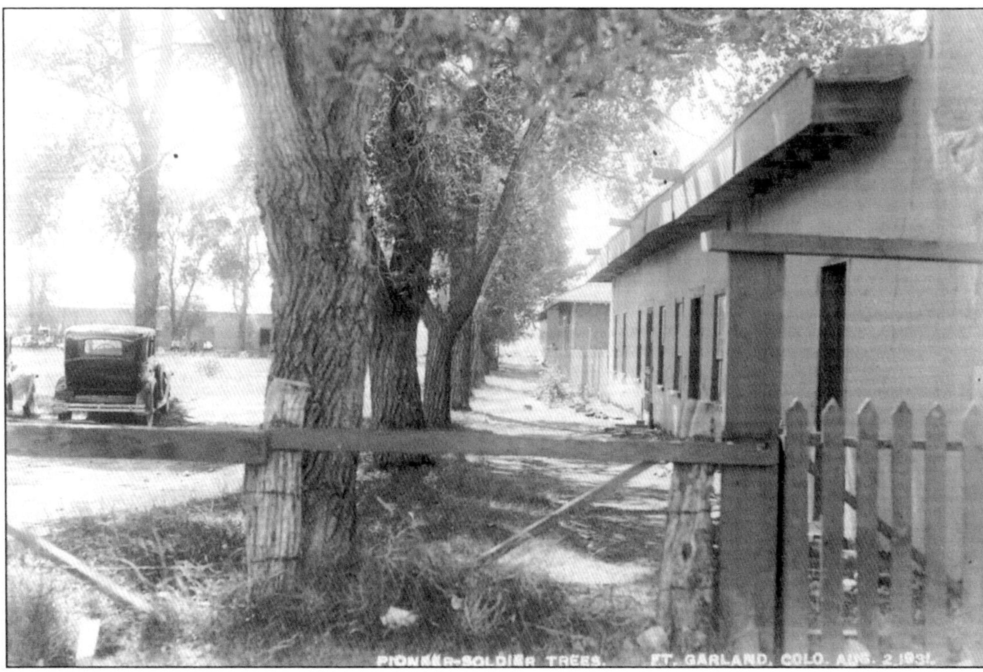

Fort Garland, August 2, 1931. These "Pioneer Soldier" trees next to the officers' quarters were planted early in the fort's history. The Colorado Historical Society acquired the fort in 1945 and restored all the adobe buildings. The fort was then opened as a museum in 1948, with the commandant's quarters furnished to reflect the 1866–1867 command period of Kit Carson.

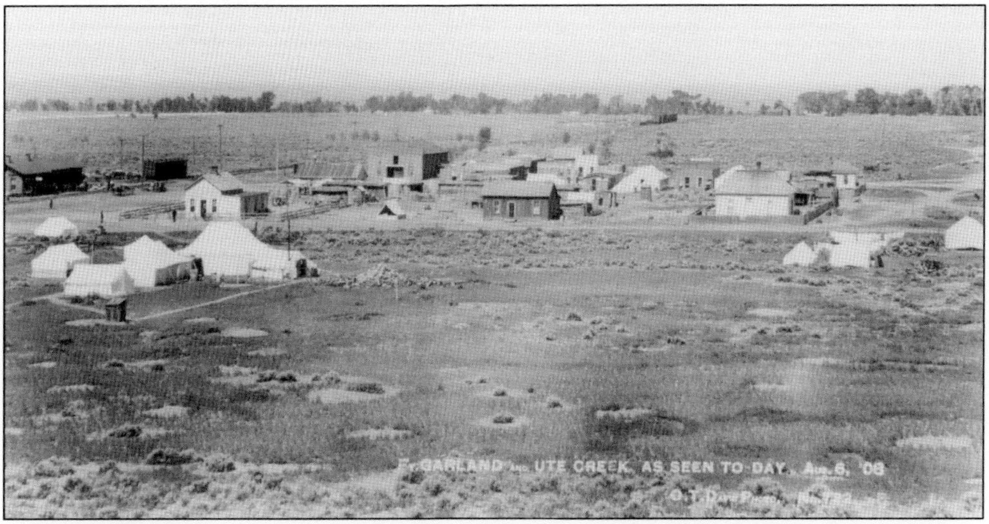

Town of Fort Garland, August 6, 1908. When the Army pulled out of the fort in 1883, the departing soldiers took their spending money with them, and the town of Fort Garland suffered. The D&RG line (seen from top left to right) still brought revenue to the town, but Fort Garland never grew much more. The line of trees at the top of the photograph marks the location of Ute Creek.

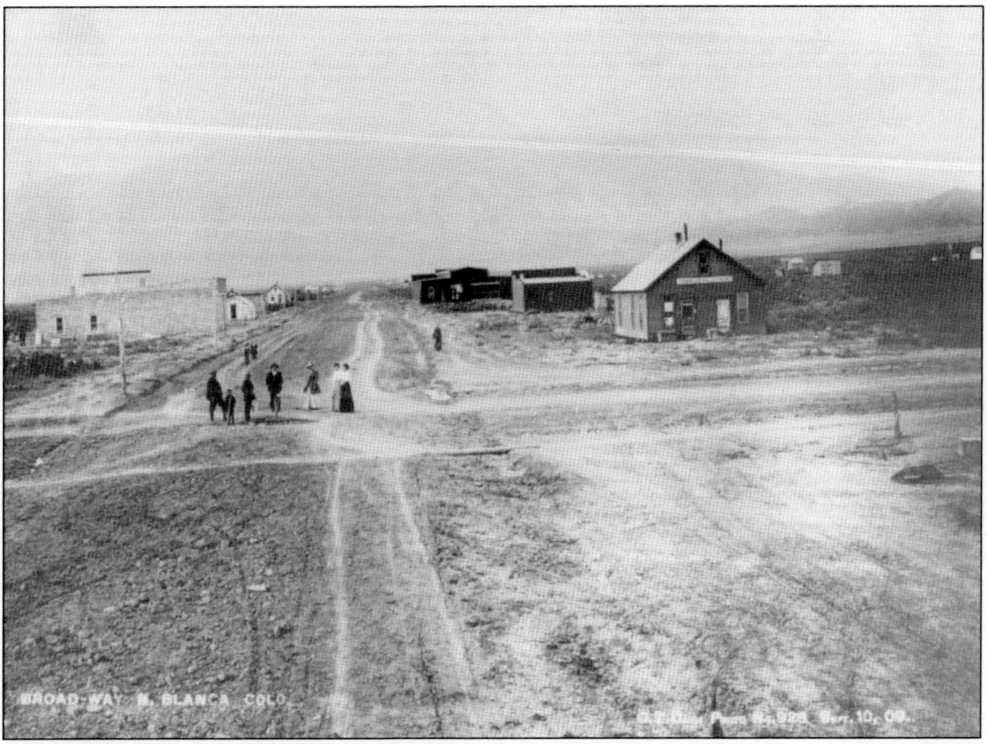

Town of Blanca, September 10, 1909. Looking north on Broadway Street toward Blanca Peak, the new town was just over a year old at this time. On August 12, 1908, a land developer held a lottery to sell lots, and people lined up for the opportunity to purchase land. The building on the right housed the *San Luis Valley News*, published by George E. Wood.

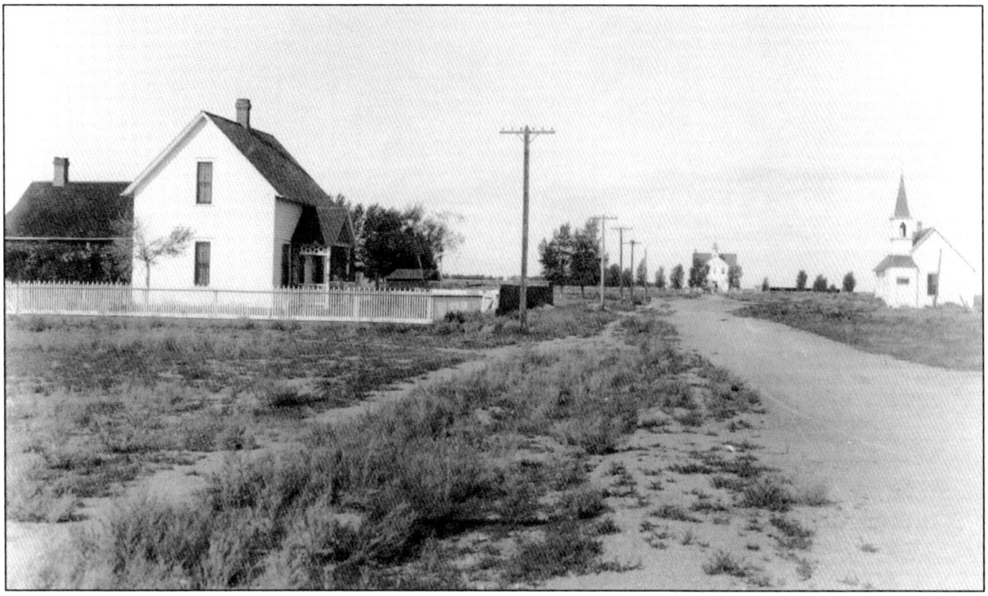

Town of Mosca, 1912. In 1890, the D&RG Railroad built a narrow-gauge line south from Villa Grove to Alamosa. New towns soon arose along the 54-mile rail line. Eight miles north of Alamosa, the Mosca Town Company was organized in 1890 to sell land there. From left to right are the home of Jesse Booth, the school, and the church.

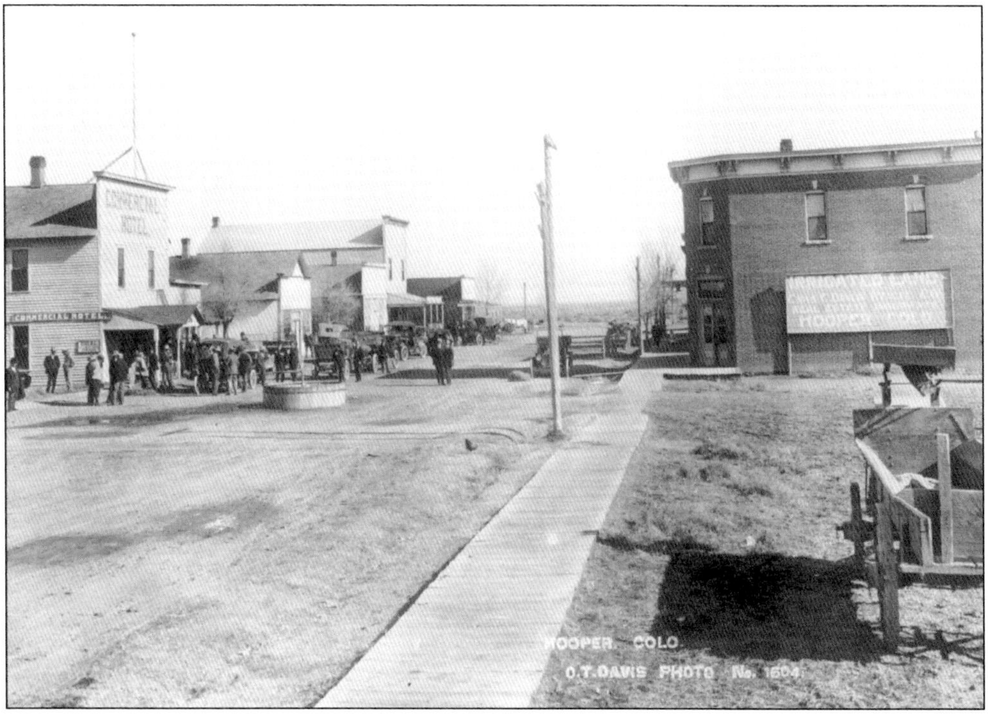

Town of Hooper, November 22, 1913. The town of Garrison was formed 22 miles north of Alamosa along the D&RG line in 1891. The name was changed to Hooper (after D&RG agent Shadrach K. Hooper) to avoid confusion with the town of Gunnison. On Main Street, the Commercial Hotel is seen on the left, and a realty company is on the right.

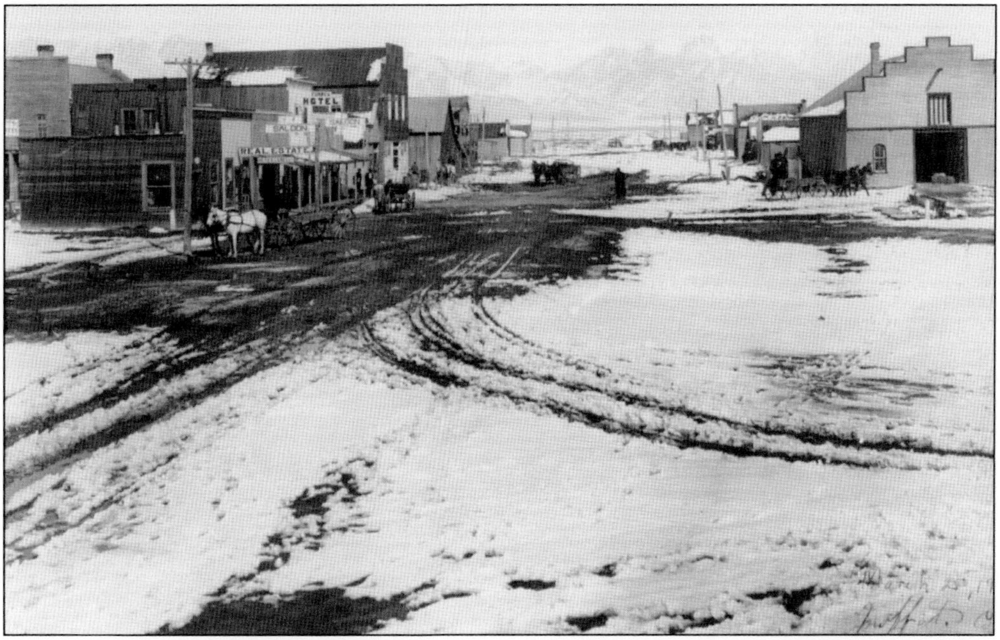

Town of Moffat, March 25, 1910. Moffat, founded in 1890, was named after D&RG president David Moffat. The town was the center of a large cattle-raising area, and it boomed with the arrival of the D&RG. By 1910, it had as many as 2,500 residents. A hotel, a saloon, and a real estate office are on the left side of Main Street in this view east toward the Sangre de Cristo Mountains.

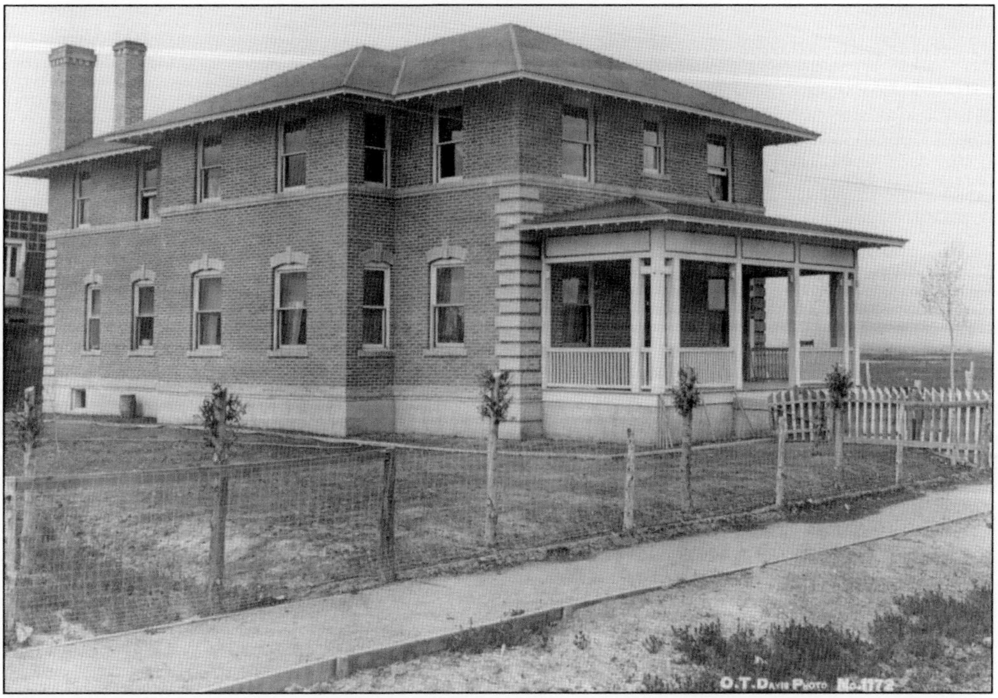

Moffat Hotel, 1911. This brick hotel looks much more substantial than the frame hotel on Main Street in the photograph above. After the cattle boom, Moffat still prospered as a center of artesian well drilling and contracting for cutting the area's hay fields.

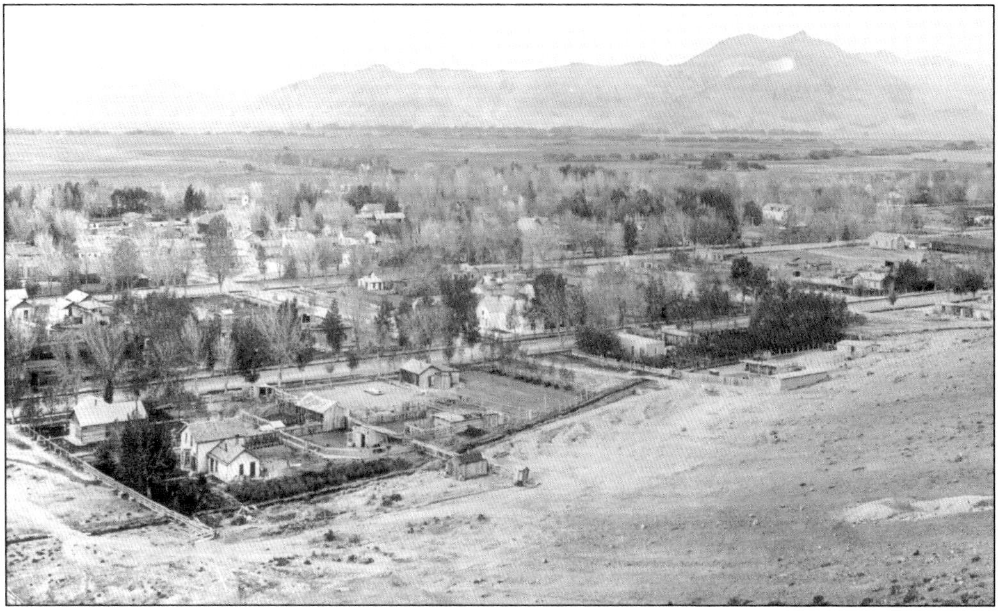

Northwest View, Town of Saguache, 1911. Saguache was one of the earliest settlements in the San Luis Valley. In 1866, gold fever brought prospectors to the area, and, by 1867, there was a new town to serve them. A number of German immigrants, mustered out of service at Fort Garland, joined the gold rush, and there were so many German settlers that one street in Saguache was named Sauerkraut Avenue.

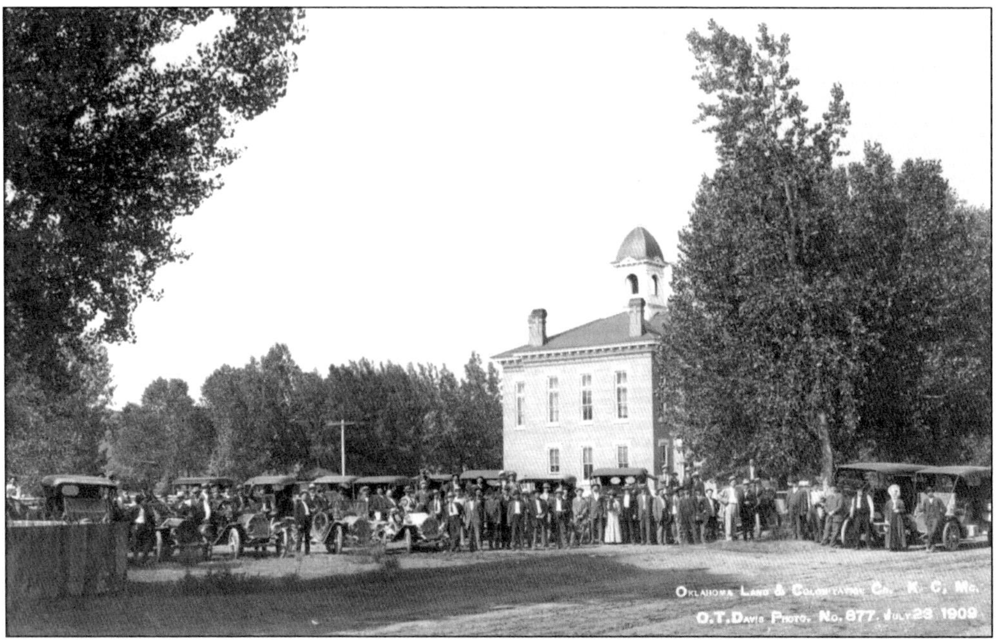

Saguache County Courthouse, July 23, 1909. Though Saguache was never served by the railroad, it prospered as a service center for mining and agriculture in the northwestern San Luis Valley. In 1909, this large group of automobiles and people from the Oklahoma Land & Colonization Company gathered outside the courthouse. Perhaps they were looking for more prosperous land to settle on than Oklahoma could offer.

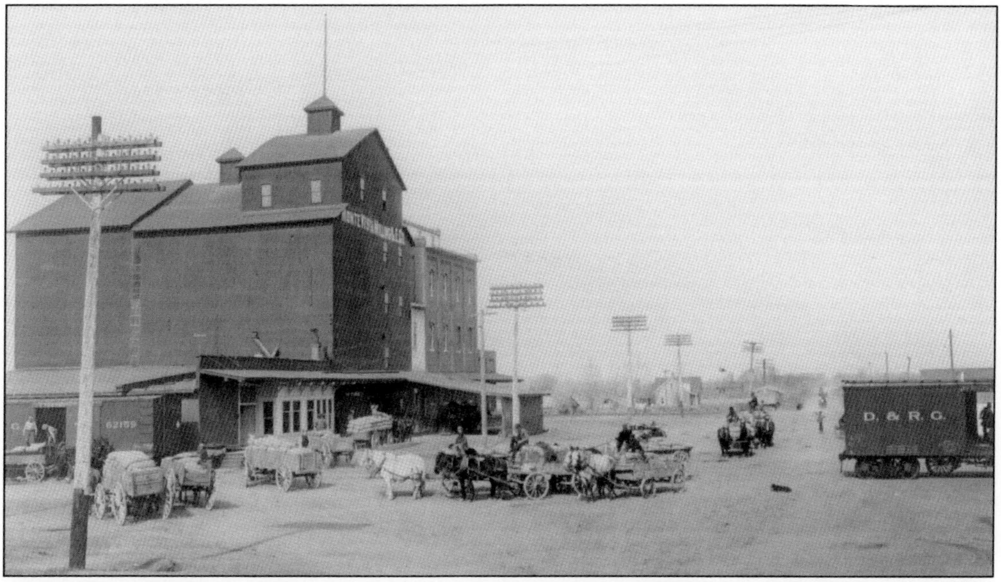

MONTE VISTA MILLING & ELEVATOR COMPANY, NOVEMBER 15, 1911. Originally founded as the Lariat siding of the D&RG Railroad in 1881, the settlement was renamed Monte Vista (Spanish for "Mountain View") in 1886. This large flour mill was built in 1892. Area farmers hauled wheat in wagons to the mill. The milled flour was then shipped out on the D&RG boxcars, as seen in the photograph. The mill was torn down in 1983.

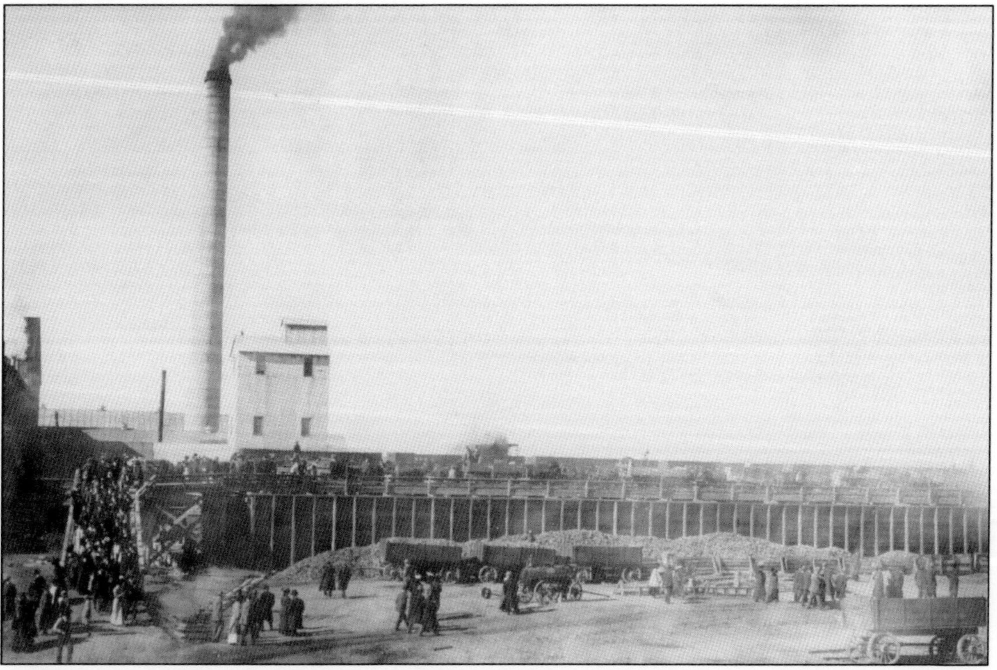

SAN LUIS VALLEY BEET SUGAR FACTORY, NOVEMBER 15, 1911. This was opening day for the new factory in Monte Vista. Sugar beets are almost totally dependent on irrigation, and while that was readily available in the San Luis Valley, other irrigated crops, such as barley and potatoes, brought in more money to farmers. After only a few years, sugar beet production almost totally ceased in the San Luis Valley.

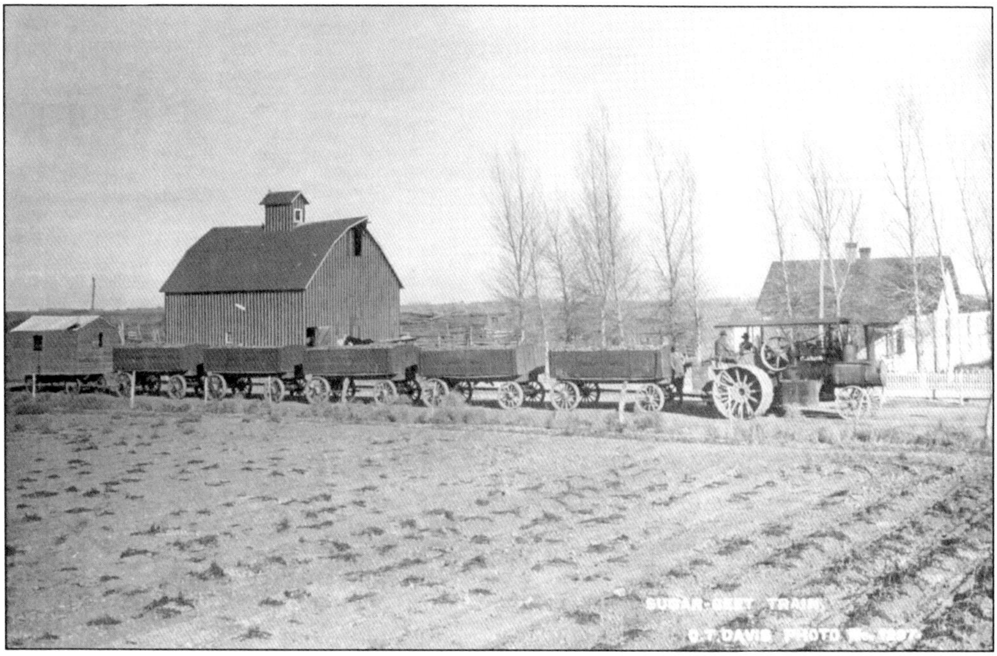

Sugar Beet Tractor Train, c. 1912. A steam tractor pulled five wagonloads of sugar beets from this farm east of Monte Vista to the new San Luis Valley Sugar Beet Factory. Sugar beets soon lost favor among farmers, who received more cash for their crops of barley and potatoes.

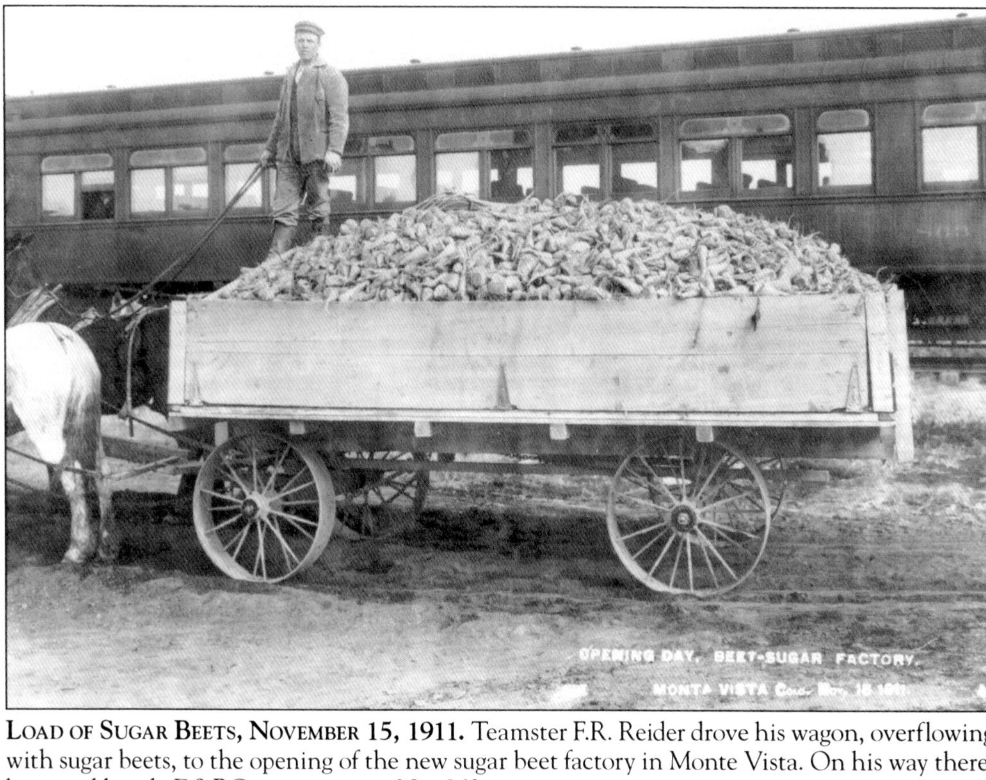

Load of Sugar Beets, November 15, 1911. Teamster F.R. Reider drove his wagon, overflowing with sugar beets, to the opening of the new sugar beet factory in Monte Vista. On his way there, he posed beside D&RG passenger car No. 863.

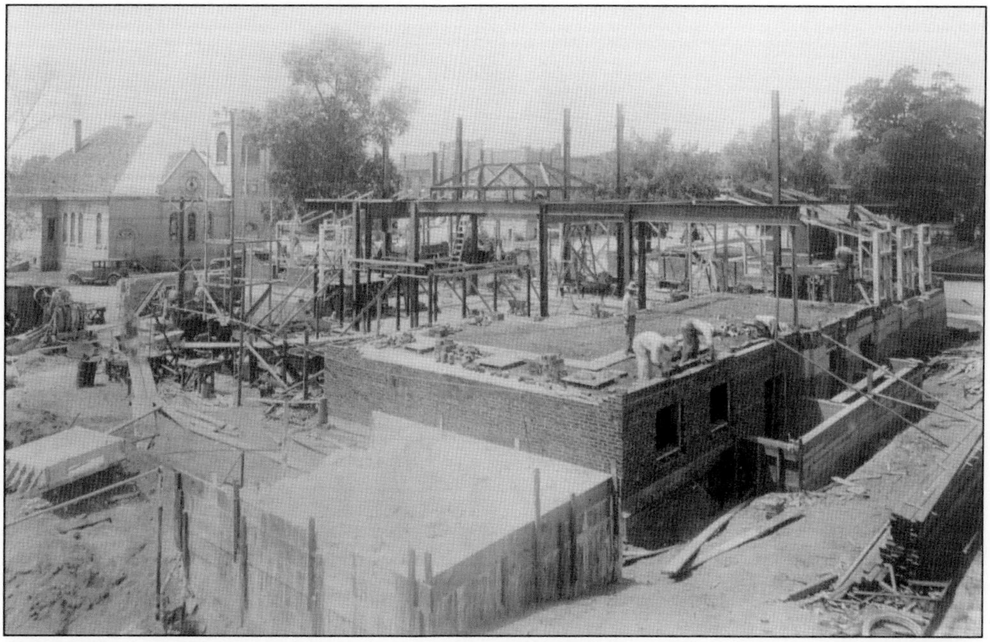

Monte Vista Post Office Construction, June 27, 1932. Foundation work and steel erection for a new post office in Monte Vista occurred in the summer of 1932. The First Christian Church is on the left. Monte Vista's growth was based on the processing and shipment of barley, wheat, and potatoes. The Adolph Coors Brewing Company built a 10-story elevator building to hold barley for shipment to its breweries.

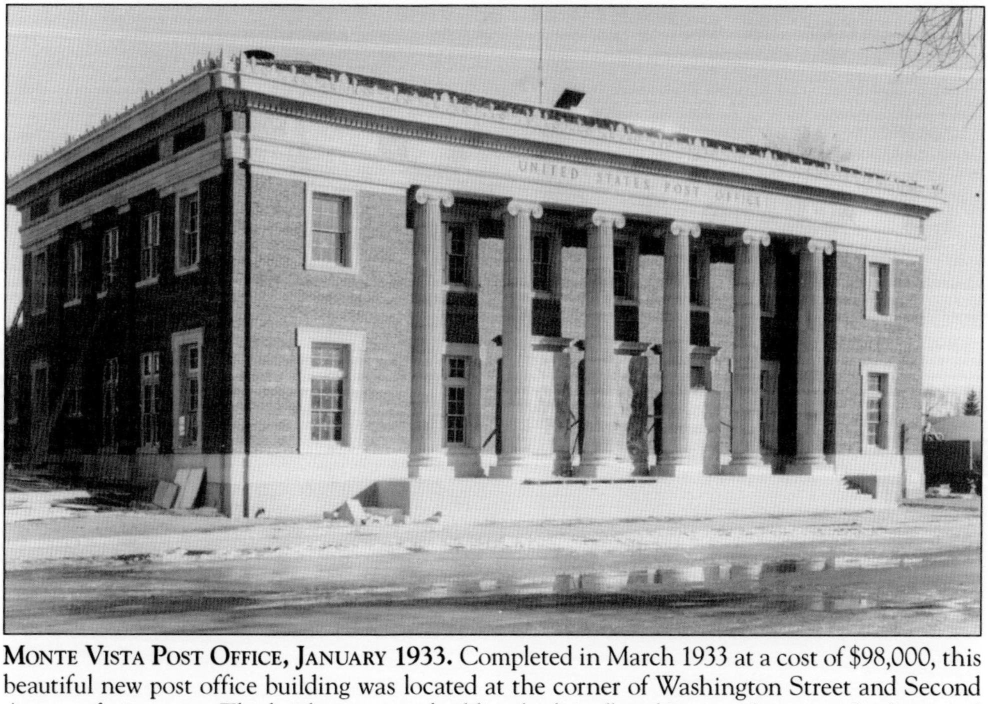

Monte Vista Post Office, January 1933. Completed in March 1933 at a cost of $98,000, this beautiful new post office building was located at the corner of Washington Street and Second Avenue, facing west. The brick two-story building had six fluted Ionic columns at the front and three bronze entry doors behind the columns.

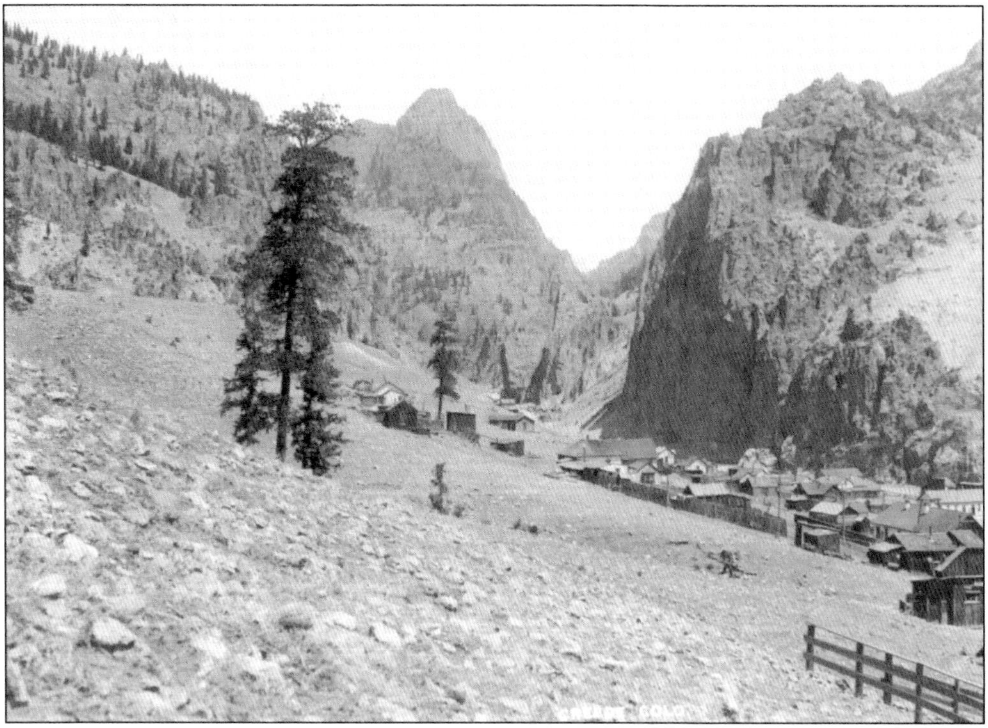

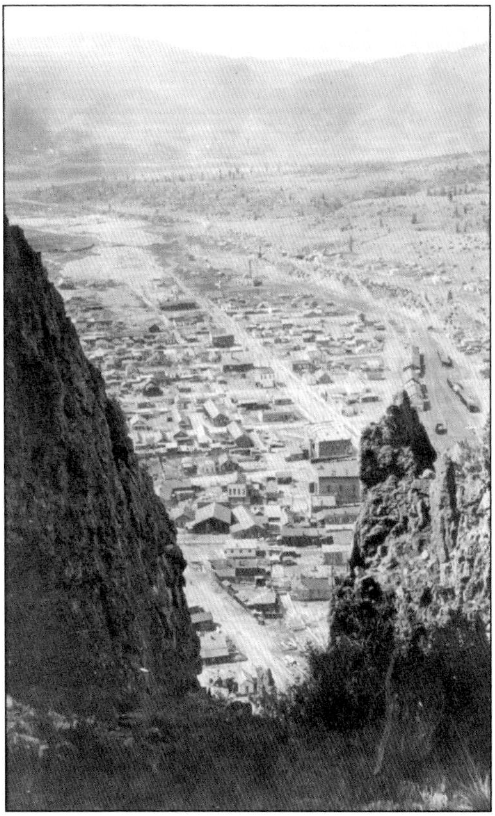

CREEDE, C. 1900. Not really a part of the San Luis Valley, Creede is located in a steep valley of the San Juan Mountains surrounded by volcanic basalt cliffs. The discovery of silver there by Nicholas Creede in 1890 prompted the D&RG Railroad to extend its line north from Wagon Wheel Gap to Creede.

OVERVIEW OF CREEDE, C. 1900. O.T. Davis climbed high among the basalt cliffs to obtain this spectacular view of Creede to the south. Creede boomed with the silver mines, but today, it has settled into a bustling summer tourist resort. The D&RG depot and rail yards are at center right.

Eight

ALAMOSA
"CLOSE TO FREEZING TO DEATH"

When Alexander C. Hunt, president of the Denver & Rio Grande Railroad Construction Company, platted streets for the railroad's newest town on the banks of the Rio Grande in 1877, he named the settlement Rio Bravo. However, a year later, when the plat was officially filed in May 1878, the town name was listed as Alamosa (Spanish for "cottonwood tree"). Rails reached the new town from Garland City on June 26, 1878. Hunt, a former territorial governor of Colorado (1867–1869), built a large house for his family on the western bank of the river. This construction was in contrast to most of the buildings in Alamosa, which had been uprooted in Garland City, placed on railcars, and hauled to Alamosa. With those buildings, Alamosa literally sprang up overnight in 1878.

At the center of the San Luis Valley and at the end of track, Alamosa prospered from the beginning. By 1880, Alamosa had a population of 800; by 1900, it had grown to 1,000. By 1913, Alamosa had boomed to 3,000, and its residents became increasingly frustrated with having to travel 28 miles south to conduct their county business at the county seat in Conejos. They began a strenuous political and legal battle to have Alamosa become the seat of its own county. The Alamosans won the battle but paid a steep price when Alamosa County was created in 1913. The new county, the last county created in Colorado, was formed from portions of Conejos and Costilla Counties, and Alamosa had to agree to share the bonded indebtedness of Conejos County. This heavy financial burden delayed the construction of a courthouse in Alamosa for 25 years, until 1938.

With temperatures at times reaching 50 degrees below zero, Alamosa has always been one of the coldest cities in the United States in winter. In his book *Alamosa: A Quick History*, Leland Feitz noted, "In Alamosa, you could learn to play bridge, sing and tap dance. And, God knows, you could come close to freezing to death!"

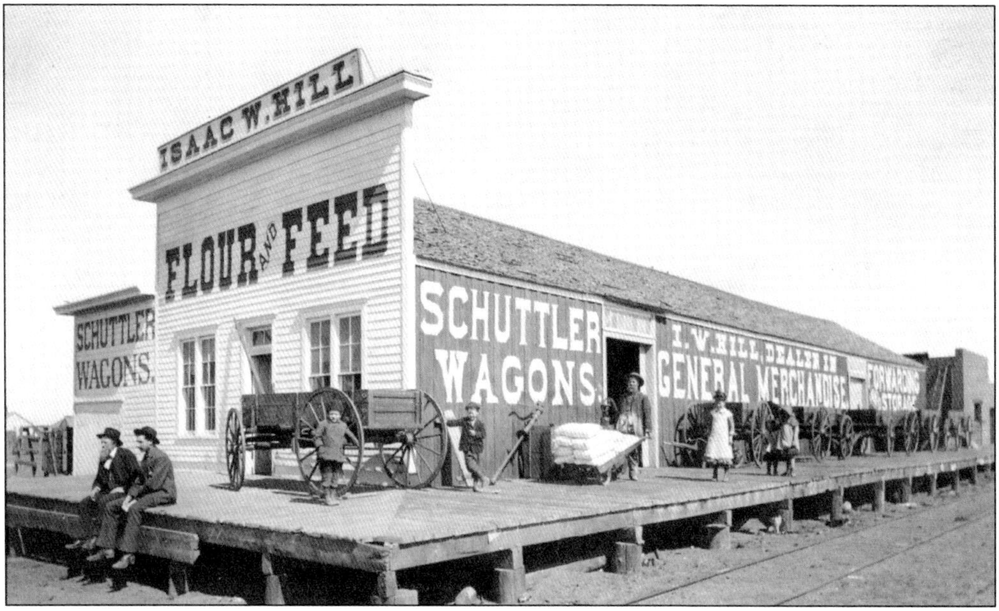

Isaac W. Hill Store, 1880s. The Hill store was a general merchandise shop specializing in the sale of Schuttler Wagons and flour and feed. Hill was a very prosperous merchant, selling supplies to land developers, irrigation companies, and miners.

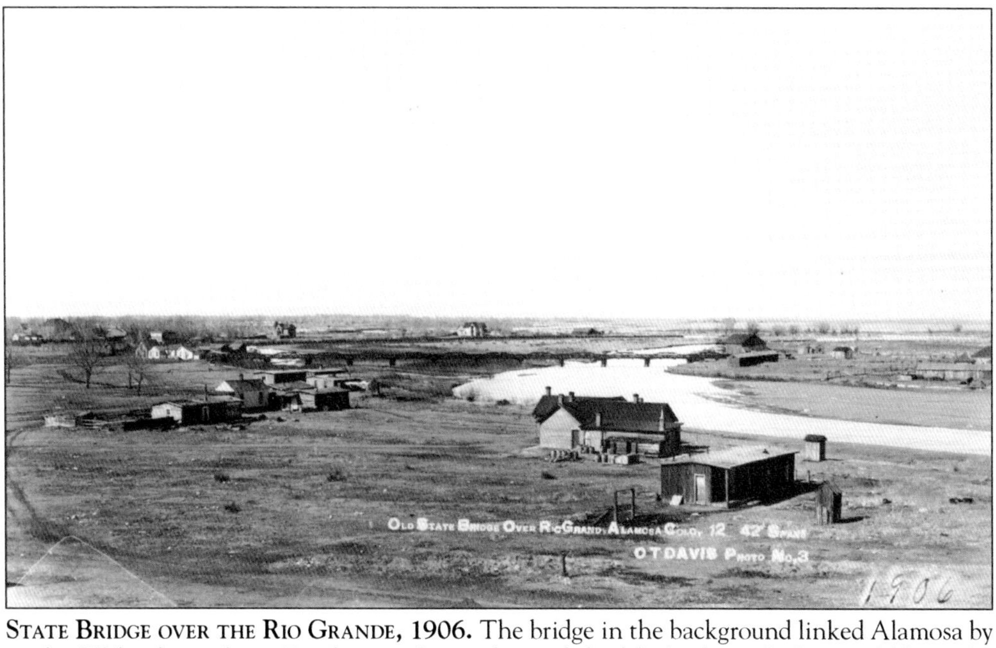

State Bridge over the Rio Grande, 1906. The bridge in the background linked Alamosa by road to Walsenburg, about 60 miles east. Just to the top left of the bridge is the home of Alexander C. Hunt, the founder of Alamosa. This was probably one of the first photographs taken by O.T. Davis when he moved his studio to Alamosa in 1906.

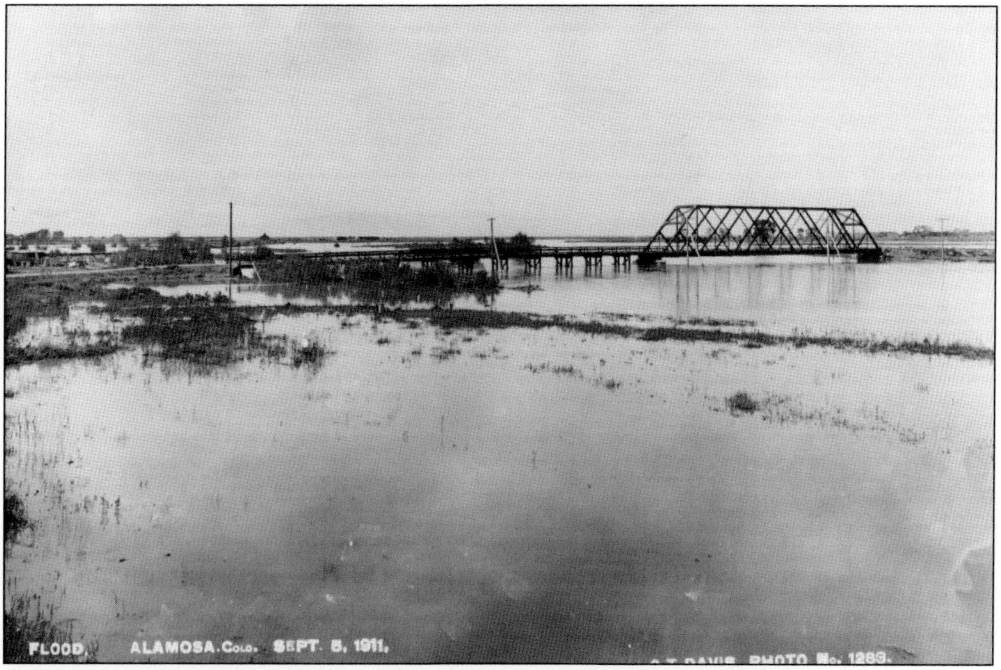

Rio Grande Flood, September 5, 1911. The State Bridge spans the Rio Grande in an unusual September flood. The river usually flooded eastern Alamosa in the spring.

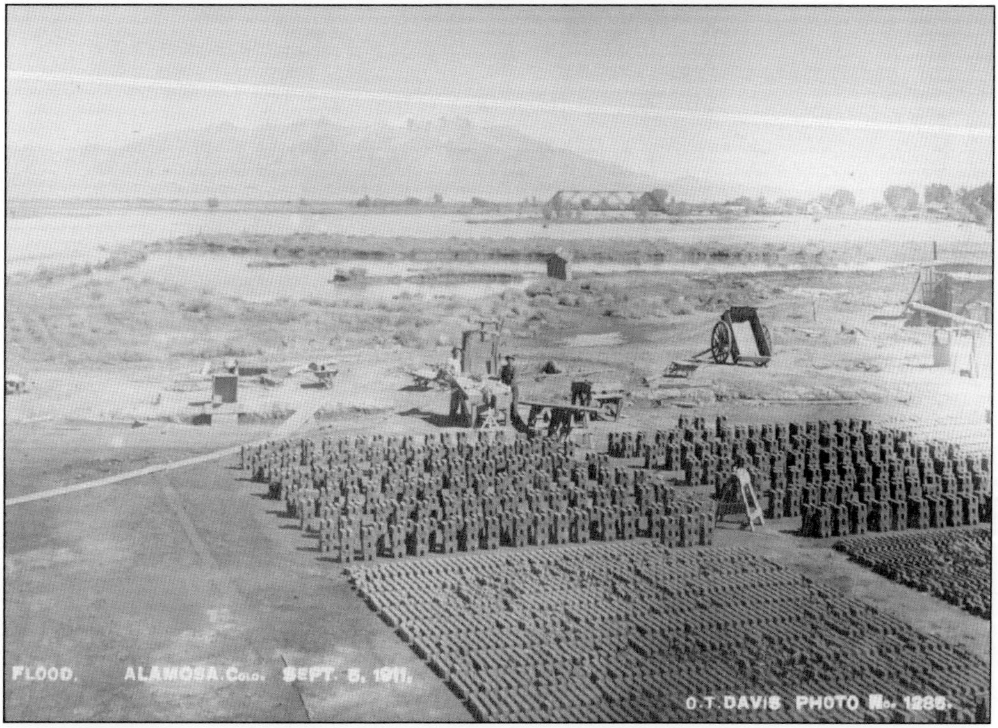

Adobe Brickyard in Alamosa, September 5, 1911. The flood of the Rio Grande came very near the brickyard. The floodwaters would have ruined the bricks drying in the sun if the water had reached there. In the distance, the State Bridge and Blanca Peak can be seen.

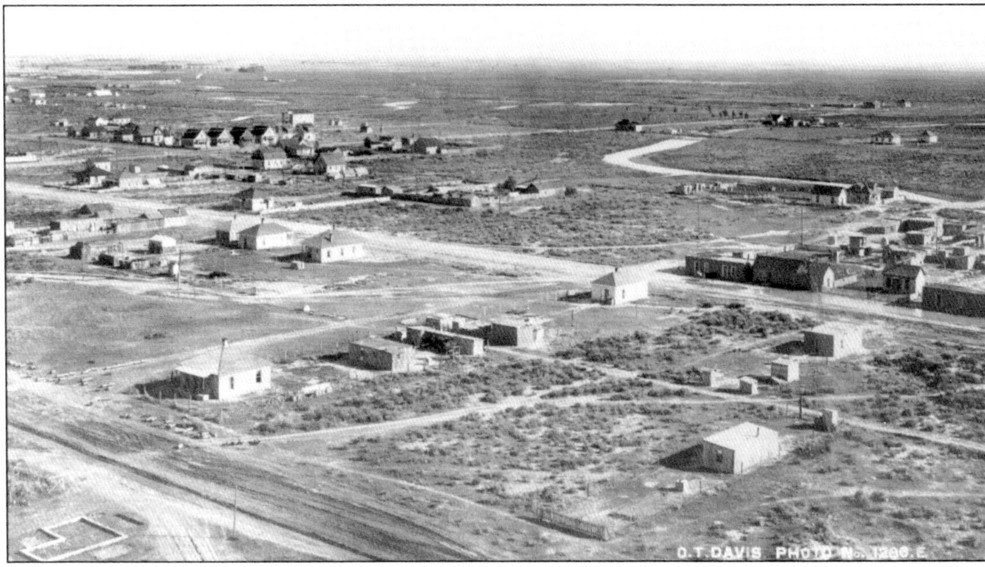

VIEW OF ALAMOSA LOOKING SOUTHEAST, OCTOBER 6, 1911. The Rio Grande floodwaters had largely subsided in this view, taken one month later. This residential area was located south and east of the D&RG depot.

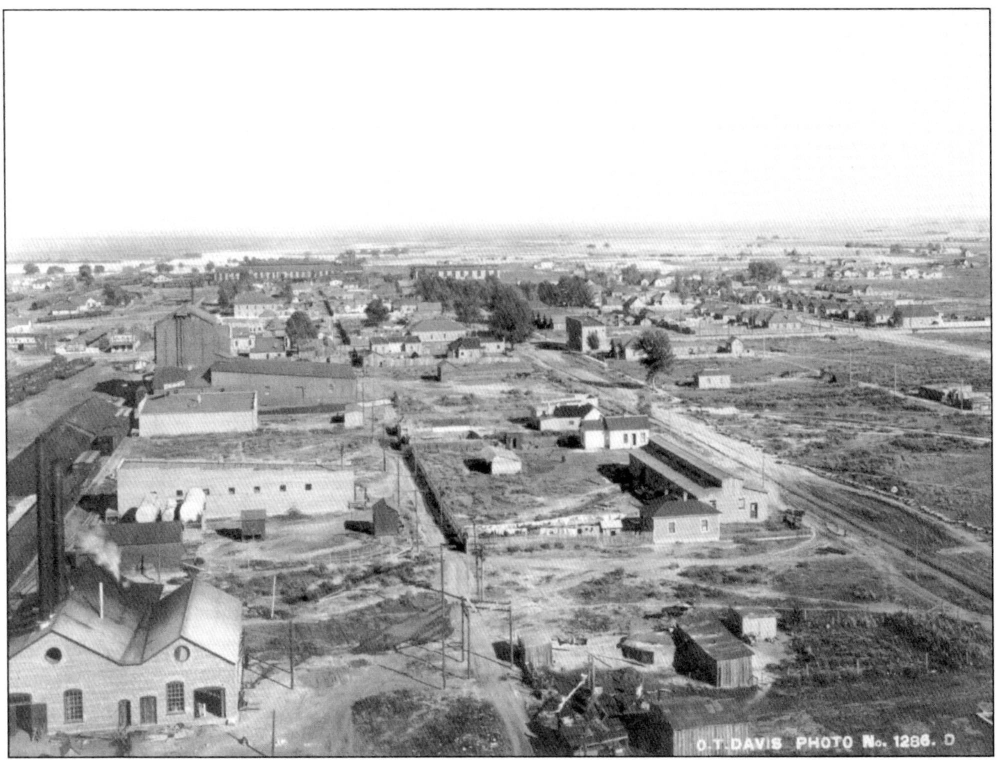

VIEW OF ALAMOSA LOOKING EAST, OCTOBER 6, 1911. O.T. Davis took this shot from the water tower (see page 30). At the base of the water tower in the left foreground is a city power plant. Three buildings beyond that is the tall Alamosa Milling & Elevator Company plant.

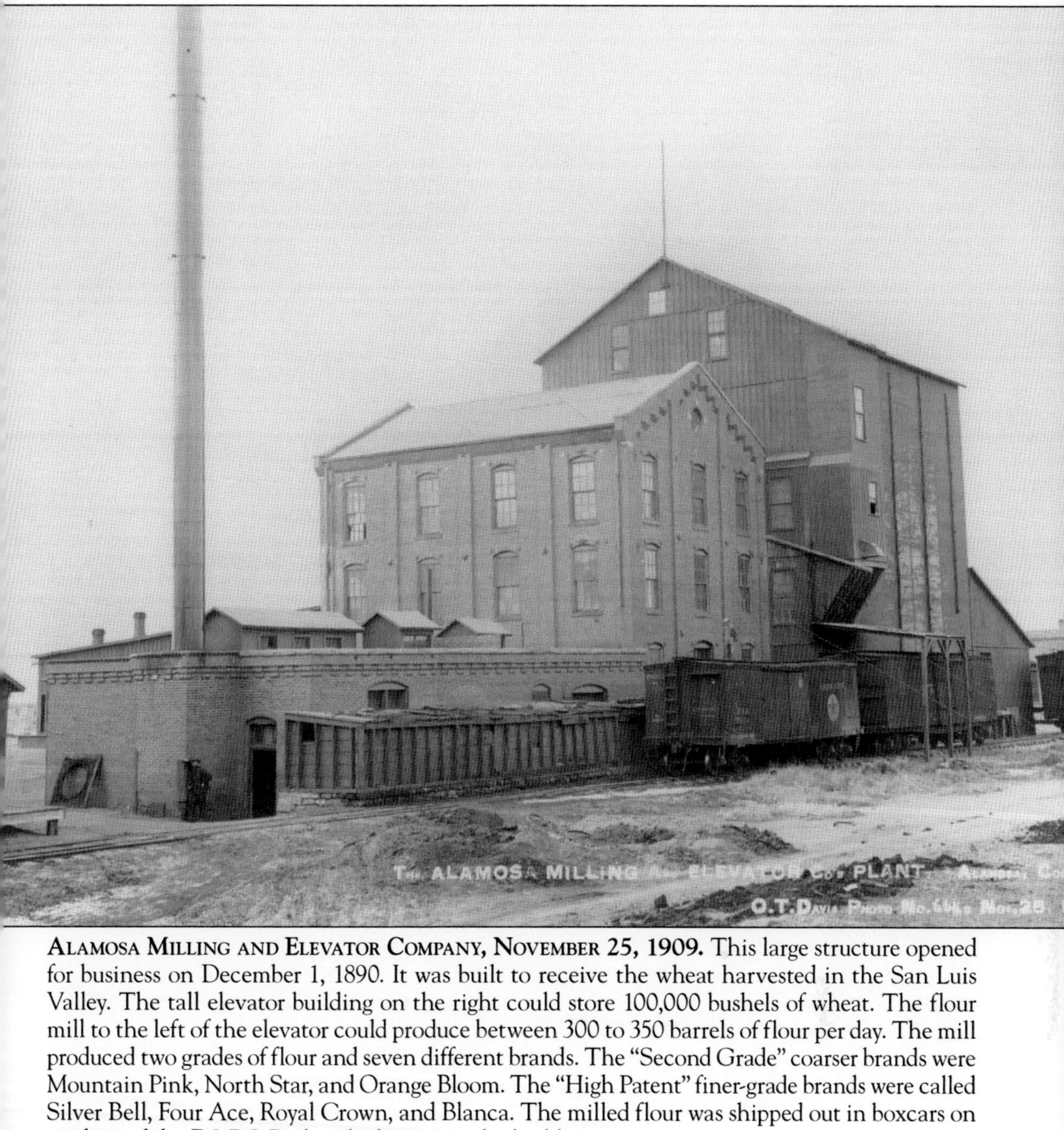

ALAMOSA MILLING AND ELEVATOR COMPANY, NOVEMBER 25, 1909. This large structure opened for business on December 1, 1890. It was built to receive the wheat harvested in the San Luis Valley. The tall elevator building on the right could store 100,000 bushels of wheat. The flour mill to the left of the elevator could produce between 300 to 350 barrels of flour per day. The mill produced two grades of flour and seven different brands. The "Second Grade" coarser brands were Mountain Pink, North Star, and Orange Bloom. The "High Patent" finer-grade brands were called Silver Bell, Four Ace, Royal Crown, and Blanca. The milled flour was shipped out in boxcars on a siding of the D&RG Railroad adjacent to the buildings.

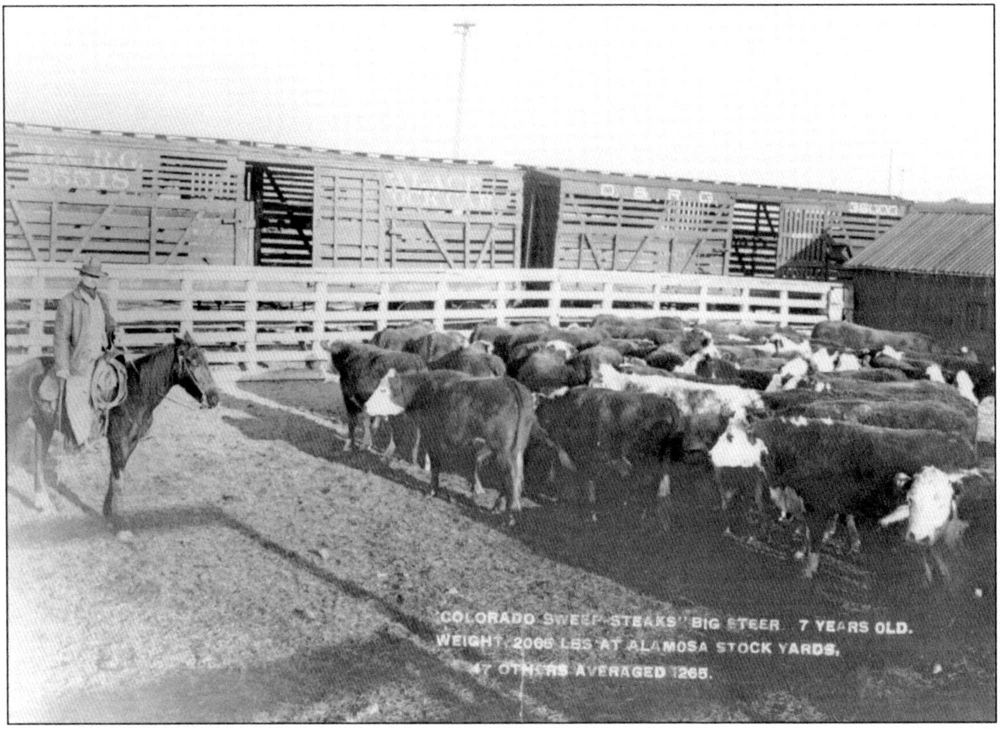

ALAMOSA STOCKYARDS, 1913. Prize cattle are waiting to be shipped on D&RG "Palace Stock Car" No. 35518 and car No. 36000. In the "Colorado Sweep Steaks" promotion, O.T. Davis noted that the largest steer weighed 2,065 pounds and was seven years old. The 47 other cattle in this herd had an average weight of 1,265 pounds.

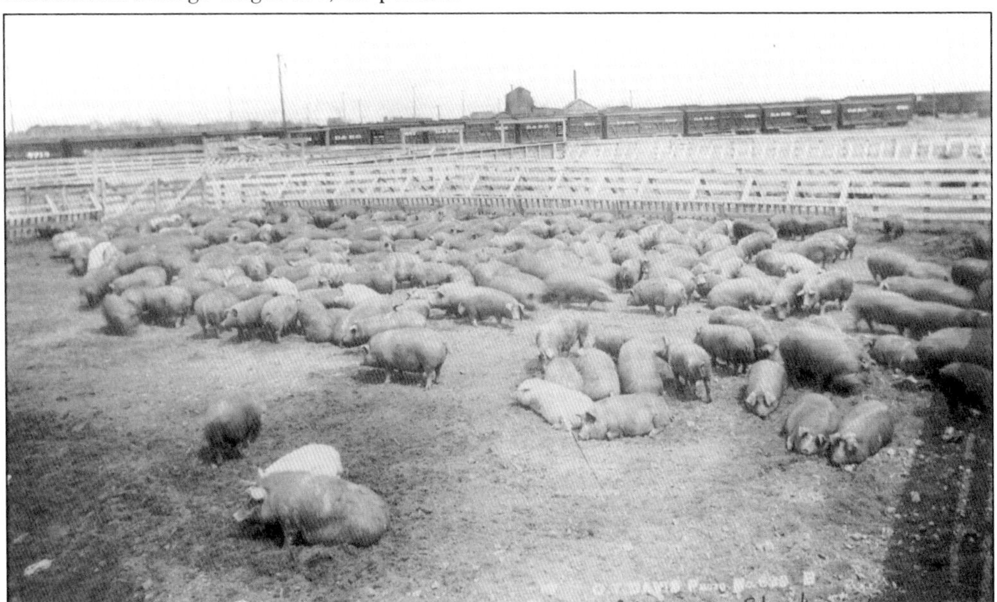

HOGS AT STOCKYARDS, 1907. These San Luis Valley hogs, well-fattened on peas and grains, were ready for shipment on the D&RG stock cars in the background. At least 10 stock cars await their cargo. The Alamosa Milling & Elevator Company can also be seen in the background.

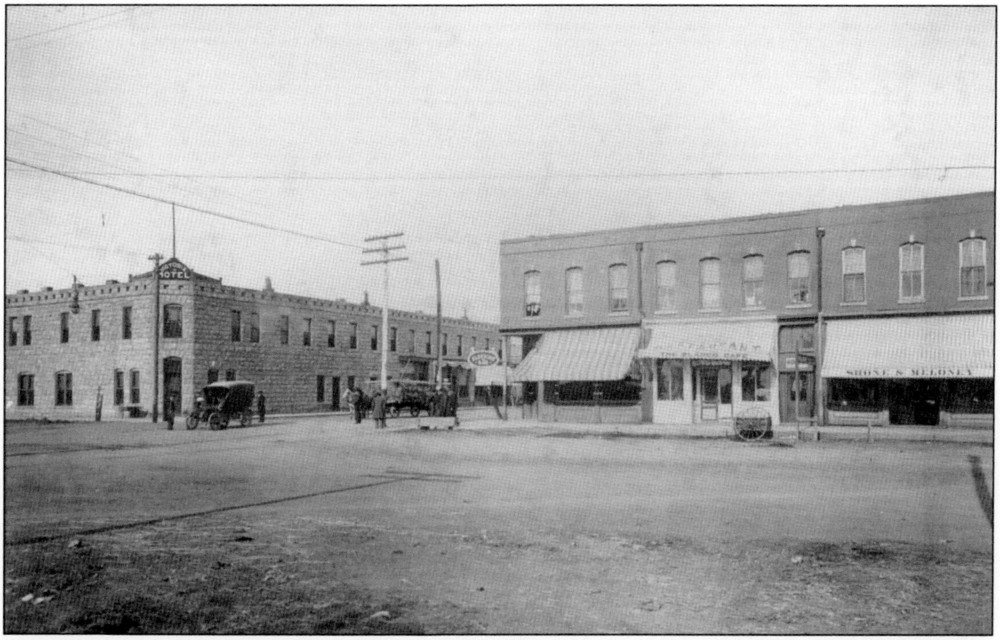

Alamosa Street Scene, 1908. This northwest view at the corner of State Avenue and Sixth Street shows some prominent Alamosa businesses. To the left is the Victoria Hotel. The next three businesses are Slavick's Bar, the Blanco Café, and Shone & Meloney Men's Furnishings. Slavick's Bar opened in 1889.

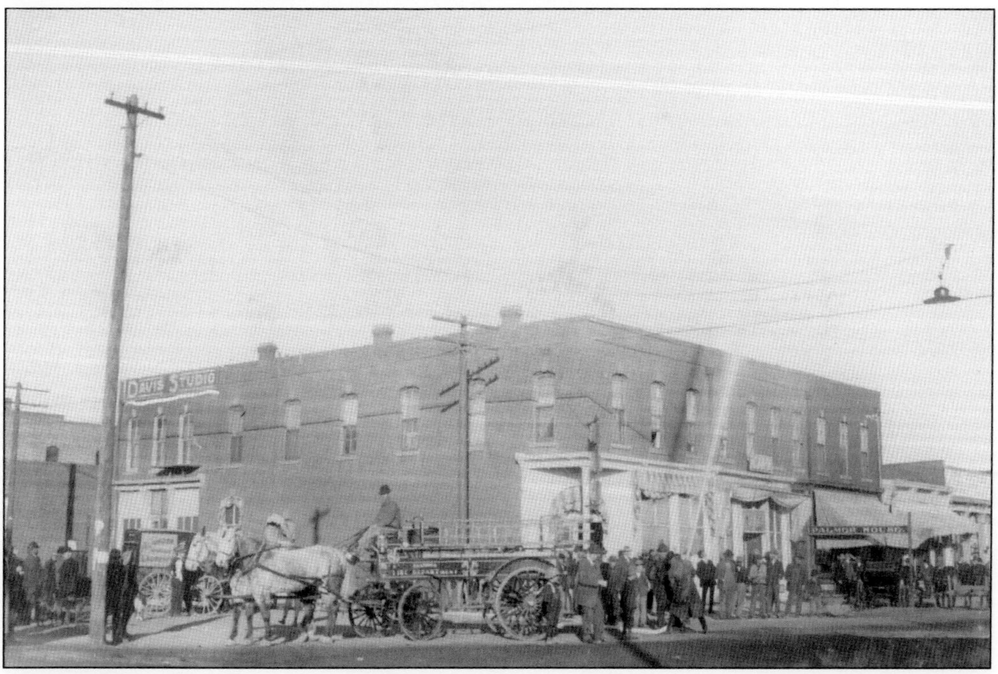

Horse-Drawn Fire Wagon on Display, c. 1910. At the northeast corner of State Avenue and Sixth Street, O.T. Davis set up his first studio (sign at left) in Alamosa, in rooms over Ambler's real estate office. At the front of this building were the three businesses noted above—Slavick's Bar, the Blanco Café, and Shone & Meloney.

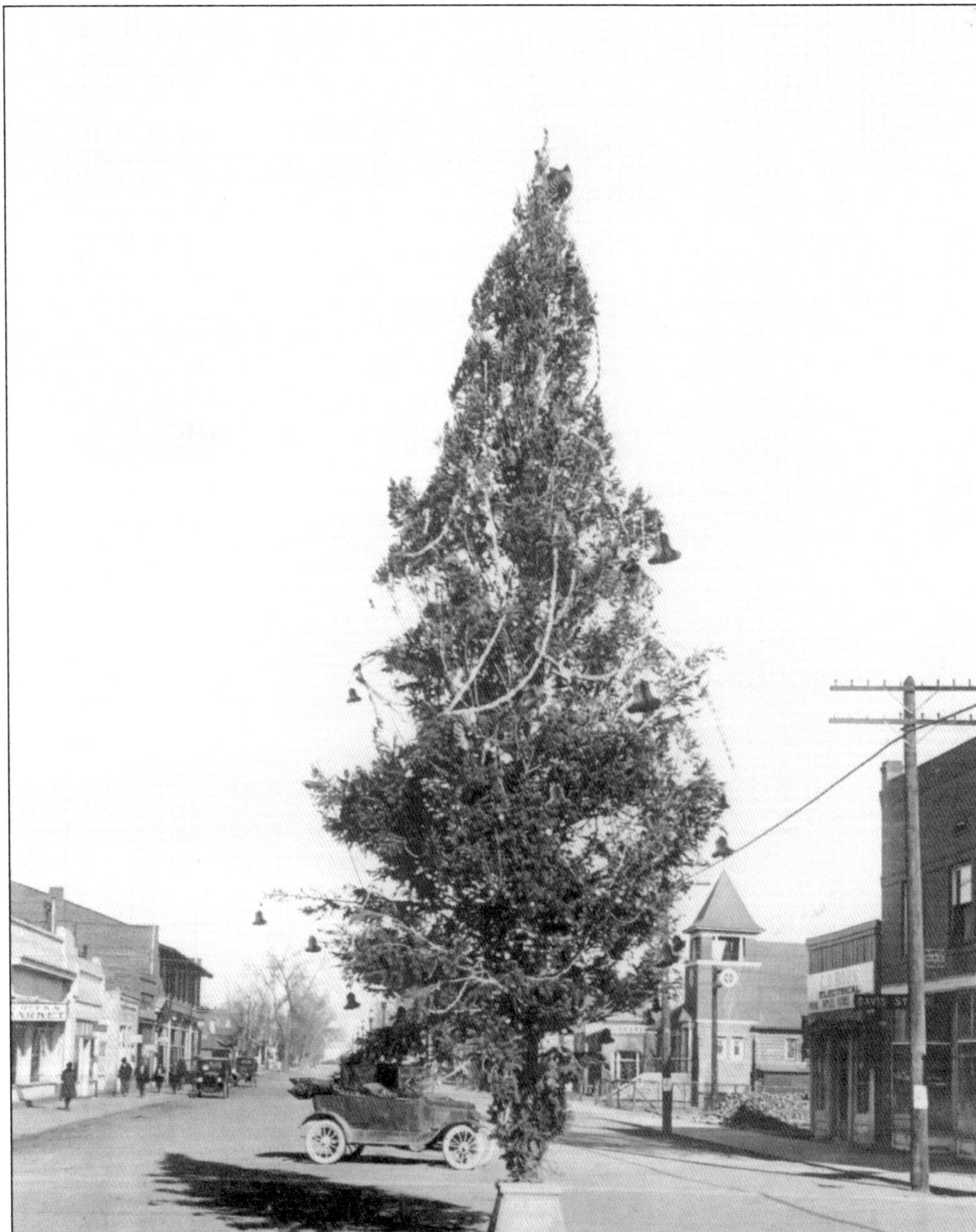

CHRISTMAS TREE, c. 1917. This large decorated Christmas tree was located at the intersection of State Avenue and Main Street. The view looks north toward Fourth Street. The sign at the base of the tree reads, "Close your mufflers." Local author Leland Feitz recalls, "Each Christmas, Alamosa became one of the most beautifully decorated little cities in Colorado, largely through the efforts of Carl Johnson of the Public Service Company." In the first building on the right, the Emperius Building, at 422 State Avenue, O.T. Davis's second Alamosa studio was on the ground floor. Next to it was the C.D. Born Electrical Supply Store. The First Baptist Church, built in 1907, is just past that, followed by the Carnegie library, which opened in 1910. On the left side of the street, Creeks Market can be seen.

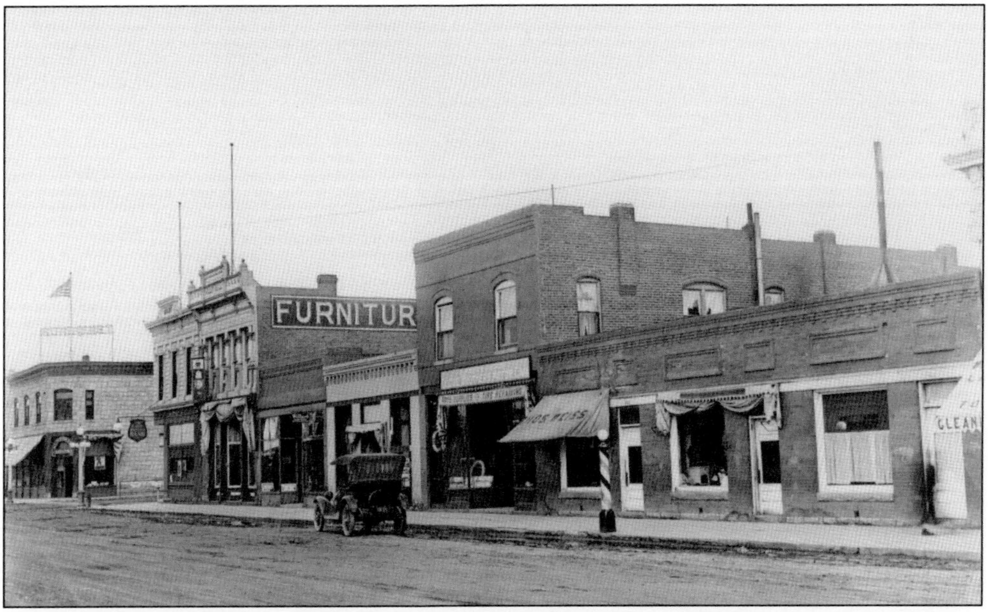

Main Street, Alamosa, c. 1910. The view looks west on Main Street between State and San Juan Avenues. Businesses include, from left to right, Sundquist Brothers general merchandise, Alamosa National Bank, a furniture store, Dodge Brothers Motor Car Company, offering supplies and tire repairs, a barbershop, and a cleaners.

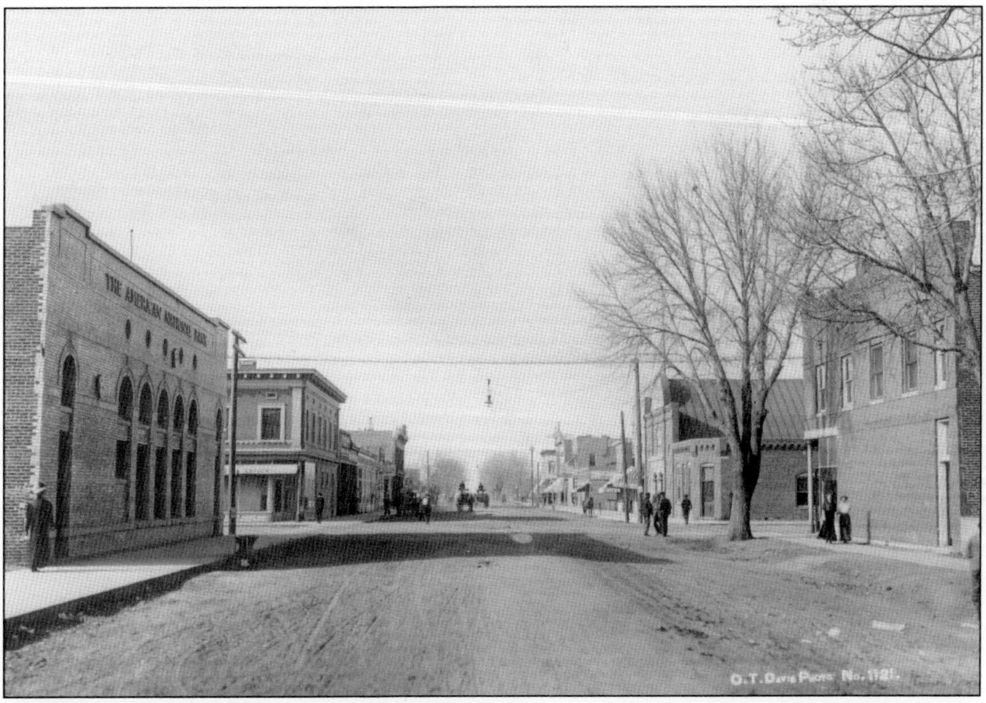

American National Bank, January 10, 1911. The view west from Main Street at the corner of State Avenue shows a rare mild January day with shoppers on the sidewalks and horses and buggies on the street. The American National Bank occupied the handsome brick building on the left.

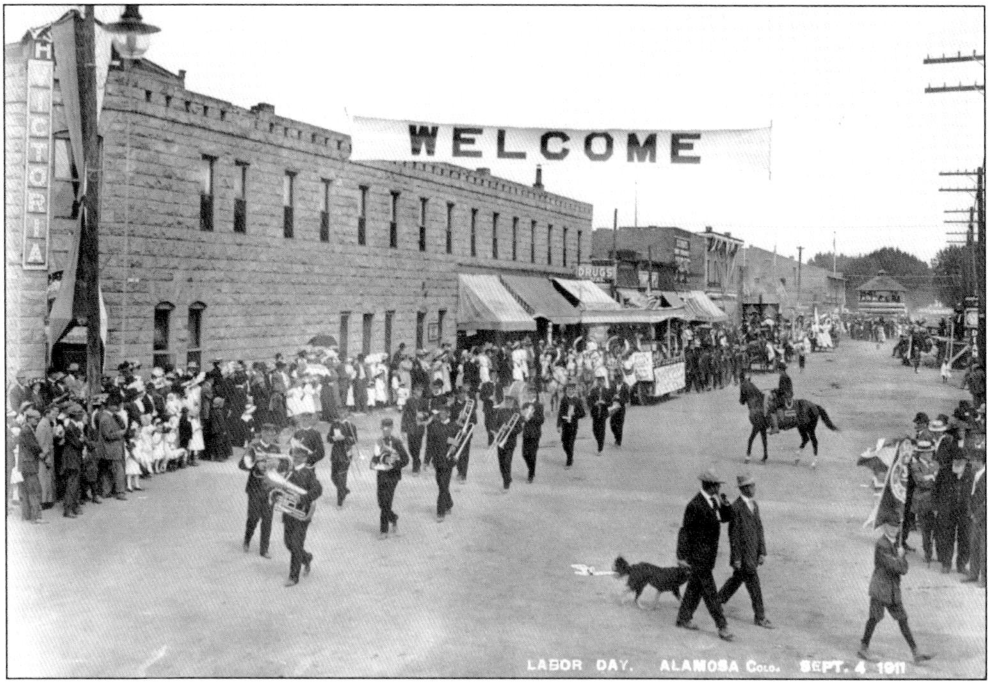

LABOR DAY PARADE, SEPTEMBER 4, 1911. A band leads the parade down State Avenue past the Victoria Hotel, on the left. Built in 1900, the Victoria burned down in 1981. It was famous for the breakfasts it served to D&RG passengers arriving at the depot across the street on the overnight train from Denver. It was also said to be known for all-night poker games.

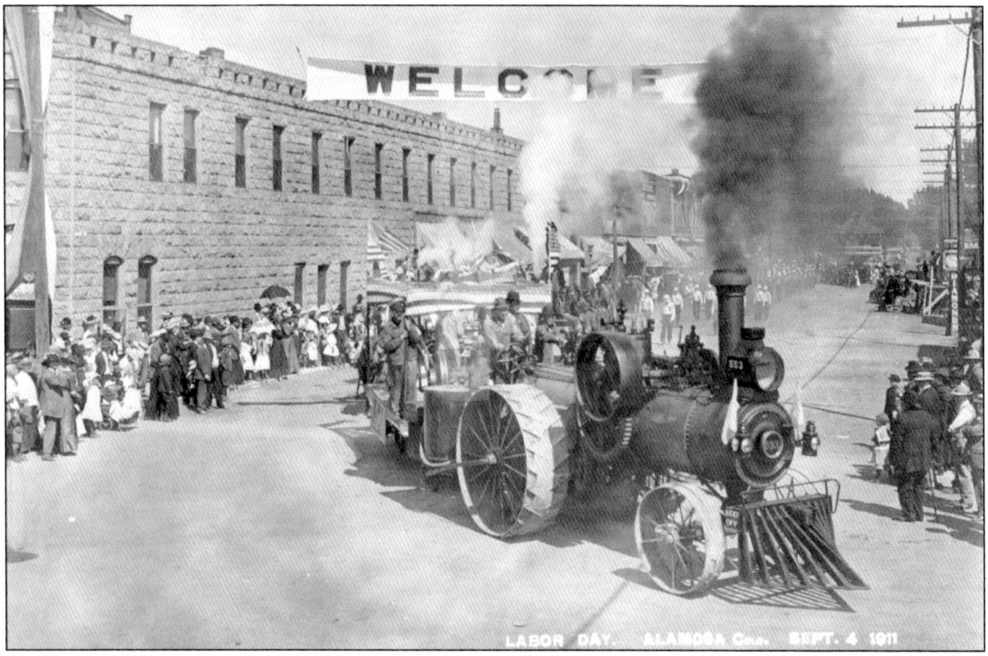

STEAM TRACTOR/LOCOMOTIVE, SEPTEMBER 4, 1911. The Labor Day parade featured this steam tractor gussied up with a cowcatcher and headlight. International Association of Machinists Mount Blanca Lodge No. 553 created it to replicate a D&RG steam locomotive.

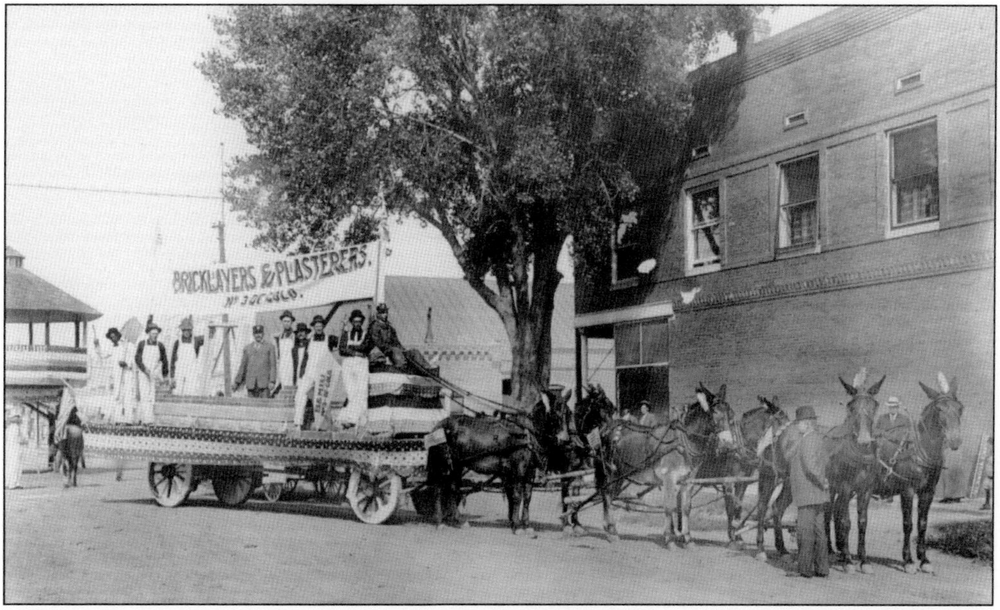

Bricklayers and Plasterers Float, September 4, 1911. This group used a six-mule team to pull its float in the Labor Day parade. Note the bandstand at the left, which is also seen at the far end of State Avenue in the photograph on the top of the previous page. This seemed to be the starting point for the parade.

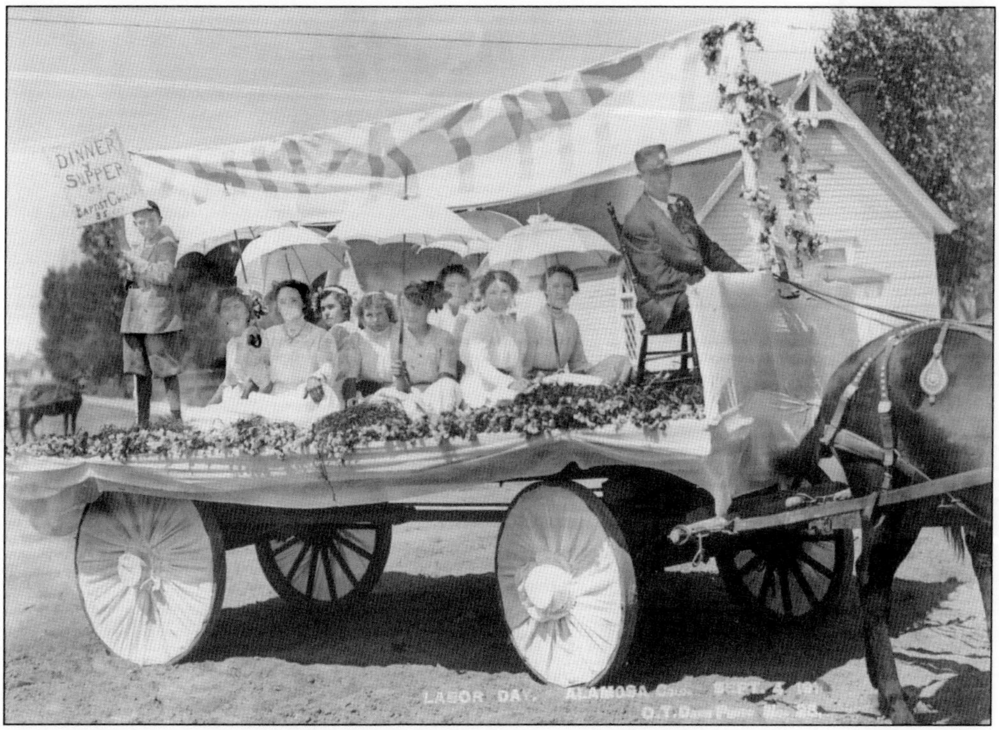

Baptist Church Float, September 4, 1911. Ladies of the First Baptist Church rode in shaded comfort under their parasols on this horse-drawn wagon. The boy at the rear holds a sign that reads, "Dinner and Supper at Baptist Church, 35 cts."

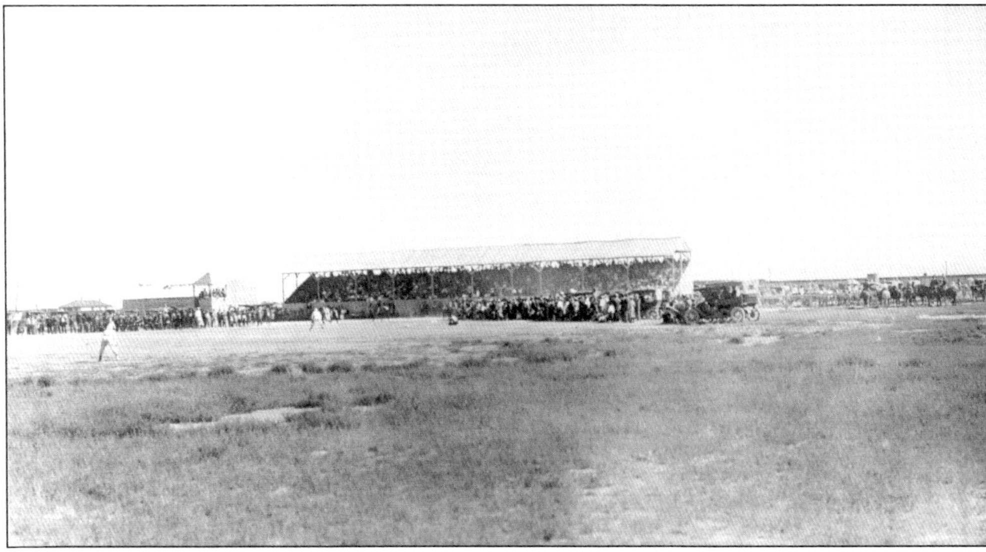

Labor Day Baseball Game, September 4, 1911. After the parade, the crowds moved out to the Alamosa fairgrounds to watch the traditional Labor Day baseball game.

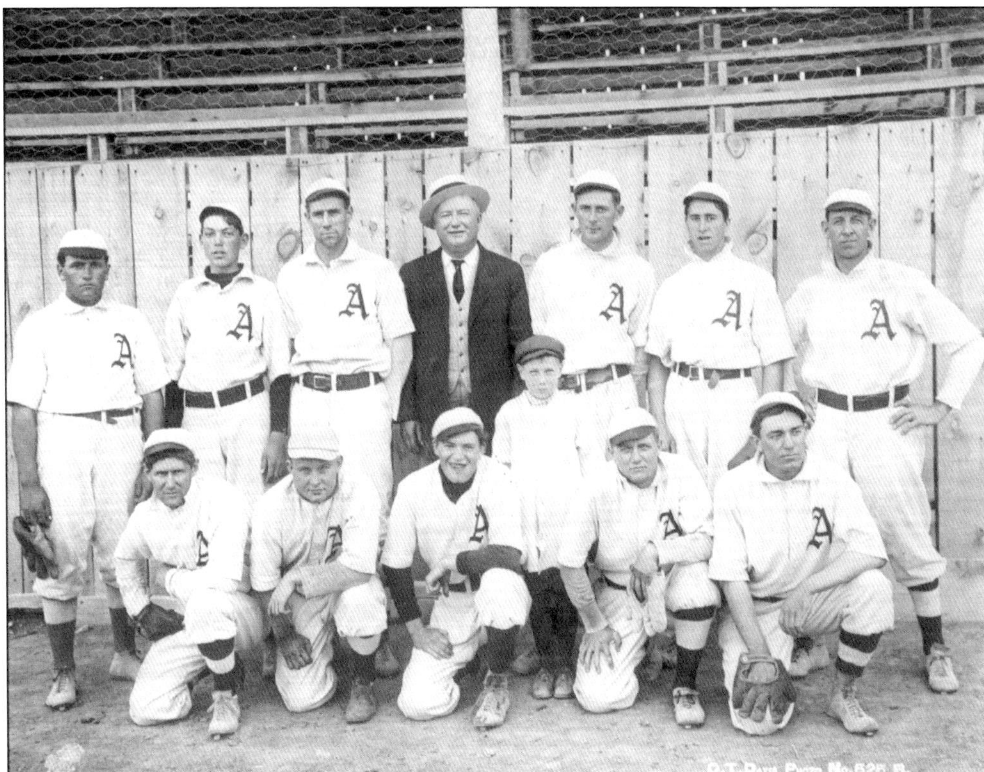

Alamosa Baseball Team, April 1910. Photographed here along with members of the team are manager H.L. Nathan, in the suit and tie, and team mascot Ford Ginn, the boy standing in the first row.

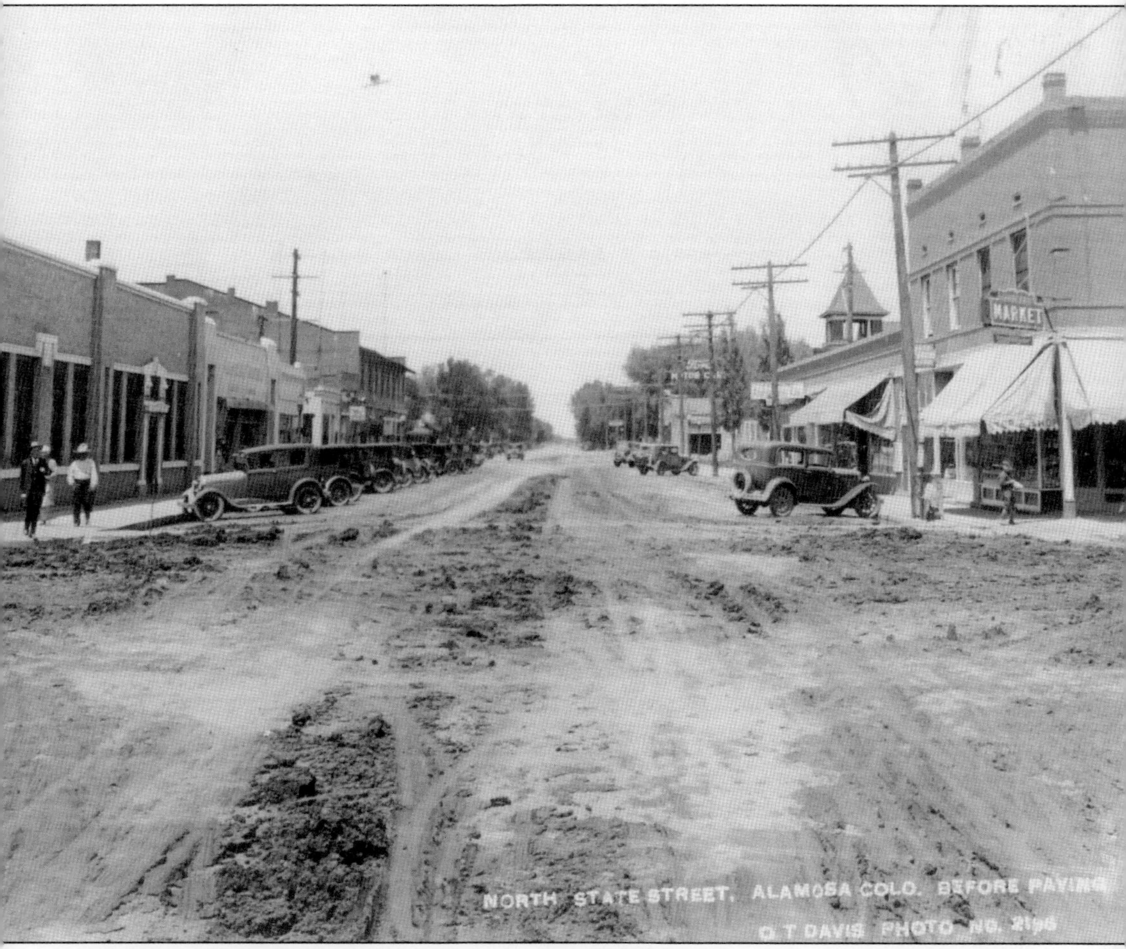

Muddy Streets, September 20, 1930. Alamosa's streets were in definite need of paving as motorcars churned up the mud after a September rainstorm. This is at the corner of Main Street and State Avenue looking north on State Avenue. The pedestrians at the left corner may be pondering how to get across the mud. The horses, buggies, and wagons seen in earlier Alamosa street scenes had disappeared by this time, replaced by automobiles, some of which were probably purchased at the Ford Motor Car dealership seen at the right rear.

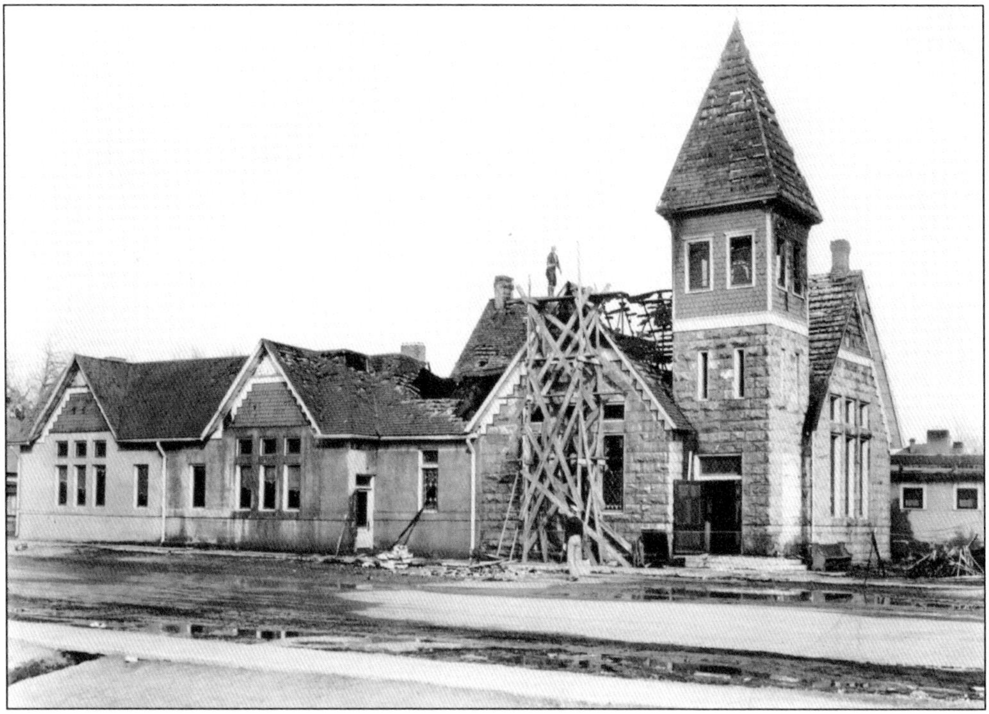

First Presbyterian Church, February 19, 1933. This church, located at the corner of Fourth Street and San Juan Avenue, was constructed in 1896. The interior and the roof were gutted by fire in 1933. Restoration and reconstruction began immediately after the fire.

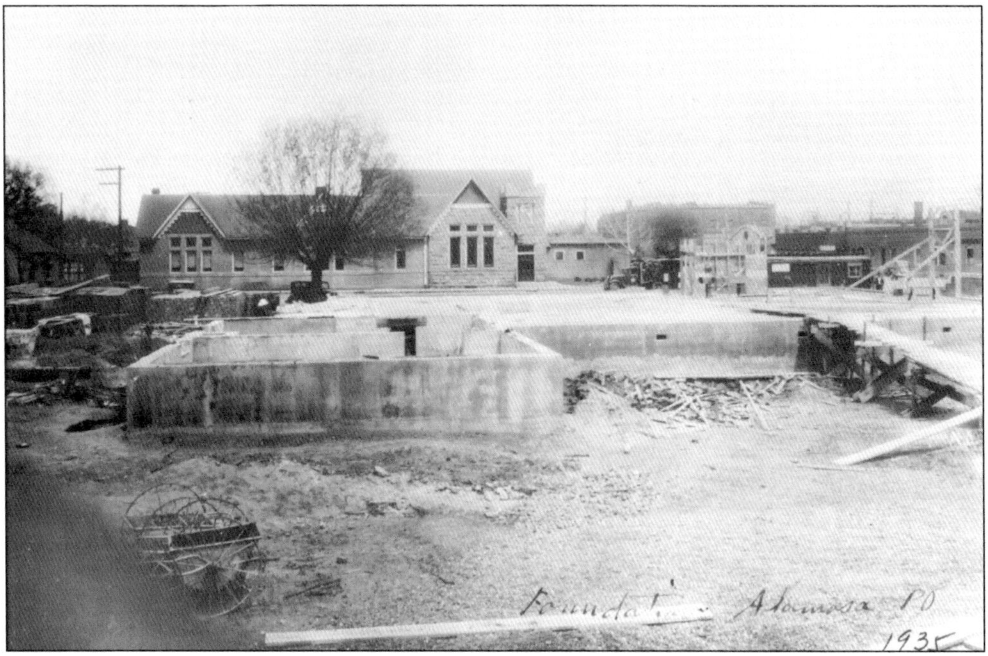

First Presbyterian Church, 1935. By 1935, the church had recovered from the effects of the fire. Note, however, that the steeple shown in the photograph above was not rebuilt. In the foreground is the foundation for the new Alamosa post office under construction.

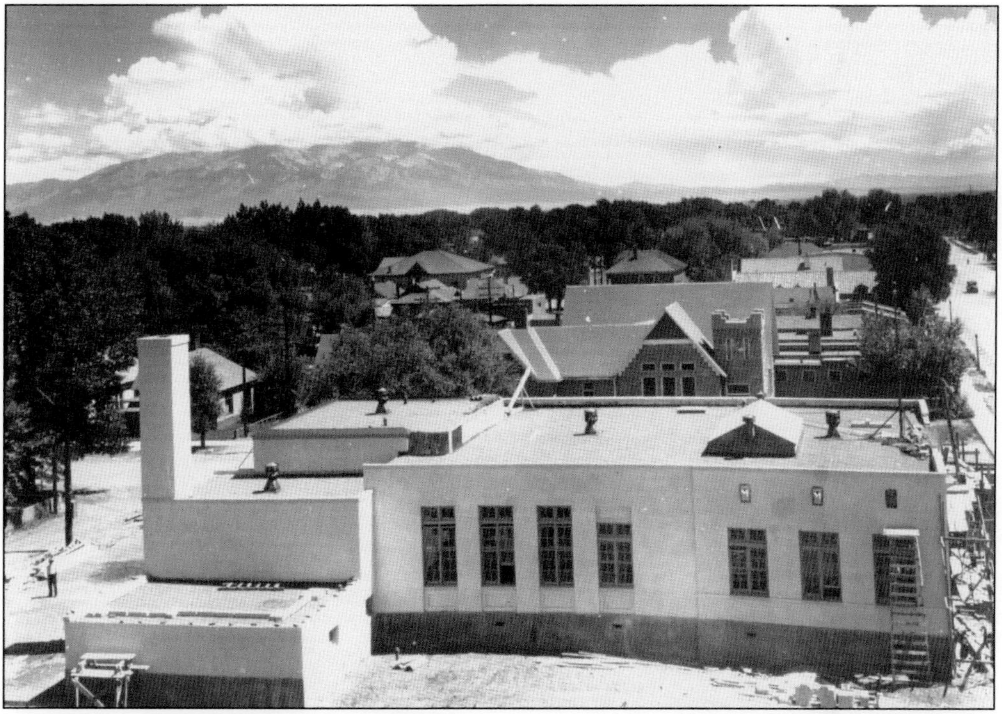

Post Office Construction, 1935. This view, looking west along Fourth Street toward Blanca Peak, shows construction of the post office nearing completion. The First Presbyterian Church can be seen next to the post office.

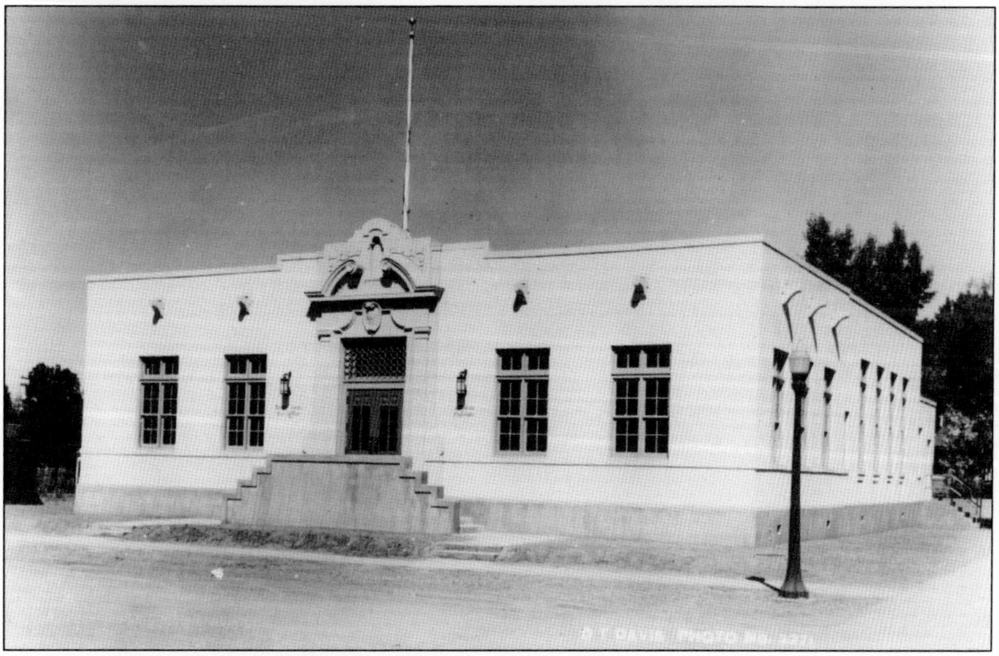

Alamosa Post Office Completed, 1935. This view of the front of the post office from Fourth Street shows the newly completed building. The building's simple design is in stark contrast to the ornate Monte Visa post office, shown on page 87.

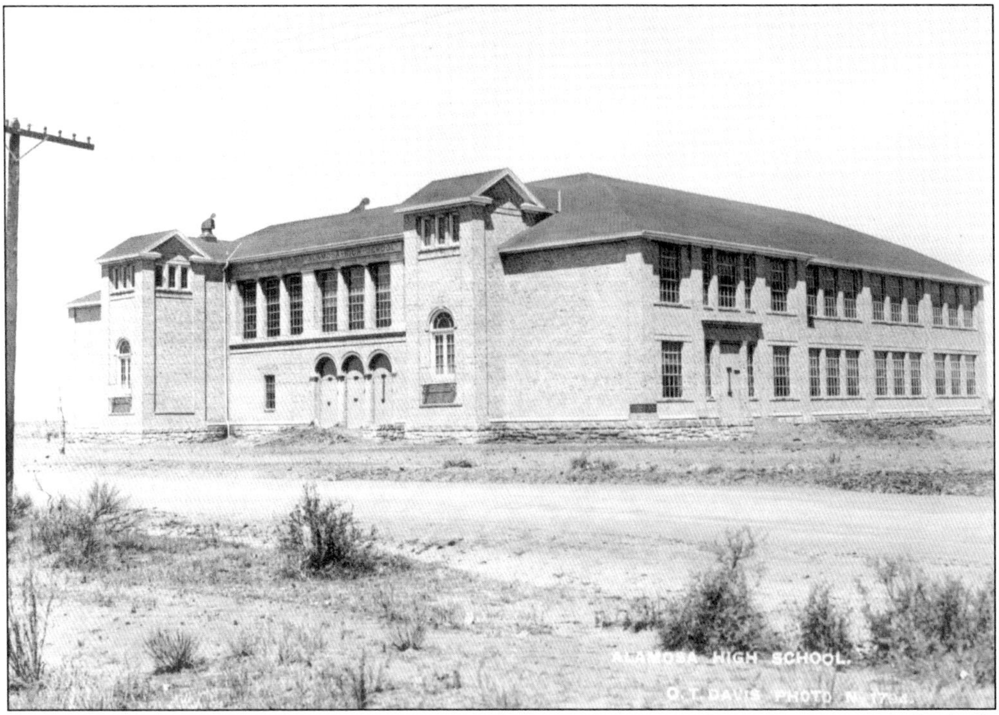

ALAMOSA HIGH SCHOOL, APRIL 1921. Located at Main Street and La Veta Avenue, the high school building was nearing completion when this photograph was taken. Only nine years later, it would suffer the same fate as the First Presbyterian Church—destruction by fire.

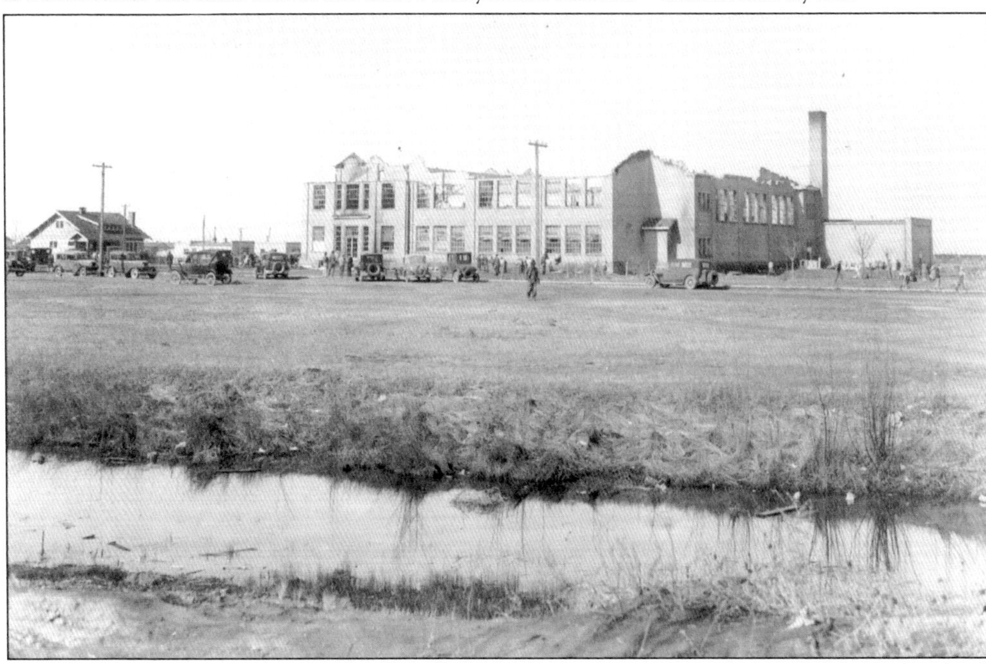

ALAMOSA HIGH SCHOOL, APRIL 1930. Fire destroyed most of the building, leaving only a brick shell, as shown in this photograph taken the morning after the fire. Classes were moved to Richardson Hall at Adams State Normal School.

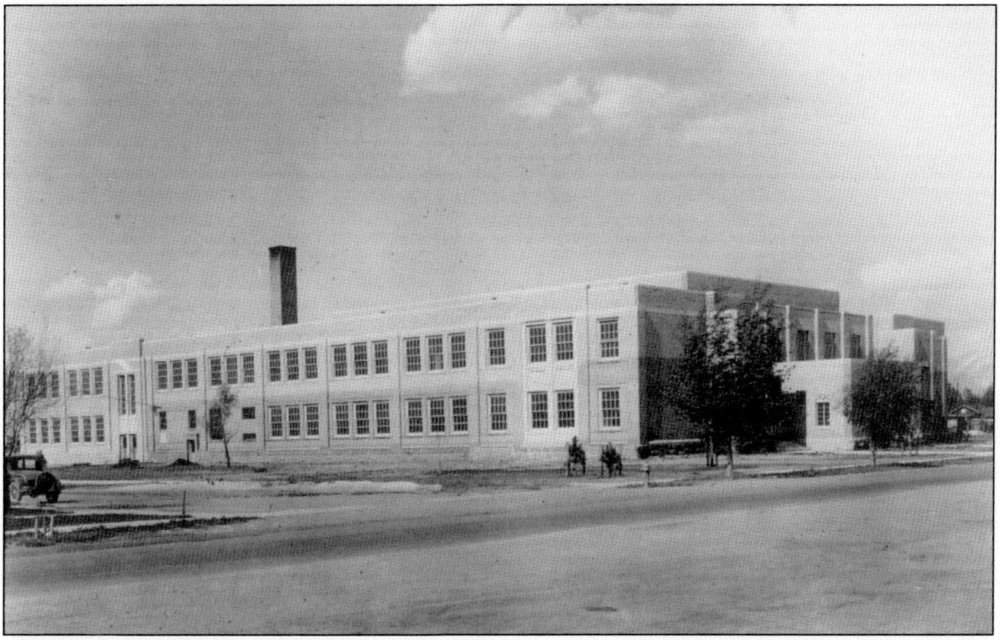

New Alamosa High School, 1931. Located on the same site as the school that burned down in April 1930, this new school building served Alamosa and its students faithfully for 70 years. It was finally torn down in 2000.

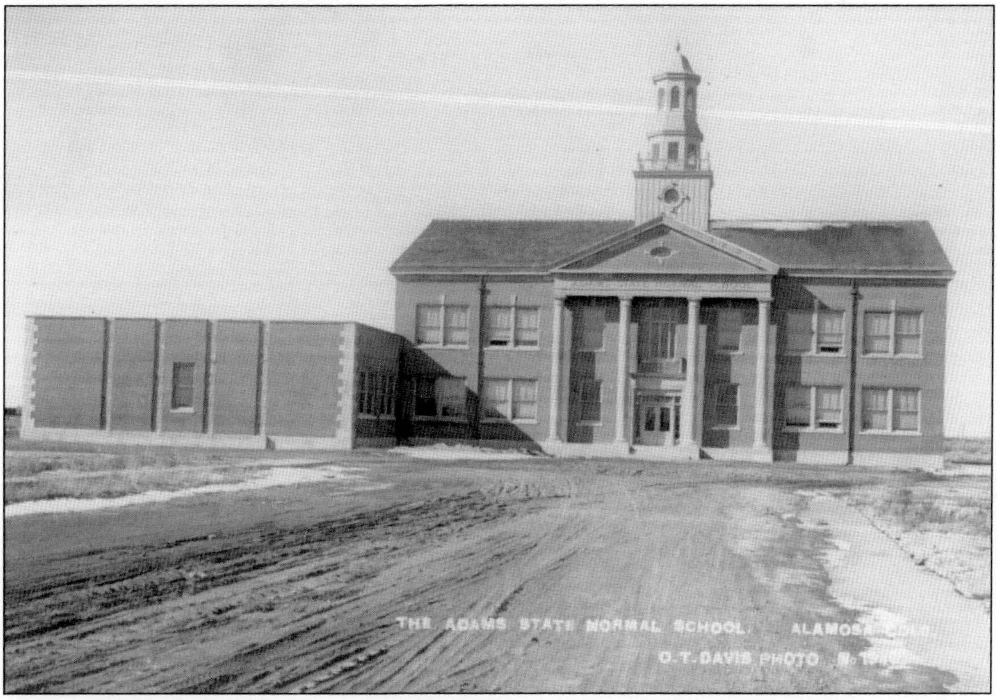

Adams State Normal School, 1929. In 1921, state senator William "Billy" Adams, a San Luis Valley rancher, introduced legislation to build a normal school, or teacher's college, in Alamosa. Construction began in 1923, and the first classes were held in Richardson Hall (right) in September 1925. The square building on the left is an auditorium and gymnasium completed in 1929.

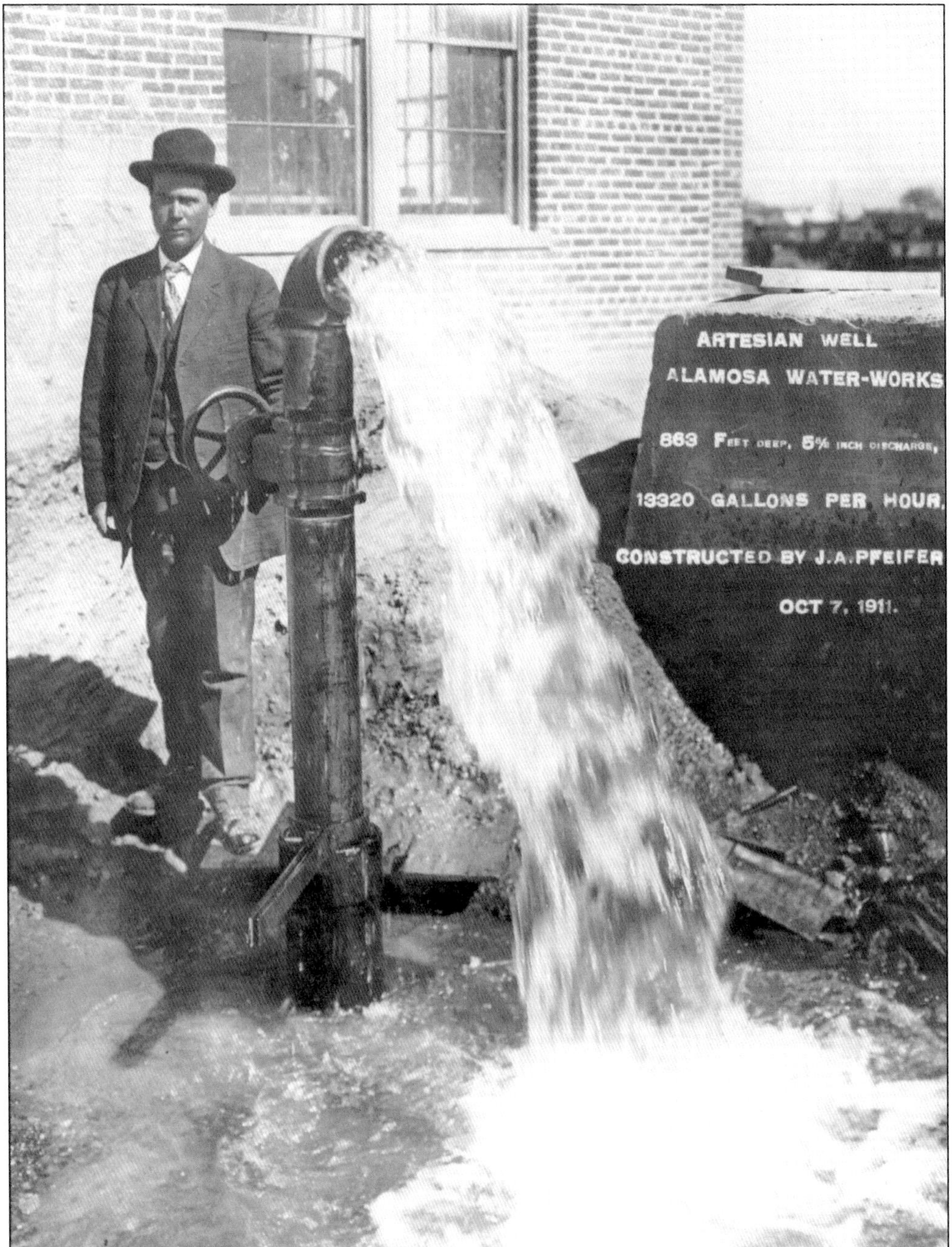

ALAMOSA ARTESIAN WELL, OCTOBER 7, 1911. Water is the lifeblood of the San Luis Valley. Artesian wells and irrigation canals met the needs of growing towns and thirsty croplands. Here, at the Alamosa Water Works, six artesian wells fed the town water tower, seen on page 30. This particular well was 863 feet deep and discharged 13,320 gallons of water per hour. The man is not identified.

Nine

Scenic Places
"Colorado's Best Kept Secret"

As a commissioned photographer, O.T. Davis photographed railroads, mines, and agricultural lands. Scenery was not a major focus of his photographs unless it was a backdrop for one of those economic activities. However, a few strictly scenic photographs are found in his collection, and this chapter presents some of those, in particular one visit he made to the north side of Blanca Peak in 1899.

Blanca Peak is easily visible from the south and west from various transportation corridors. The north side of the peak, where O.T. Davis took his photographs, is very difficult to reach even today. Traversing back roads requiring four-wheel drive is necessary to approach this section of today's Sangre de Cristo Wilderness Area. There are several versions of the origin of the name of these mountains. The main thread of the story is that a wounded and dying Spanish priest in the 1600s looked toward these mountains at sunset when they were bathed in a red glow, and he uttered "sangre de Cristo," Spanish for "blood of Christ." Congress created the Sangre de Cristo Wilderness Area in 1993 to preserve this spectacular scenery for generations to come.

O.T. Davis called Blanca Peak "Sierra Blanco," Spanish for "white mountain." At 14,345 feet elevation, the mountain is indeed clothed in white snow for much of the year. Hikers today can retrace O.T.'s route to the north side of Blanca Peak by driving west on County Road 550 from the small town of Gardner and then south on Forest Road 580 to the trailhead to Lily Lake. The three-mile hiking trail to Lily Lake passes by many of the places photographed by O.T. Davis in this chapter.

The trail to Lily Lake encompasses some of Colorado's most beautiful scenery, with soaring jagged peaks, cirque lakes, and glacial valleys filled with rushing streams. The Huerfano (Spanish for "orphan") River has its origin at Lily Lake. In this spectacular and remote setting, it is easy to see why the Alamosa Chamber of Commerce called the San Luis Valley and the Sangre de Cristo Mountains "Colorado's Best Kept Secret."

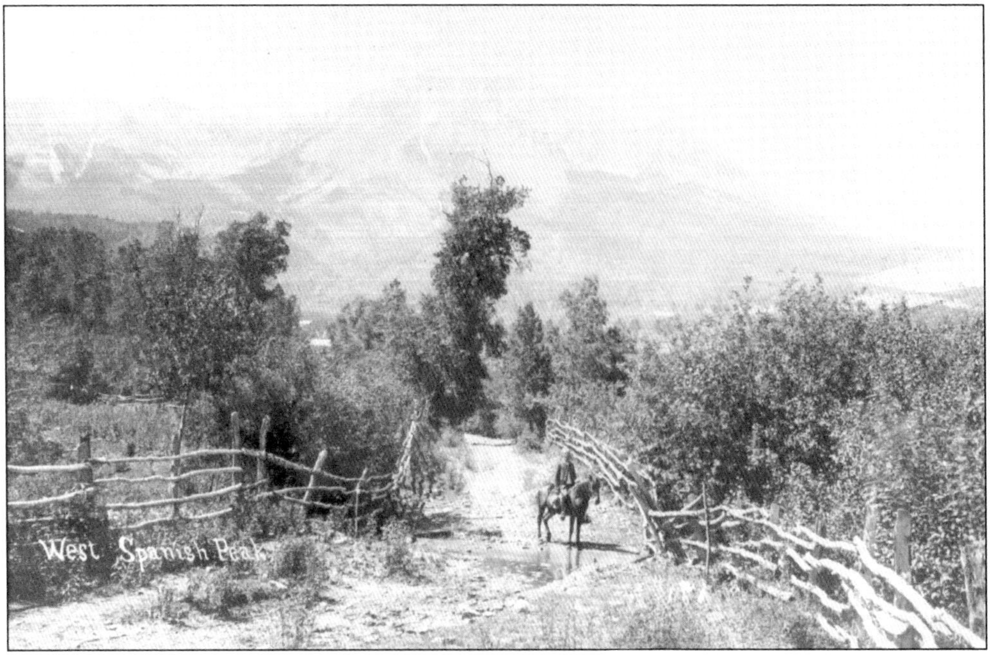

WEST SPANISH PEAK, 1890. From his base in La Veta, O.T. Davis traveled over the surrounding area, including the Spanish Peaks and Blanca Peak. In this view looking south toward the north face of West Spanish Peak, Davis encountered a lone rider on the road.

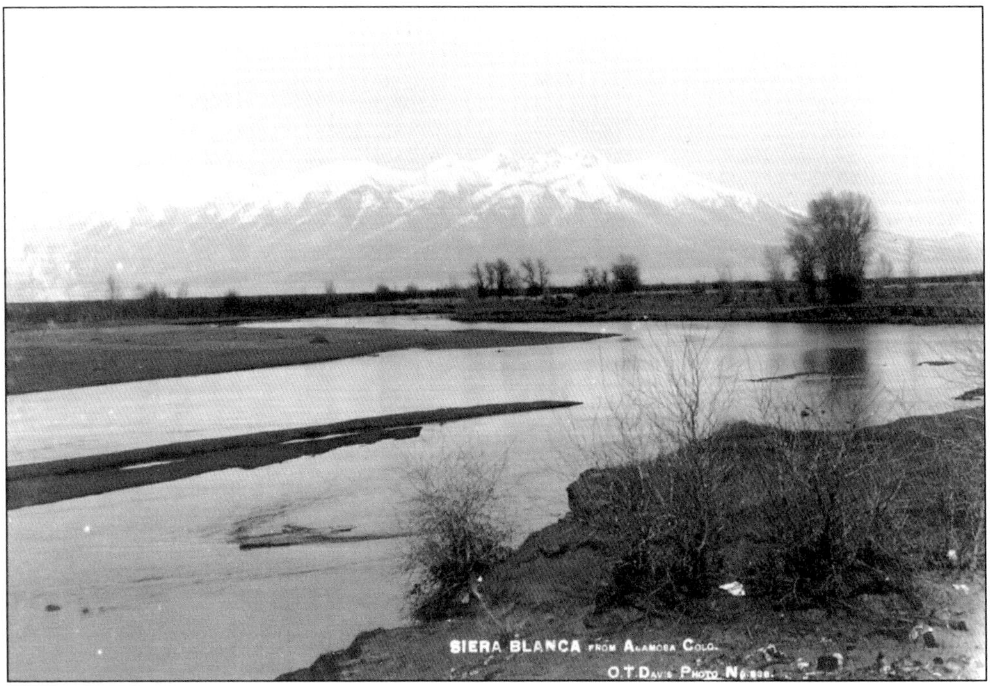

VIEW OF BLANCA PEAK FROM ALAMOSA, 1907. O.T. Davis captured this beautiful view of the Rio Grande and Blanca Peak after he moved his studio to Alamosa in 1906. This was the view seen by travelers arriving in Alamosa on the D&RG train and along the primitive roads in the area. Very few people at that time saw the north face of Blanca Peak, as presented in the following pages.

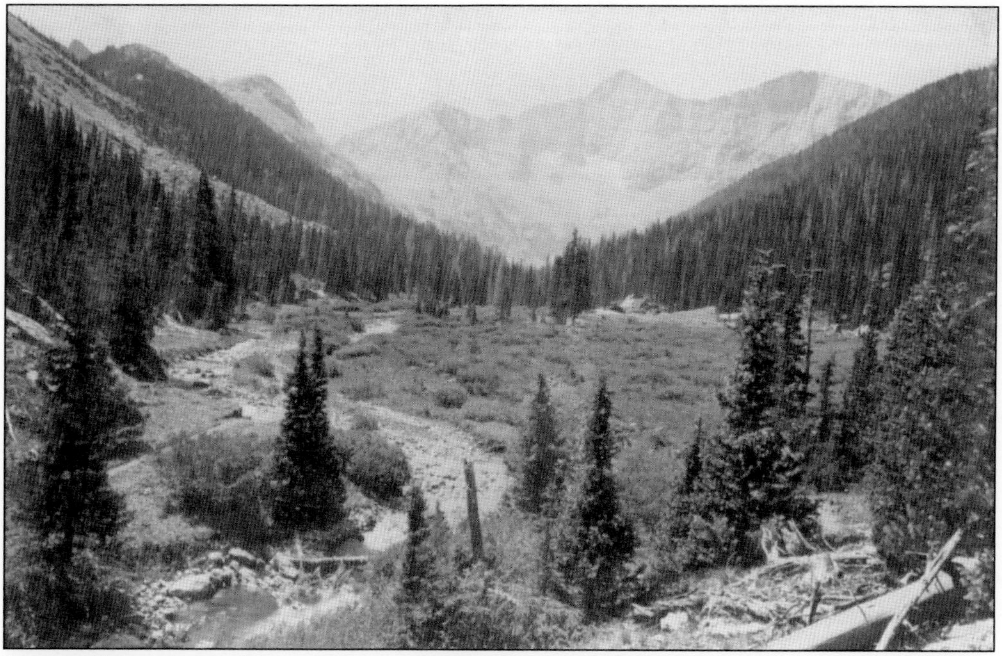

Shingle Park, Sierra Blanco, August 1899. The trail to Lily Lake follows along the Huerfano River through Shingle Park and then up the forested slope to the right. Blanca Peak is the highest peak at the right center. Perhaps Shingle Park was named after all the loose rocks on the slope at the left, resembling a shingled roof.

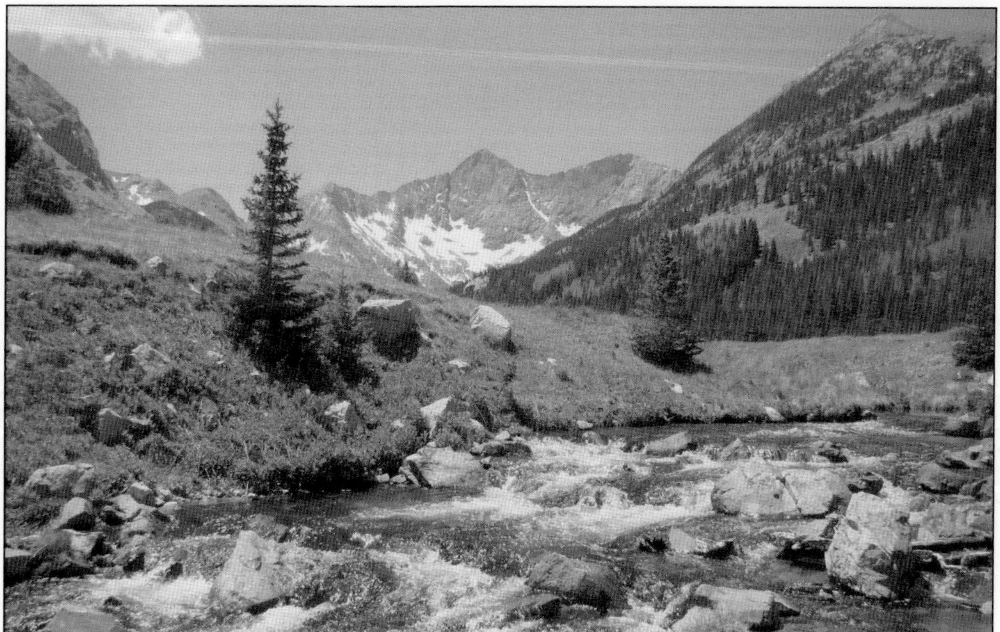

Shingle Park and Blanca Peak, June 17, 2013. From the banks of the Huerfano River, the author shot this scene of the Shingle Park area with Blanca Peak dominating the center background. Note how the outline of the peaks match the O.T. Davis photograph above. This beautiful place is now preserved in the Sangre de Cristo Wilderness Area. (Photograph by author.)

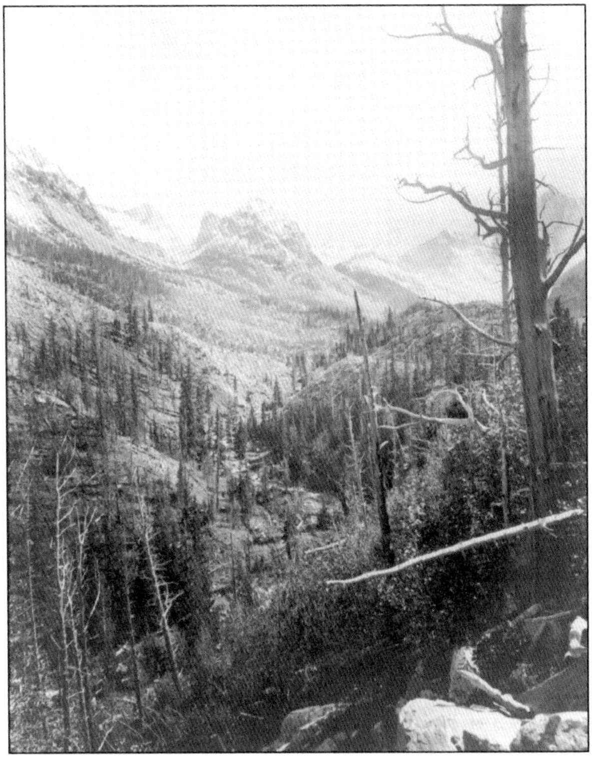

Canyon on Sierra Blanco, August 1899. This is not the Huerfano River canyon; it is a branching canyon to the southeast. A primitive trail leads to Mount Lindsey (14,042 feet). The mountain in the center is Iron Nipple, with Lindsey off in the left background.

Henderson-Hawkins Park, Sierra Blanco, August 10, 1899. Blanca Peak is directly in the center of the photograph. This log cabin on the Huerfano River was undoubtedly home for some of the miners working higher up the face of the mountain at the Hawkins Lode (see page 40).

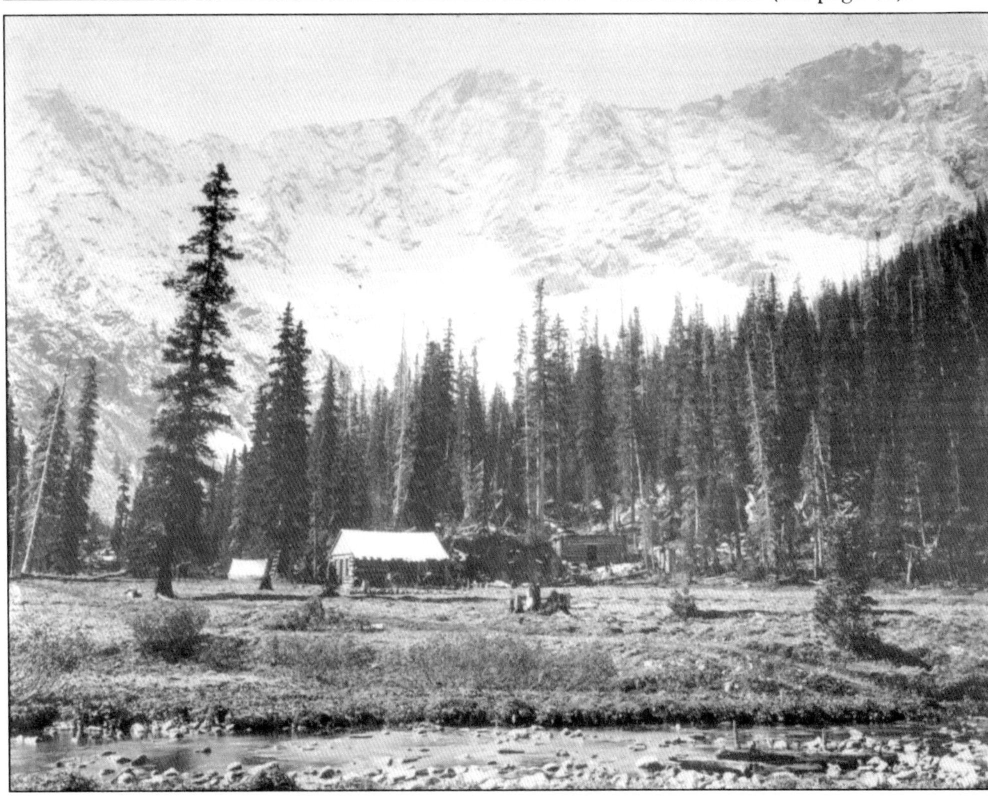

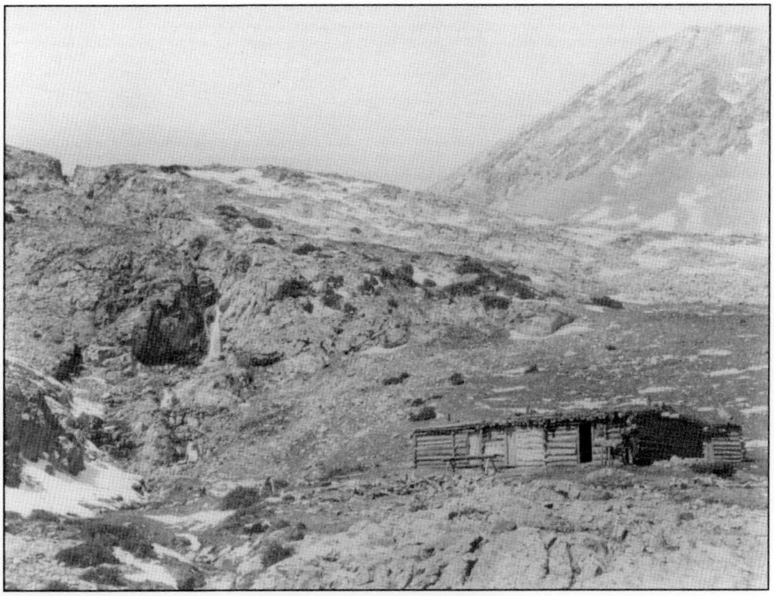

LILY CABIN, AUGUST 1899. The Lily family's rustic log cabin provided some shelter from the elements at this extremely high elevation (approximately 12,000 feet). This cabin was most likely built to house miners working at the nearby Hawkins Lode. Lily Lake is a bit farther up the mountain beyond the cabin.

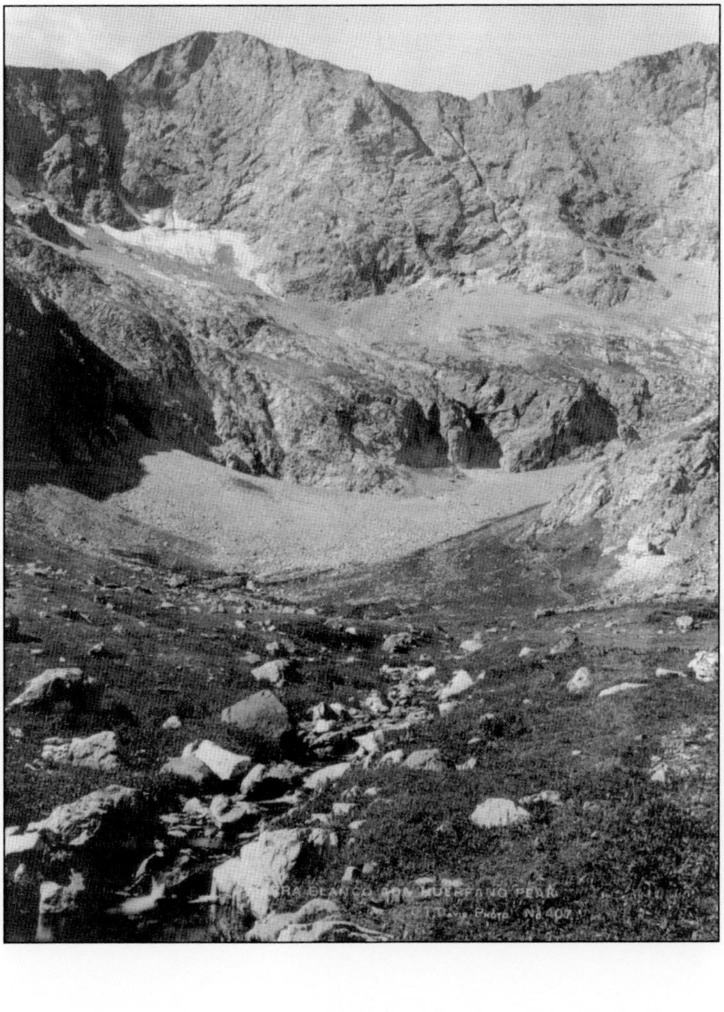

SIERRA BLANCO AND HUERFANO PEAK, AUGUST 10, 1899. Huerfano Peak is not found on today's maps. It was probably a part of the Blanca Peak massif. The patch of snow on the mountain seems to correspond with the "glacier" shown on the next page.

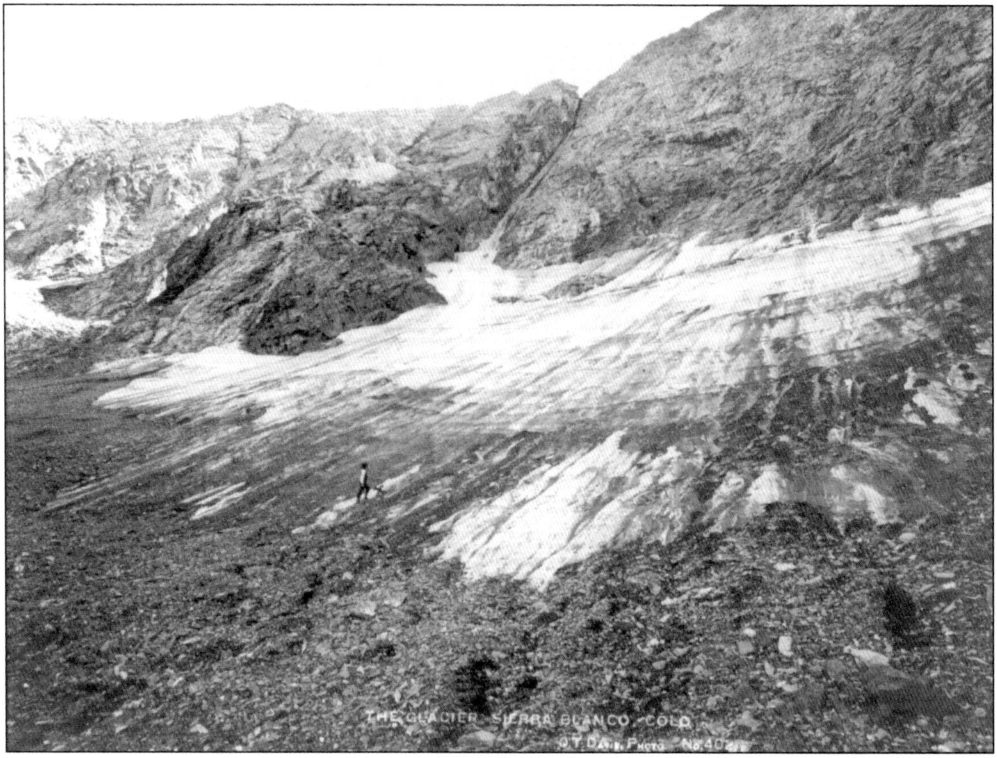

GLACIER ON SIERRA BLANCO, AUGUST 1899. It is difficult to tell if this was a glacier or a snowfield. A glacier is a mass of year-round ice, while a snowfield is an accumulation of snow that generally melts off by the end of each summer. The man in the center is identified as Sylvester J. Davis, the father of O.T. Davis and his brother Corin F. Davis.

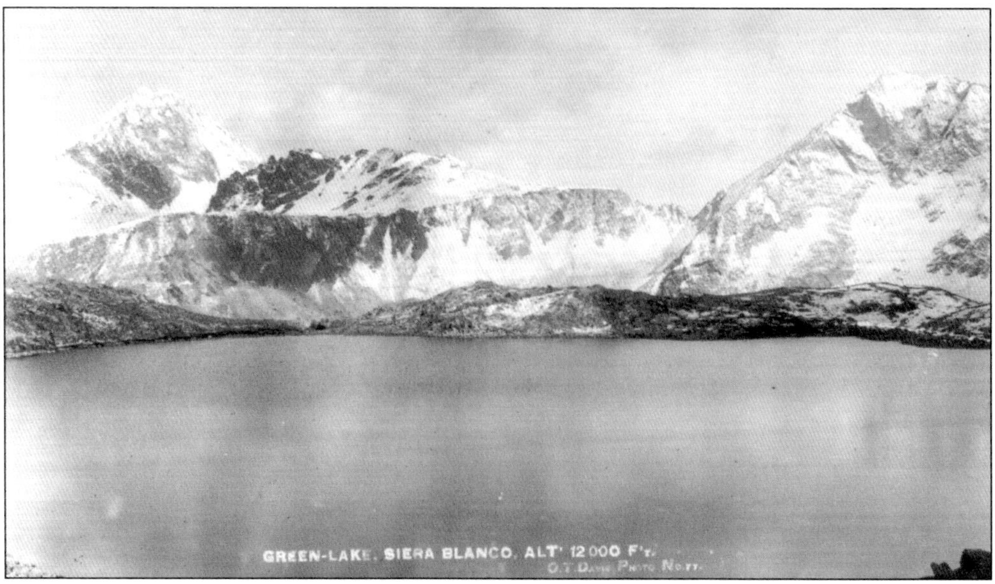

GREEN LAKE, SIERRA BLANCO, AUGUST 1899. The lake is known today as Lily Lake, and it can be reached by hiking the 3.2-mile trail from the trailhead along the Huerfano River. This spectacular view to the east shows Mount Lindsey on the left.

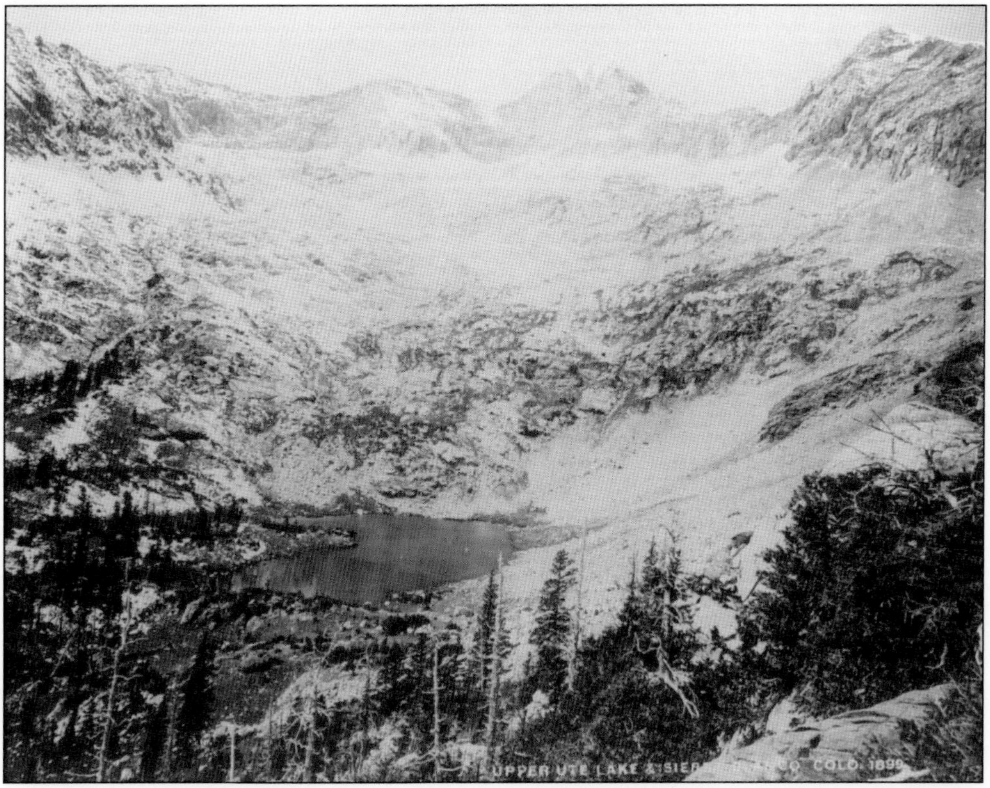

Upper Ute Lake and Sierra Blanco, August 1899. This small lake above Lily Lake was identified by O.T. Davis as Upper Ute Lake, but the name does not appear on maps today.

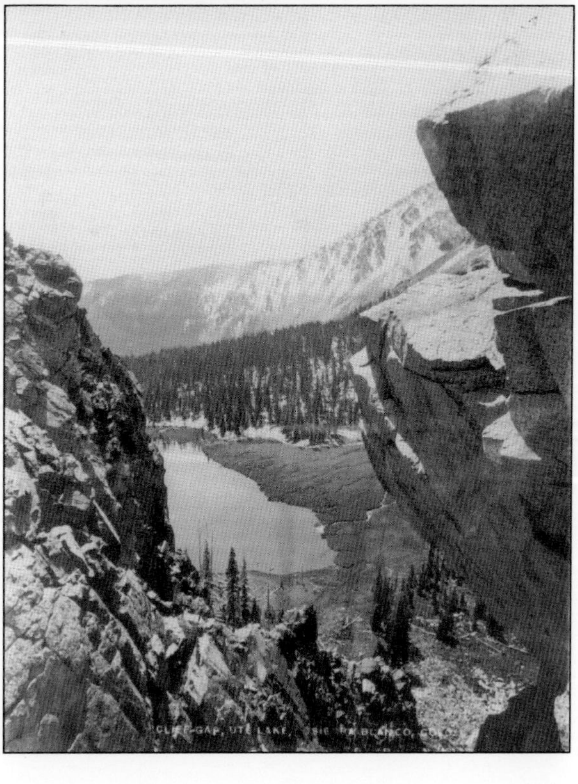

Cliff Gap, Ute Lake, Sierra Blanco, August 1899. O.T. Davis climbed above the lake to take this shot looking east through the gap in the rocks.

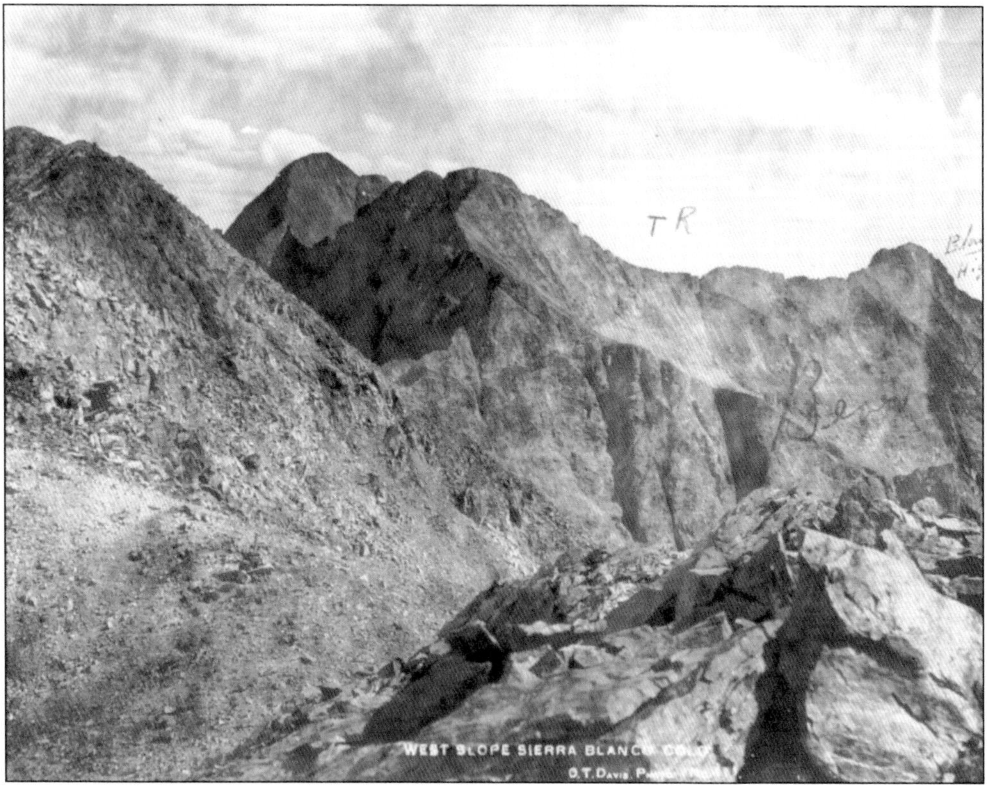

West Slope, Sierra Blanco, August 1899. O.T. Davis's notations identify the high point of Blanca Peak at the right. Below that, the word "Bear" is written, perhaps referring to what is today known as Little Bear Peak (14,037 feet). The "TR" above the peak may refer to the Trinchera Ranch (see page 54), which was located on the south side of Blanca Peak.

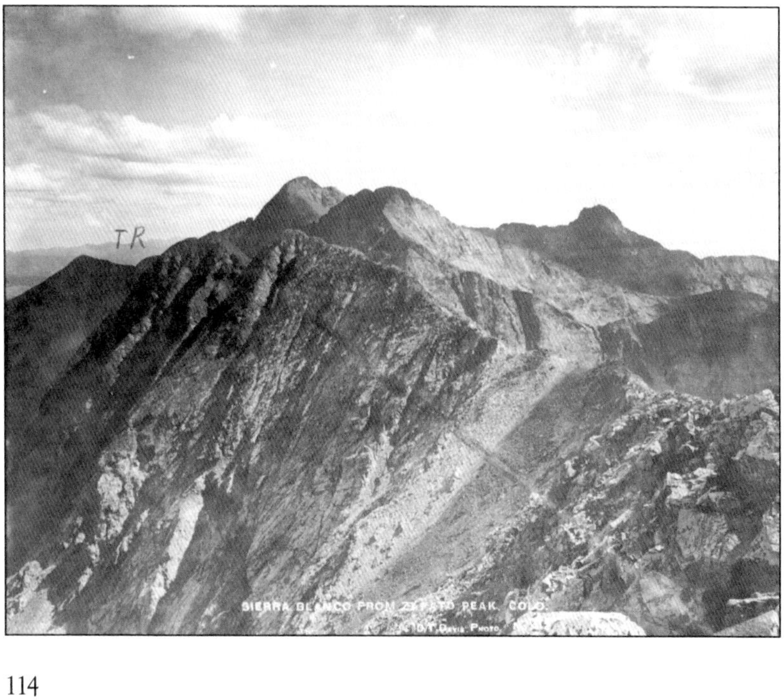

Sierra Blanco from Zapato Peak, August 1899. This is the same ridgeline of peaks shown above, just taken from a farther distance back. O.T. Davis stated that he was on Zapato Peak, but that name is not on today's maps. Today, there is a South Zapata Lake located to the northwest of Blanca Peak.

Ten

Automobiles and Roads

"Off for Good Roads Inspection"

The advent of the automobile in the early 1900s made as big an impact on the San Luis Valley as the arrival of the railroad had in 1878. Isolated farms and ranches could now be connected with towns much more quickly than in horse-and-buggy days. Henry Ford's Model T was introduced on October 1, 1908, and, with a price tag of $825, it could be afforded by most ranchers. Ford promoted the vehicle extensively and created dealerships across the country to sell it. In Alamosa, the Ford dealership on State Avenue did a booming business. As Ford developed his assembly line production of Model Ts, cost efficiencies were achieved, which eventually allowed the price of the Model T to be lowered to $360, well within the price range of almost all families.

With an efficient advertising and distribution system, Ford sold 250,000 cars in 1914, and 472,000 in 1916. By 1918, half of all cars in the United States were Model Ts. Ford promoted not just his cars but also the concept of driving. Local motor clubs, such as the Alamosa Boosters Club, sprang up to help novice drivers and to encourage the exploration of local roads. O.T. Davis followed this club on several excursions, noting that they were "Off for Good Roads Inspection." Their adventurous November 24, 1910, trip is chronicled by his photographs in this chapter.

Davis was also present for an outing on the recently completed Wolf Creek Pass Road on August 6, 1916. This torturous path had stymied surveyors of the Denver & Rio Grande Railroad in their search for a route to Durango and Silverton. They chose instead the gentler grade of Cumbres Pass to the south. Travelers today marvel at the road over Wolf Creek Pass, which has now been widened to four lanes in most places. On the east side of the pass, however, the steep, narrow canyon along the south fork of the Rio Grande is still only two lanes wide. In 1916, O.T. Davis photographed this canyon with Model Ts slowly picking their way up the rocky road.

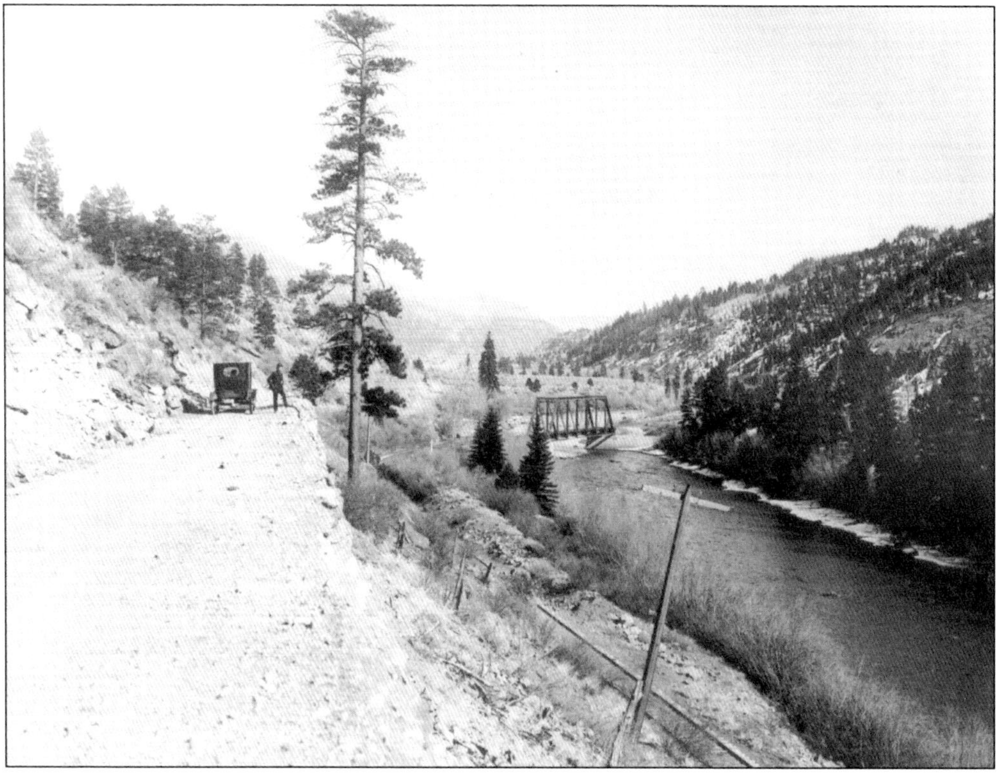

Creede Road, June 1922. The view faces south along the Rio Grande between Wagon Wheel Gap and Masonic Park. It illustrates the two types of transportation, railroad and automobile, which played such a large role in the development of southern Colorado in the 19th and 20th centuries.

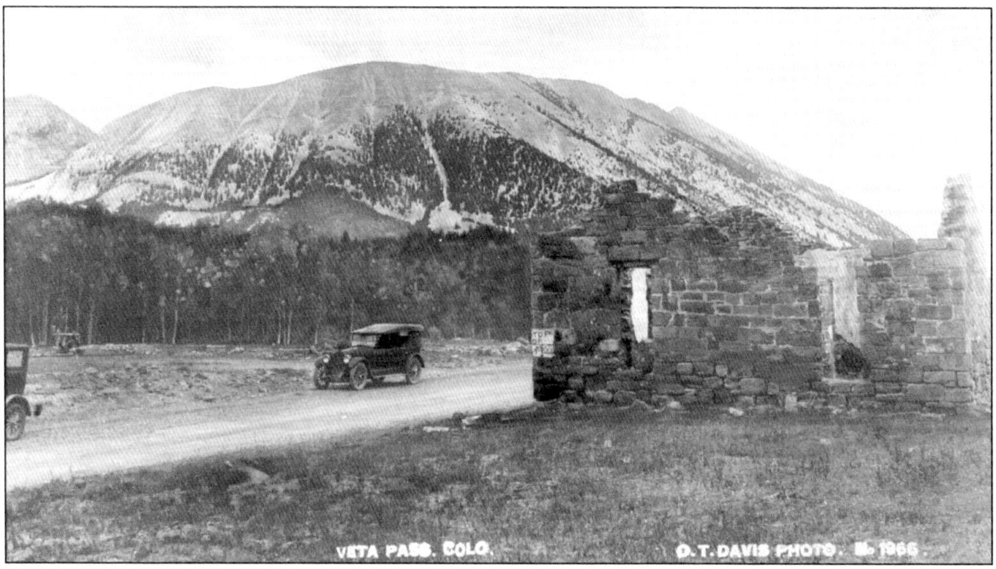

Top of Veta Pass, 1925. A fairly good gravel road over Veta Pass was built on the old roadbed of the D&RG narrow gauge when the narrow gauge was abandoned in 1899. The stone narrow-gauge depot on the right was in ruins by 1925, but it has since been restored. Mount Mestas rises in the background.

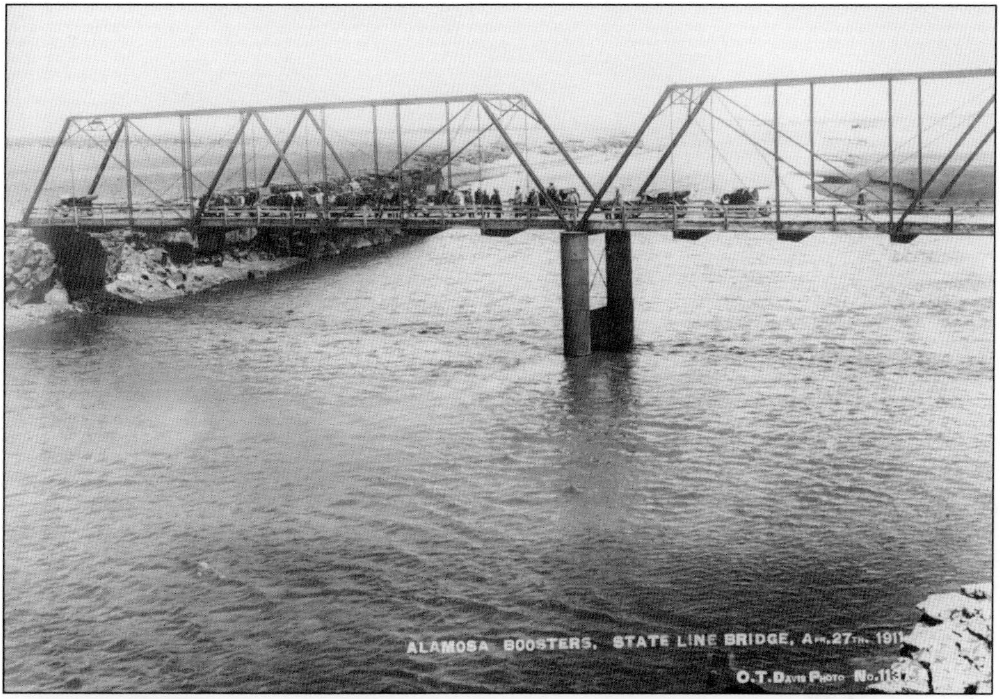

State Line Bridge, April 27, 1911. Alamosa Boosters Club members massed their automobiles on the bridge during one of their exploratory trips around the San Luis Valley. The bridge crosses the Rio Grande about six miles north of the Colorado–New Mexico border, linking Conejos County with Costilla County.

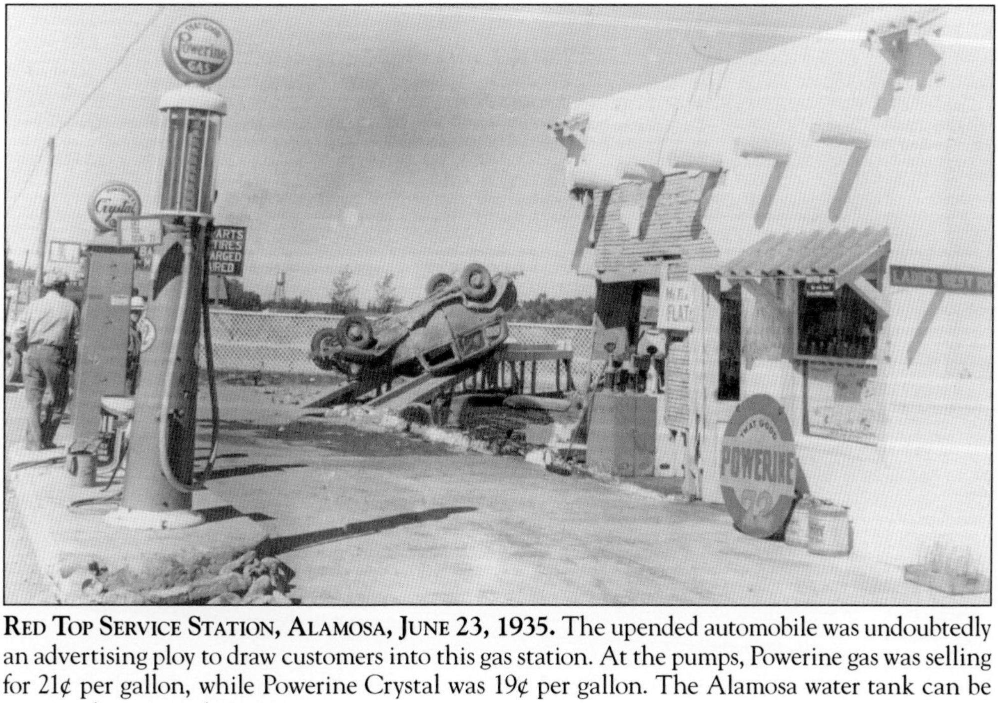

Red Top Service Station, Alamosa, June 23, 1935. The upended automobile was undoubtedly an advertising ploy to draw customers into this gas station. At the pumps, Powerine gas was selling for 21¢ per gallon, while Powerine Crystal was 19¢ per gallon. The Alamosa water tank can be seen in the center distance.

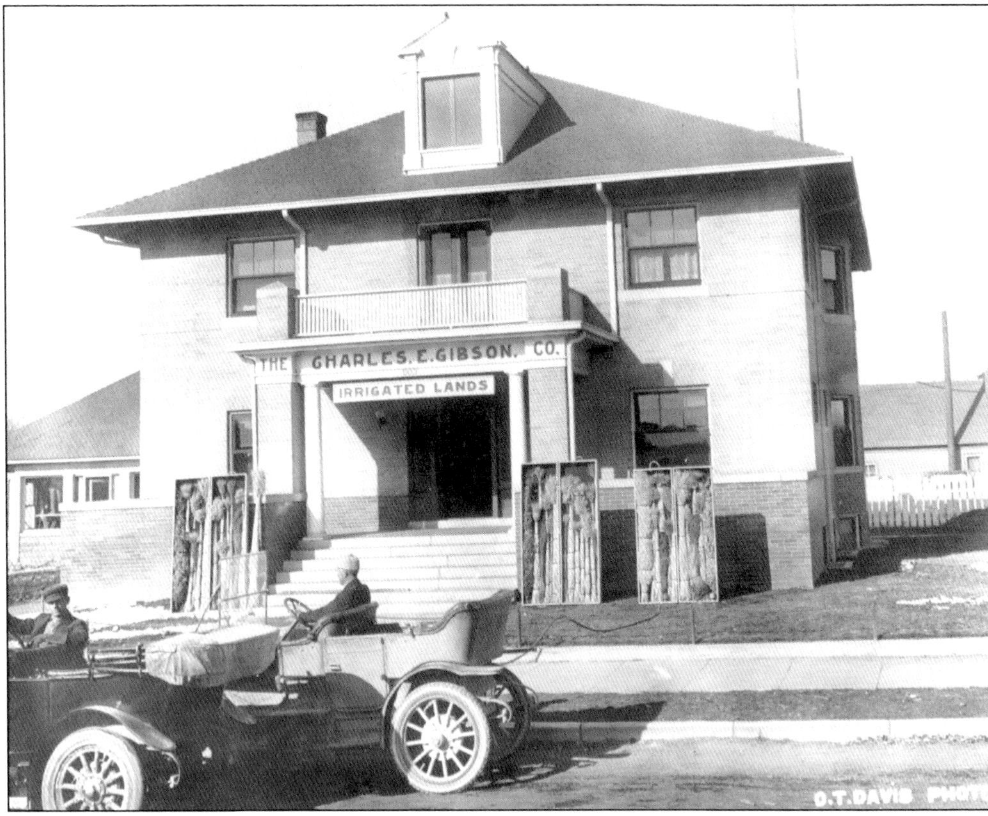

Charles Gibson Land Office, 1912. This real estate office was located at 503 Main Street in Alamosa, in the former Alamosa hospital building. Local realtors, hoping to entice buyers, commissioned O.T. Davis to photograph their buildings and their land offerings. The automobiles are probably waiting to take customers out to view land for sale.

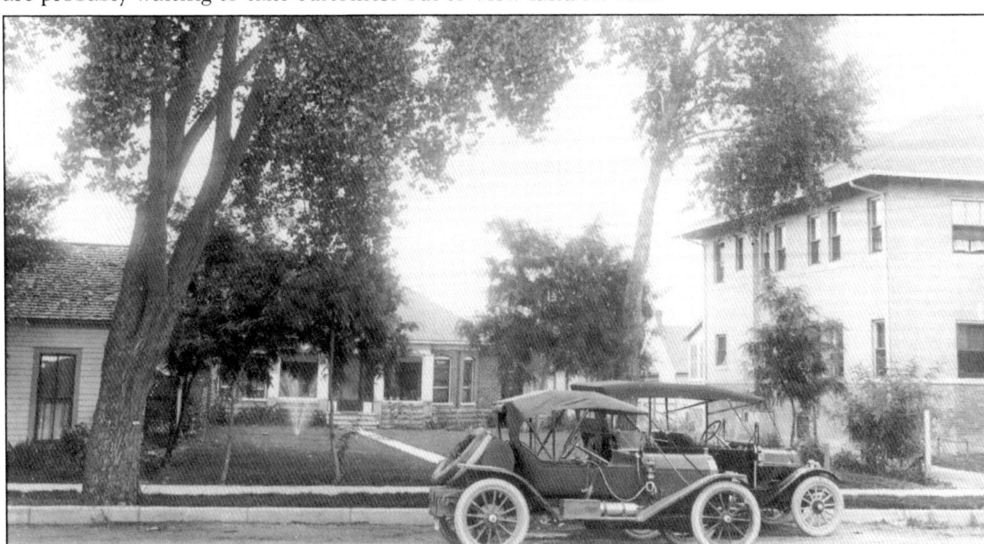

Red Cross Hospital, Alamosa, August 13, 1913. These automobiles are double parked outside the Red Cross Hospital on State Avenue. The hospital is the building on the right.

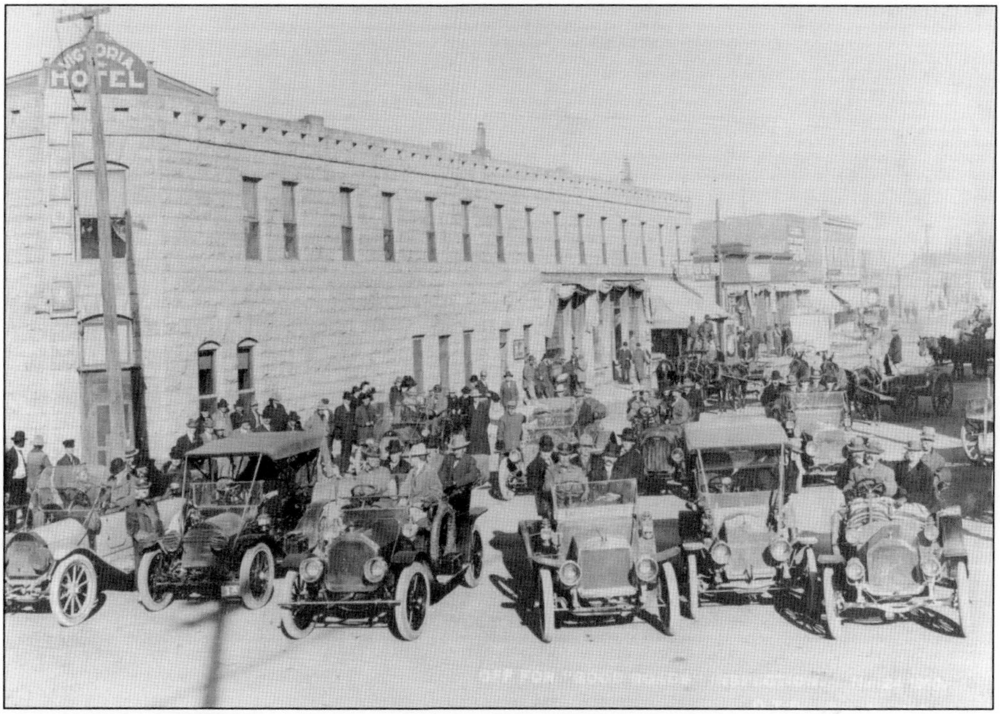

"Off for Good Roads Inspection," November 24, 1910. The Alamosa Boosters lined up their automobiles on the corner of State Avenue and Sixth Street as they prepared to head out of town on an excursion to inspect the roads. The Victoria Hotel is on the left.

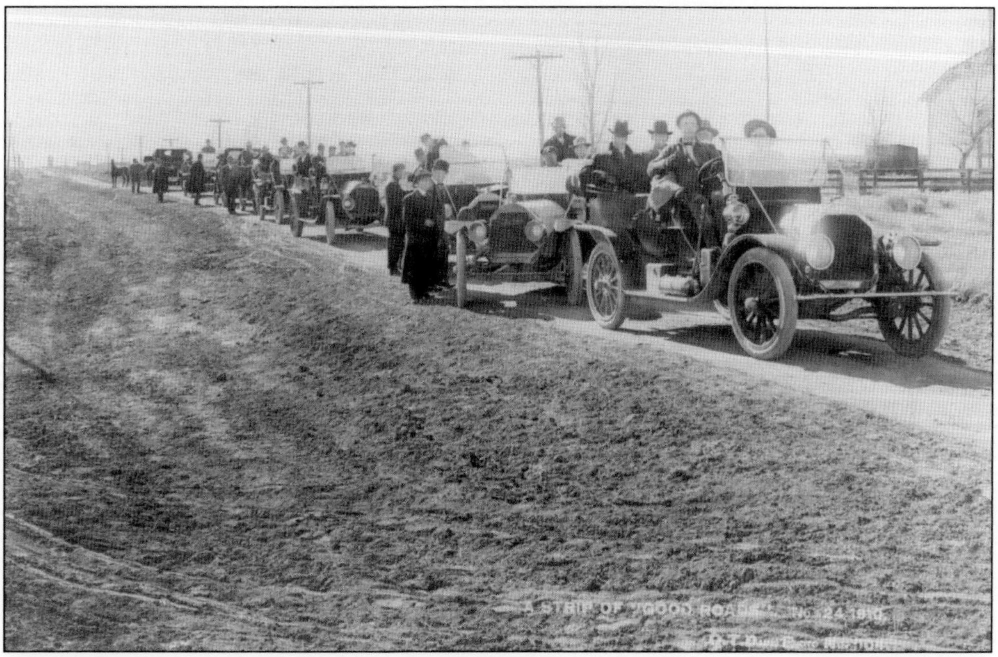

Testing Road near Alamosa, November 24, 1910. The "road inspectors" paused for a photograph on a strip of good road. There appears to be a church or school in the right background, and a horse and buggy bring up the rear.

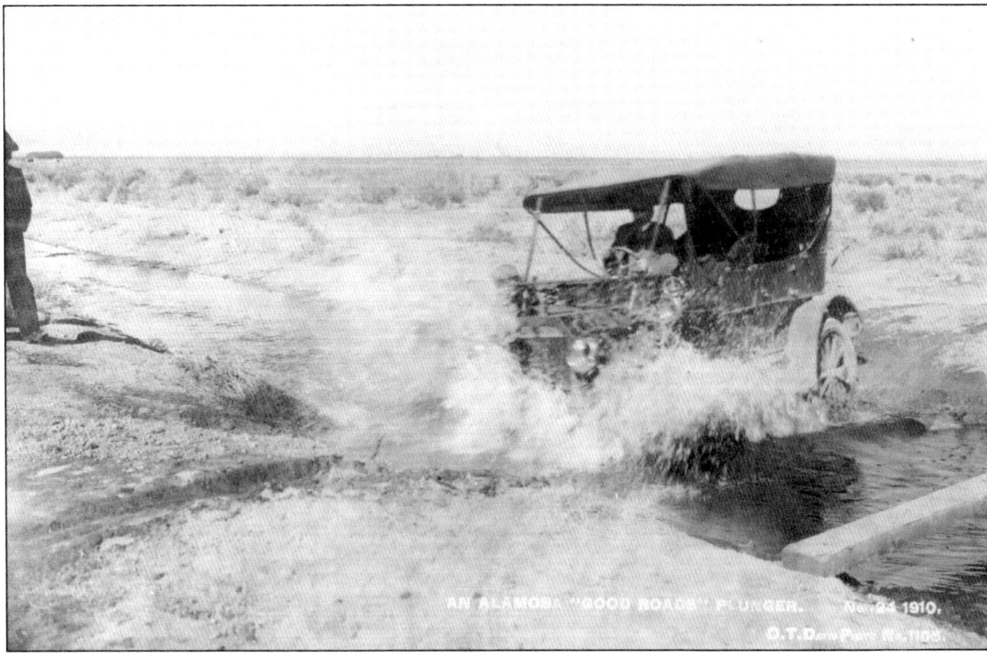

"AN ALAMOSA 'GOOD ROADS' PLUNGER," NOVEMBER 24, 1910. An adventurous driver plunges his automobile into an irrigation ditch. Will he make it through? See the next photograph for the result.

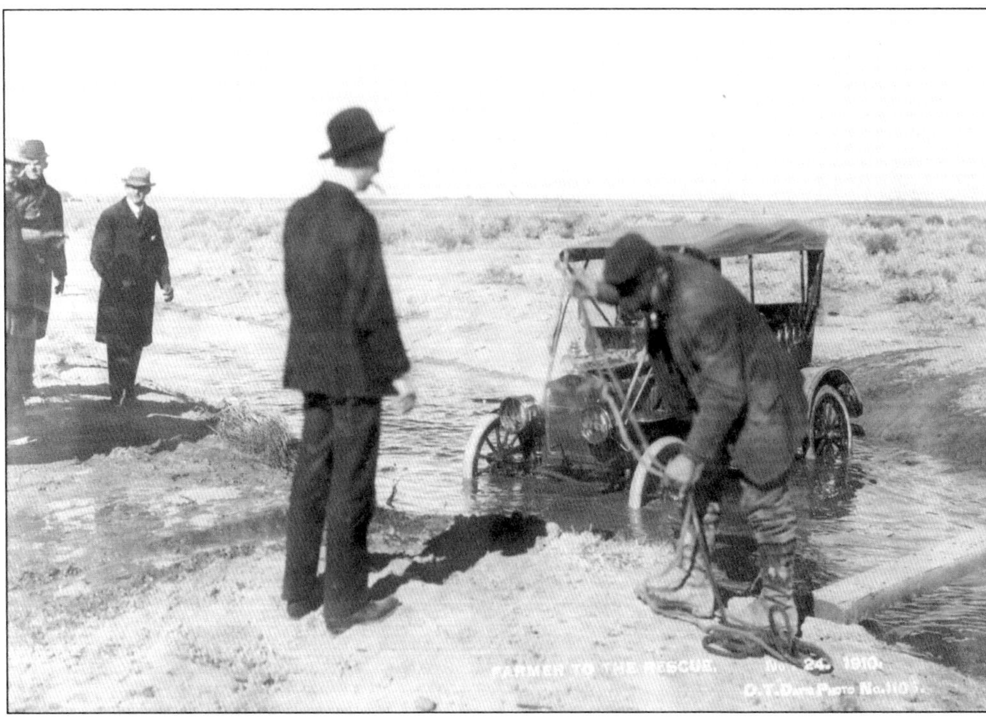

STUCK IN THE DITCH, NOVEMBER 24, 1910. The chagrined driver has marooned his automobile in the irrigation ditch. A local farmer comes to help out by tying a rope to the car. Will he use horses to pull it out? See the next photograph for the answer.

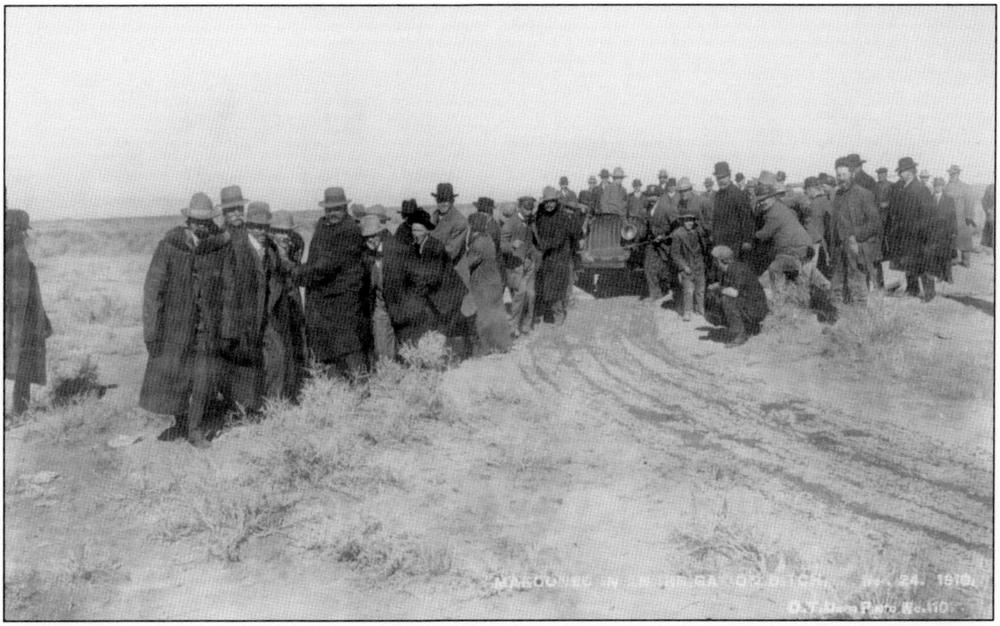

ARM STRONG POWER RESCUES CAR, NOVEMBER 24, 1910. With no horses in sight, the "good roads inspectors" were enlisted to pull on the ropes to get the automobile out of the irrigation ditch. It is a good thing there were so many of them to help!

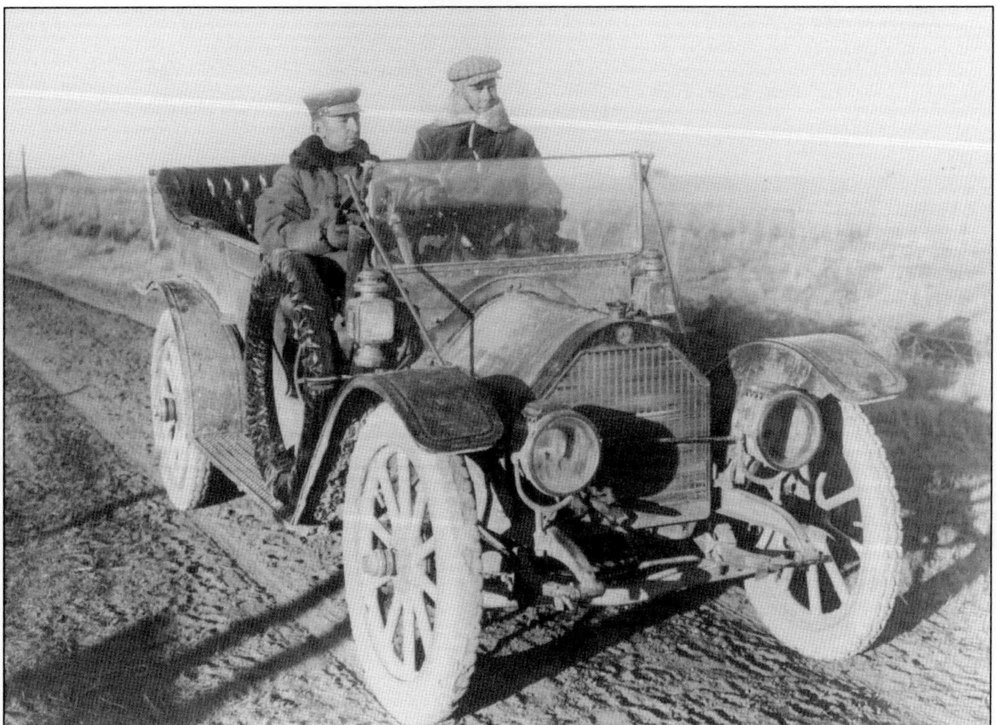

ROY SHAHAN, REAL ESTATE AGENT, 1911. Roy Shahan (left), manager of the Charles E. Gibson Company, shown on page 118, drives an unidentified passenger out to look at some land. It must have been a cold day, as both men were heavily bundled in coats and caps.

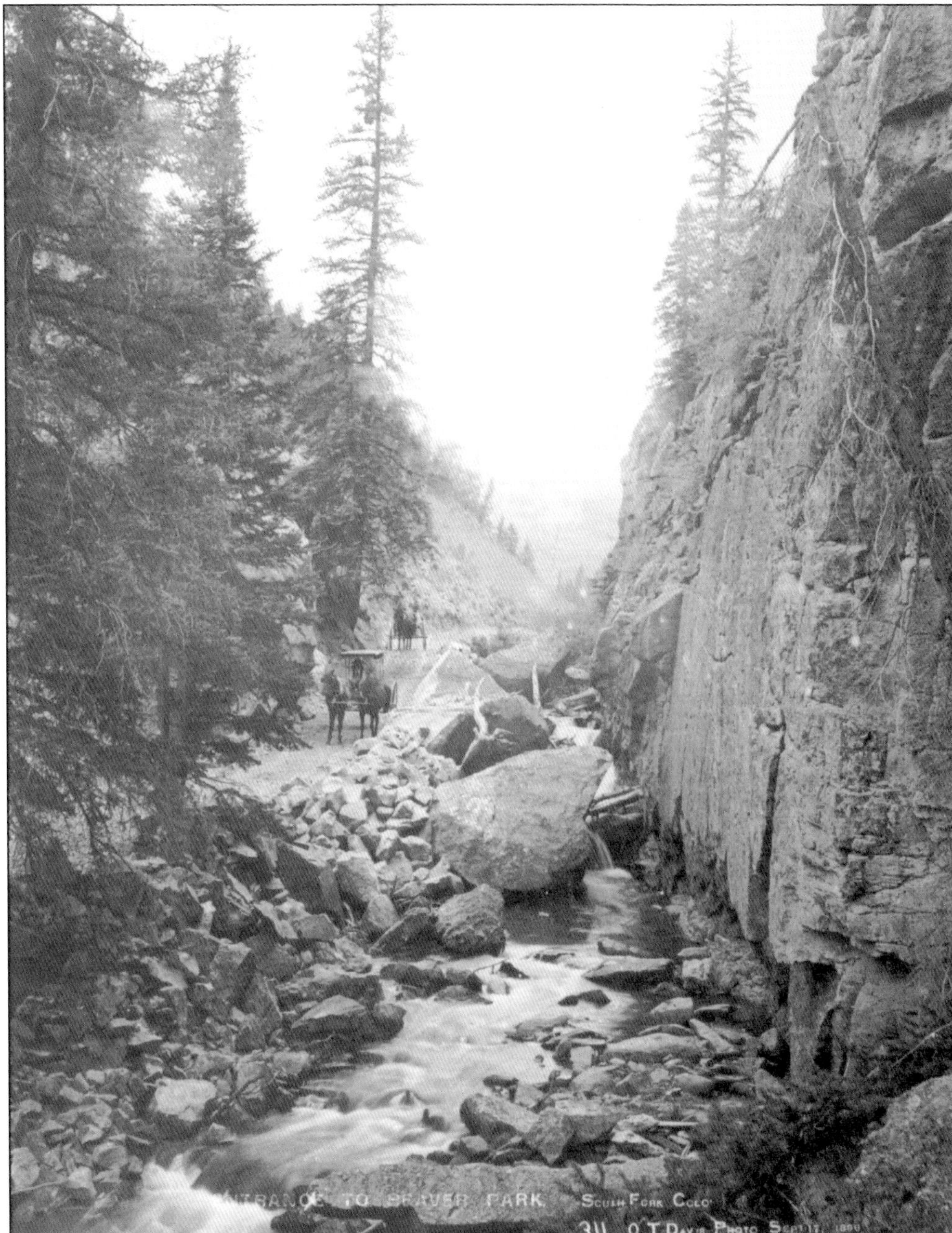

Entrance to Beaver Park, September 17, 1890. Beaver Park is on Beaver Creek south of the town of South Fork. This photograph is a bit of a puzzle. It is one of O.T. Davis's earliest photographs, taken at a time when most of his photographs were of the La Veta–Walsenburg area. Perhaps he rode the D&RG train to South Fork. He then would have taken this primitive road to Beaver Park and then farther south to the mines at Summitville or Jasper. This road branches off the road to Wolf Creek Pass just about a mile southwest of South Fork. The canyon is similar to what road builders faced in the canyon of the south fork of the Rio Grande as they built west up Wolf Creek Pass, as seen on the following pages.

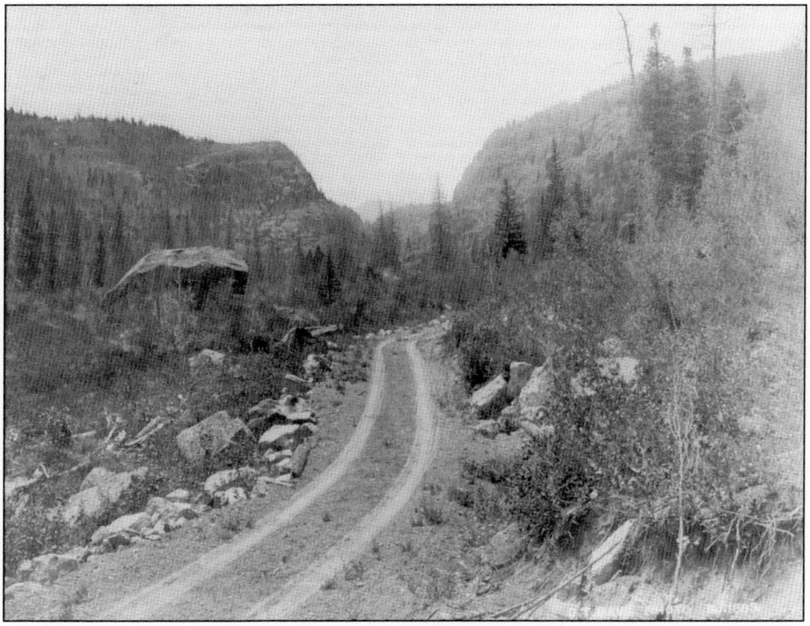

Box Canyon, Wolf Creek Road, August 6, 1916. This view west up the canyon illustrates the rugged terrain that had to be conquered by road builders. The south fork of the Rio Grande cannot be seen, but it is on the left behind the large boulder.

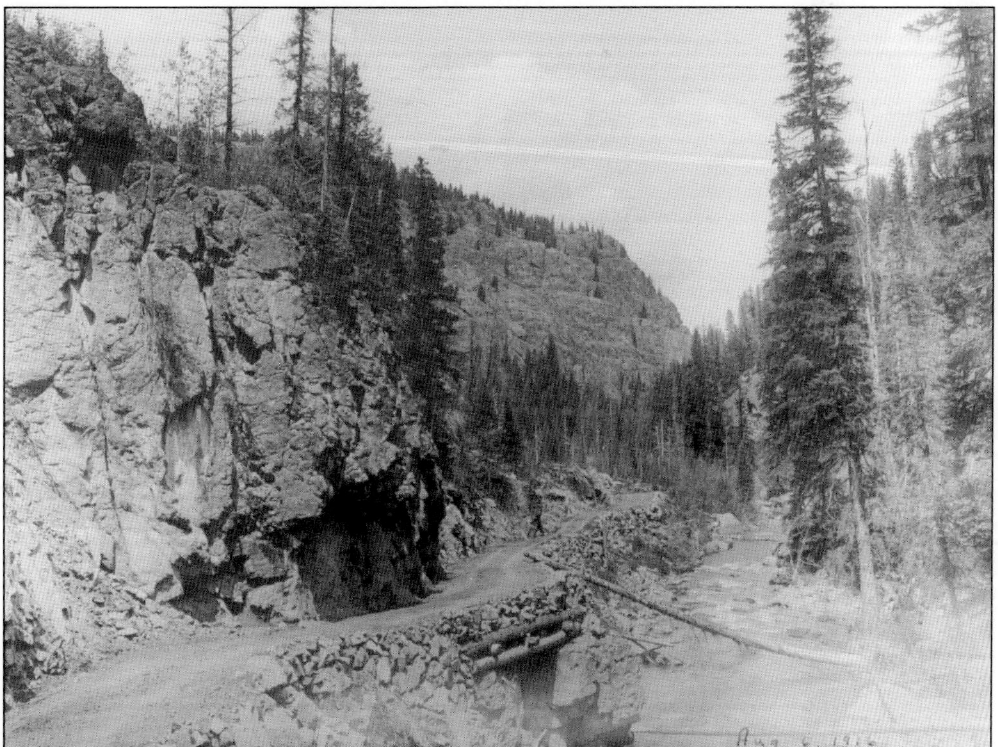

Upper Entrance, Box Canyon, August 6, 1916. This view at the top of the canyon looks east where Park Creek (under the bridge) joins the south fork of the Rio Grande. This narrow stretch through the canyon is still only two lanes wide today.

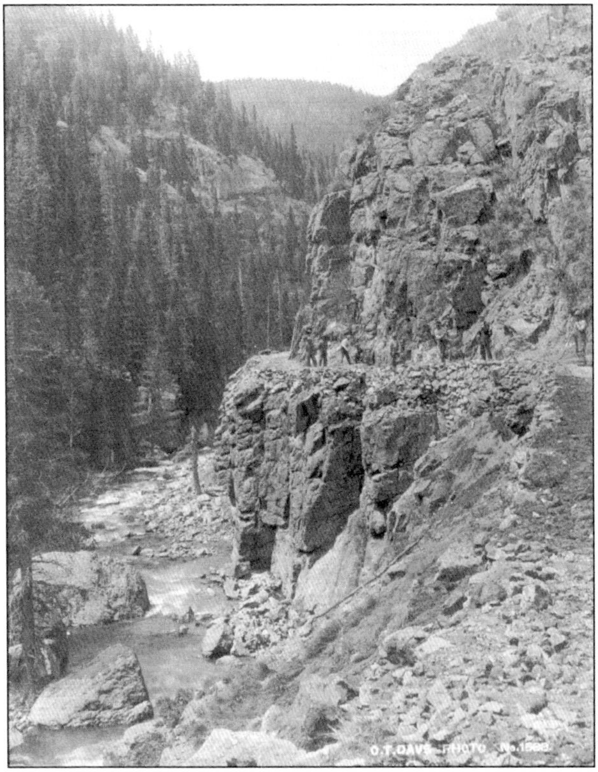

WOLF CREEK ROAD, AUGUST 6, 1916. Workers clear rock fall off the road in advance of the caravan of approaching automobiles seen on the next page. The precipitous drop-off to the south fork of the Rio Grande still exists along US Highway 160 today.

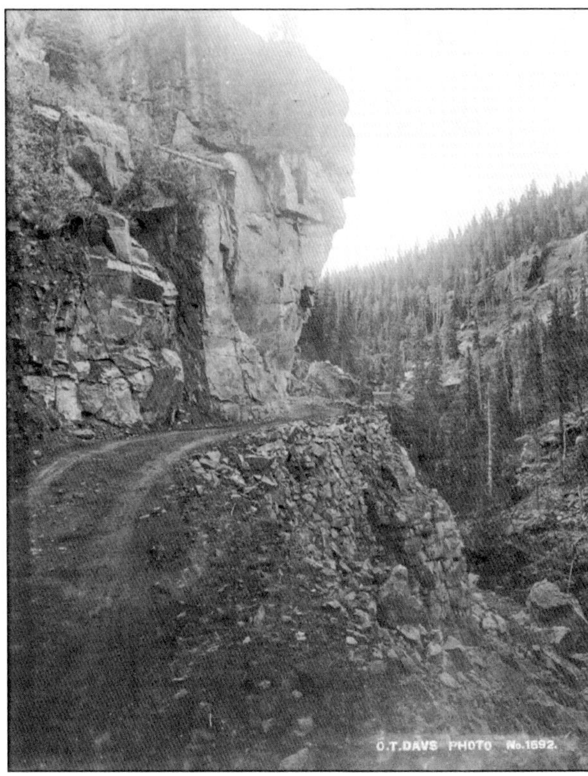

UPPER END, BOX CANYON, AUGUST 6, 1916. By this point, the road has crossed over the south fork of the Rio Grande and is headed toward the upper reaches of Wolf Creek Pass.

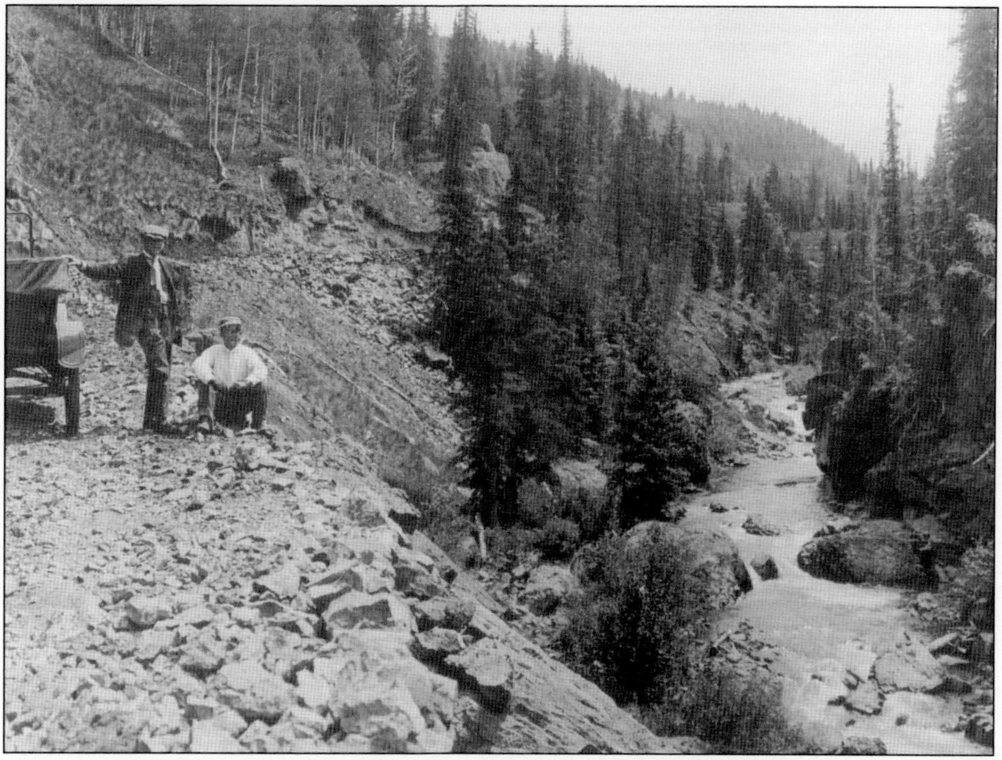

PHOTOGRAPH STOP, AUGUST 6, 1916. These gentlemen parked their automobile on the Wolf Creek road so that O.T. Davis could take their photograph. The view looks east downstream on the south fork of the Rio Grande.

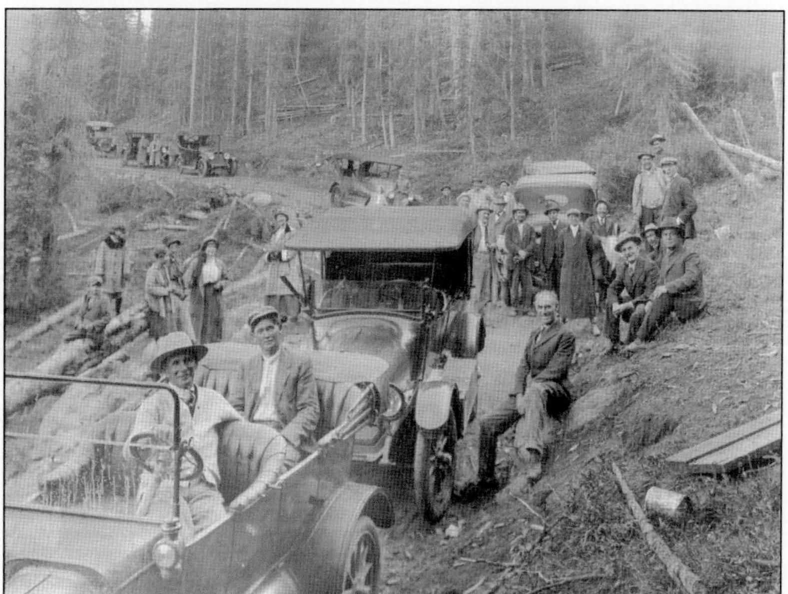

GROUP ON WOLF CREEK ROAD, AUGUST 6, 1916. This group looks pretty happy after surviving the harrowing drive up the box canyon. The contingent of eight automobiles and passengers takes a well-deserved break. Included among the women on the left side were Nina Weiss, Mary Wiley, and Prudence Ewing.

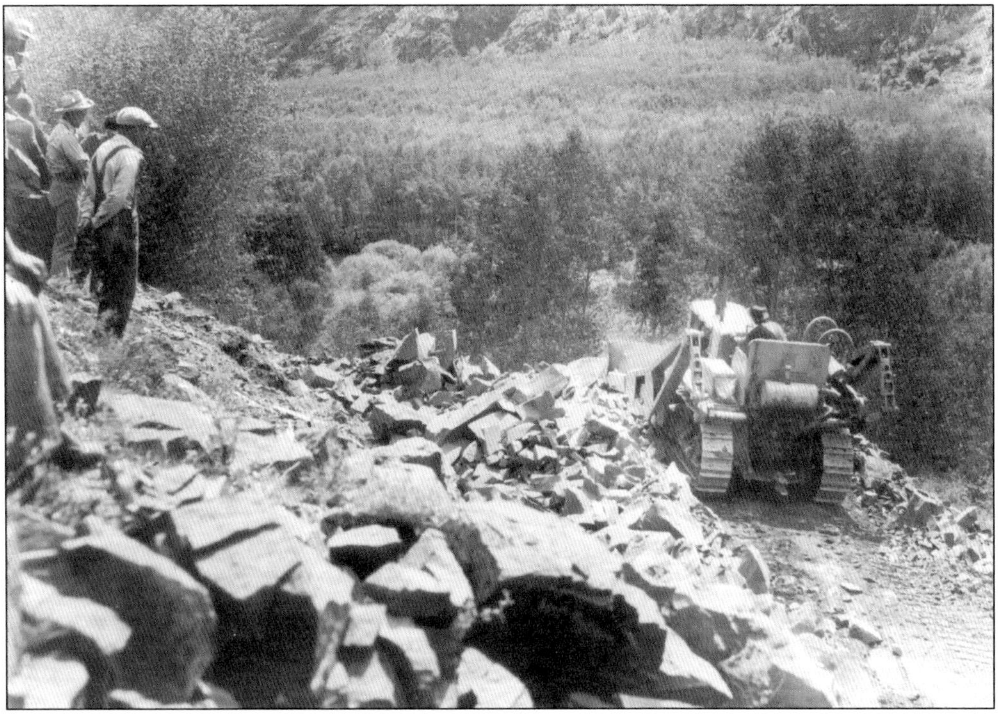

Road Work, Undated. This bulldozer is hard at work moving boulders to create a mountain road in southern Colorado. O.T. Davis left no date or location for this photograph.

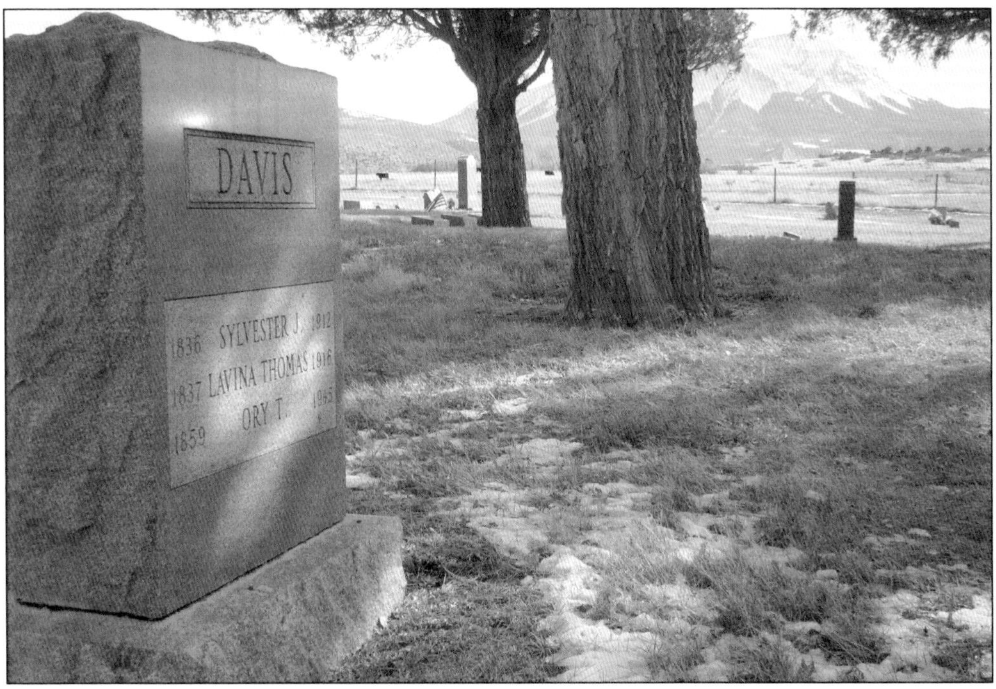

Rest in Peace, Ory T. Davis. When O.T. Davis died in 1945, he had been living in Alamosa for 39 years. He was buried in La Veta with his parents. The beautiful West Spanish Peak, photographed often by O.T., rises in the background south of the cemetery. (Photograph by the author.)

Bibliography

Athearn, Robert G. *Rebel of the Rockies: A History of the Denver & Rio Grande Western Railroad.* New Haven, CT: Yale University Press, 1962.

Feitz, Leland. *Alamosa: A Quick History.* Colorado Springs, CO: Little London Press, 1977.

———. *Platoro, Colorado: Mining Camp and Resort Town.* Denver: Golden Bell Press, 1969.

Griffiths, Mel and Lynnell Rubright. *Colorado: A Geography.* Boulder, CO: Westview Press, 1983.

Griswold, P.R. *Colorado's Loneliest Railroad: The San Luis Southern.* Boulder, CO: Pruett Publishing, 1980.

Harlan, George. *Postmarks and Places.* Monte Vista, CO: Adobe Village Press, 2002.

Kempner, Helen A. *Bonanza! A Pictorial History of Colorado's Kerber Creek Country.* Colorado Springs, CO: Little London Press, 1978.

Kessler, Ron. *San Luis Valley Place Names.* Monte Vista, CO: Adobe Village Press, 2002.

McAdow, Beryl. *From Crested Peaks: The Story of Adams State College of Colorado.* Denver: Big Mountain Press, 1961.

Noel, Thomas J. *Buildings of Colorado.* New York: Oxford University Press, 1997.

———. Introduction to *The WPA Guide to 1930s Colorado,* by Federal Writers Project. Lawrence, KS: University Press of Kansas, 1987.

Rasmussen, Stephen. *The Rio Grande's La Veta Pass Route.* Burlington, VT: Evergreen Press, 2000.

Simmons, Virginia McConnell. *The San Luis Valley: Land of the Six-Armed Cross.* Boulder, CO: Pruett Publishing, 1979.

Trautmann, Debra Davis and Karen Mitchell. "Huerfano County Ory T. Davis." www. kmitch.com/Huerfano/orydavis.html.

Wilkins, Tivis E. *Colorado Railroads Chronological Development.* Boulder, CO: Pruett Publishing, 1974.